Popular culture and working-class taste in Britain, 1930–39

MANCHEStER
1824

Manchester University Press

STUDIES IN POPULAR CULTURE

General editor: Professor Jeffrey Richards

Recently published

Healthy living in the Alps:
the origins of winter tourism in Switzerland, 1860–1914
Susan Barton

Leisure, citizenship and working-class men in Britain, 1850–1945
Brad Beaven

British railway enthusiasm
Ian Carter

Darts in England, 1900–39: a social history
Patrick Chaplin

History on British television: constructing nation,
nationality and collective memory
Robert Dillon

Songs of protest, songs of love: popular ballads
in eighteenth-century Britain
Robin Ganev

The BBC and national identity in Britain, 1922–53
Thomas Hajkowski

From silent screen to multi-screen:
a history of cinema exhibition in Britain since 1896
Stuart Hanson

Juke box Britain: Americanisation and youth culture, 1945–60
Adrian Horn

Popular culture and working-class taste in Britain, 1930–39

A round of cheap diversions?

ROBERT JAMES

Manchester University Press

Manchester and New York

distributed exclusively in the USA by Palgrave Macmillan

Published by Manchester University Press
Oxford Road, Manchester M13 9NR, UK
and Room 400, 175 Fifth Avenue, New York, NY 10010, USA
www.manchesteruniversitypress.co.uk

Distributed in the United States exclusively by
Palgrave Macmillan, 175 Fifth Avenue,
New York, NY 10010, USA

Distributed in Canada exclusively by
UBC Press, University of British Columbia, 2029 West Mall,
Vancouver, BC, Canada V6T 1Z2

British Library Cataloguing-in-Publication Data is available

Library of Congress Cataloging-in-Publication Data is available

ISBN 978 0 7190 9552 8 *paperback*

First published by Manchester University Press in hardback 2010

This paperback edition first published 2014

The publisher has no responsibility for the persistence or accuracy of URLs for any external or third-party internet websites referred to in this book, and does not guarantee that any content on such websites is, or will remain, accurate or appropriate.

Printed by Lightning Source

STUDIES IN POPULAR CULTURE

There has in recent years been an explosion of interest in culture and cultural studies. The impetus has come from two directions and out of two different traditions. On the one hand, cultural history has grown out of social history to become a distinct and identifiable school of historical investigation. On the other hand, cultural studies has grown out of English literature and has concerned itself to a large extent with contemporary issues. Nevertheless, there is a shared project, its aim to elucidate the meanings and values implicit and explicit in the art, literature, learning, institutions and everyday behaviour within a given society. Both the cultural historian and the cultural studies scholar seek to explore the ways in which a culture is imagined, represented and received, how it interacts with social processes, how it contributes to individual and collective identities and world views, to stability and change, to social, political and economic activities and programmes. This series aims to provide an arena for the cross-fertilisation of the discipline, so that the work of the cultural historian can take advantage of the most useful and illuminating of the theoretical developments and the cultural studies scholars can extend the purely historical underpinnings of their investigations. The ultimate objective of the series is to provide a range of books which will explain in a readable and accessible way where we are now socially and culturally and how we got to where we are. This should enable people to be better informed, promote an interdisciplinary approach to cultural issues and encourage deeper thought about the issues, attitudes and institutions of popular culture.

Jeffrey Richards

To my parents, Alfred and Patricia James,
for their love and support over the years.

Contents

General editor's introduction

In this thoughtful, well-researched and ground-breaking book, Robert James advances a revisionist interpretation of working-class taste in 1930s Britain. In doing so, he seeks to merge the often antipathetic structuralist and culturalist approaches to the subject in an analysis of both text and context, production and consumption. He examines the cultural assumptions and attitudes of the largely middle-class authorities and arbiters of taste, and compares them with the evidence of popular choice, derived from a range of important primary sources such as Mass-Observation, the Bernstein Questionnaires and the Miners' Institute ledgers. He carefully establishes the economic, social and ideological contexts by analysing the choices and motivations of the producers and consumers of popular culture and the strategies of advertising and promotion. Having established the context, he undertakes a comparative study of Portsmouth, Derby and South Wales, chosen for their geographical spread and socio-economic differences, to assess in depth and detail the nature of working-class taste. A unique feature of the book is his examination of cinema-going and reading habits side by side. These two pastimes have normally been studied separately. His conclusion, contrary to the conventional wisdom, that the working-class consumer was an active and not a passive agent and that there were regional variations in taste rather than a single uniform national working-class taste, is consistent and persuasive. He is careful however not to reject the idea that some tastes transcended region and locality and he fascinatingly establishes that the most popular author in the tuppenny libraries and the most filmed author of the decade was one and the same – Edgar Wallace. This confident, well-informed and subtly argued study makes a significant contribution to our understanding of inter-war popular culture.

Acknowledgements

First of all, I would like to thank Jeffrey Richards for his kind and encouraging comments during the various stages of this project. Jeffrey was external examiner for my PhD thesis, on which this study is based, and kindly suggested that it should be turned into a book.

I am hugely indebted to Sue Harper. She has been a wonderful mentor over the past years, running a critical eye over, firstly, my PhD thesis, for which she was Director of Studies, and latterly, various drafts of this book. Without her guidance and support this study would not have seen the light of day. Her gentle coaching, constructive criticism and eternal optimism have made working on it a real pleasure. I should also like to thank Brad Beaven, who has also provided much welcome advice, especially during the latter stages of this project.

I am extremely grateful for the financial assistance received from the Art and Humanities Research Council which has allowed me to undertake this research.

Gratitude must also go to the numerous staff at the archives I have visited during my research. Their assistance has been most welcome. Especial thanks go to Elisabeth Bennett, archivist at the South Wales Coalfield Collection, University of Wales, Swansea; John Dallison and Trish Kenny at Derby Local Studies Centre; and Lizzie Ennion and Elisabeth Kingston at Peterborough Archives Service. All were helpful beyond the call of duty. Numerous archivists at Portsmouth Norrish Central Library and Portsmouth Records Office also deserve gratitude for their invaluable assistance. Janet Moat and Julia Bell at Special Collections, BFI, London were also adept at digging out less well-known archival material. I would also like to thank the Trustees of the Mass-Observation Archive, University of Sussex for the use of their material, and Dorothy Sheridan for her assistance in finding what I needed. I would also like to thank Emma Brennan, editor at Manchester University Press, the production staff at MUP, and the anonymous reader, for their hard work in putting this project together.

Various academics have also offered advice during the course of writing this book. I have been fortunate to gain valuable guidance from scholars at the Film History seminars, held at the Institute of Historical Research and convened by Dr Mark Glancy. Their willingness to share their wealth of knowledge in 1930s film culture has been very gratefully received. Colleagues in the History and Film Studies departments at the University of Portsmouth have also been very generous with their knowledge, especially Justin Smith. Thank you. Thanks also to my students at Portsmouth – past and present – for making me reflect on the value and relevance of my subject.

A special note of thanks go to my circle of friends, especially Colin and Sarah Walker, Emma Mooney and Maureen Wright, but also my dog-walking companions – Mike and Sue Kenward, Lynne Stagg and Pete Harding – for putting up with my discussions on 1930s working-class taste as if there was not another subject in the world that mattered. On that note, thanks also go to my family, Mum, Dad, Linda, Jeanette and Colin. Your love and support over the years have been very much appreciated. A special note of appreciation should be recorded for David and Irene Palmer, two truly inspirational teachers who gave me the encouragement to change profession. Thanks for the 'push'.

Finally, I would like to say thank you to my wife, Alison, for her love, support, patience and unflagging encouragement.

Introduction

'Giving the Public what it wants'. By a process not difficult to imagine and easily demonstrable, this has come to mean providing fiction that requires the least effort to read and will set the reader up with a comfortable state of mind.[1]

The cinematograph film is today one of the most widely used means for the amusement of the public at large. It is also undoubtedly a most important factor in the education of all classes of the community, in the spread of national culture and in presenting ideas and customs to the world. Its potentialities moreover in shaping the ideas of the very large numbers to whom it appeals are almost unlimited. The propaganda value of film cannot be over-emphasised.[2]

These quotes reveal much about British society's attitudes towards popular leisure in the 1930s. The first, written by Q.D. Leavis, reveals how society's leisure activities were believed to be contributing to a more passive, less socially aware population. The second, taken from a Government-sponsored report of the Committee on Cinematograph Films, demonstrates that some contemporaries viewed leisure as a valuable propaganda medium. Something was clearly afoot, and the authors of these remarks were attempting to deal with it. Interestingly, these remarks were made with little or no attention paid to the consumers themselves. More to the point, consumers are being identified as *passive* observers. They are being denied *agency*. This is typical of many investigations into popular leisure in the period. When scrutinising society's leisure activities, even the most vociferous critics did so very much like a stone skipping across deep water. They failed to penetrate the surface and thus did not gain any real understanding of what leisure actually *meant* to those consuming it.

This book explores the social and cultural roles of cinema-going and reading in the lives of the working classes in 1930s Britain. It aims to establish what types of material they consumed, and, more specifically, why they consumed it.

The reasons behind these choices are three-fold. Firstly, social investigators were particularly interested in the leisure activities of the working classes in the 1930s; it was this social group that caused most concern. Secondly, cinema-going and reading, as two of the most popular leisure pastimes among working-class consumers, came under greatest scrutiny. Thirdly, and finally, historians, very much like contemporaries of the period, have been rather reluctant to analyse the *meaning* of popular leisure for those consuming it. They, too, have frequently identified working-class consumers as passive observers with no individual agency. There is, then, a gap in the literature that needs redressing, and it is one which, once filled, will help to improve our understanding of the role of popular leisure in a period during which British society's engagement with it was vital

There was, in fact, a notable growth in cinema-going and reading habits in the 1930s, especially within working-class communities. This rapid growth, coupled with heightened social tensions, persuaded society's cultural elites to look more closely at them; they were eager to understand the effects these leisure activities were having on society. Their responses were generally negative. Cinema-going, as a relatively new cultural phenomenon, bore the brunt of their criticism, but reading habits were also heavily criticised.

This interest in the effects of leisure on the working classes was not a new phenomenon. From the mid-nineteenth century onwards social commentators, such as Charles Booth and Henry Mayhew, compiled studies evaluating the relationship between leisure, labour and the working class.[3] For them, much of what was wrong in society could be blamed on the type of leisure activity in which people partook. As a result of these investigations, many middle-class philanthropists sought to influence the working classes' choice of leisure activity. Attempts were made to 'improve' working-class society through 'rational recreation'; 'educational' forms of entertainment were promoted vigorously.

The majority of investigations performed during the 1930s operated along similar lines. The writings of middle-class observers George Orwell, J.B. Priestley and Seebohm B. Rowntree, along with the work of the Mass-Observation organisation and the *Scrutiny* group, are cases in point. Like Booth and Mayhew, these observers and cultural critics sought to investigate and record various aspects of working-class life. Assorted approaches were taken, but each researcher had similar aims: to gain a better understanding of society at 'grass-roots' level. The primary motivation behind these investigations was dissatisfaction with the working classes' apparent lack of interest in politics. There was widespread concern amongst left-wing intellectuals over the damaging effects on society caused by political apathy. Many believed that the working classes had, to quote Priestley, a 'brutish, fatalistic acceptance of the miserable muddle of our present society' in which they became 'the perfect subjects for an iron autocracy'.[4] Working-class leisure was thought to be drawing the working classes away from the political arena, so it was working-class leisure that came under most scrutiny.

Significantly, all of these texts are shot through with examples of the link between working-class leisure and political apathy. Priestley complained that mass, commercial leisure drew the working classes away from the political arena, and created an atmosphere 'in which autocracies flourish and liberty dies'.[5] Orwell argued that the consumption of 'cheap luxuries' ensured that the working classes became politically apathetic and 'accepted their circumstances without seriously attempting to improve them'.[6] Cinema-going and reading were chosen for specific criticism. '[N]othing but films, films, films,' complained Priestley; for him, cinema-going was merely a form of escapism for the working classes.[7] Rowntree, too, criticised cinema-going's supposed escapist qualities, claiming that it 'arrest[ed] the development' of working-class consumers.[8] Reading fared little better. '[T]he greater part of the reading among the working classes,' Rowntree noted, 'consists of books which make no demand on the minds of the readers'.[9] Q.D. Leavis, by far the most vocal critic of reading habits in the period, identified the working classes' preference for popular fiction as an 'exhibition of herd prejudice' which had 'innumerable indirect effects on the life of the nation'.[10] In fact, the *Scrutiny* group identified all popular culture as degraded, and popular tastes, as they yielded to it, as debased. To them, the growth of working-class leisure led to the cultural degeneration of society and a 'levelling down' of elite culture.[11]

Significant weaknesses pervade these investigations, however. These investigators were predominantly middle-class by origin and were often ignorant of 'mass' culture and popular forms; they would thus probably misrepresent them. In fact, Priestley admits that the social role of one leisure activity he attended, a whist drive, was not understood because 'I was a stranger and may have missed some quiet fun'.[12] His criticisms of all manner of so-called 'passive' leisure pursuits may be similarly informed. Orwell, too, observed that while he was 'among' the working classes during his time spent investigating them, he 'was not one of them'.[13] In addition, because these investigators believed that the working classes' interest in leisure detached them from the political sphere, it is likely that they would be critical of them, primarily because of their concern over the social consequences. In fact, the *Scrutiny* group believed that their movement could be the 'base-camp' from which to begin a crusade for cultural renewal.[14] Their work can thus be read as a part of this 'missionary spirit'.

Significantly, though, these investigators were falling in to the trap of straightforwardly 'reading off' working-class leisure products as evidence of class consciousness. The issue is more complex than this. These surveys offer, not a *reflection* of the consciousness of working-class consumers, but an inter-action with it, and interrogation of it. Herein lies the problem of using these sources as evidence of working-class life, and the relationship between leisure and politics within it. Significantly, an ignorance of these structural weaknesses has informed much of the historiography on working-class leisure during this period.

Indeed, like contemporary observers, many historians have linked the rise in the number of working-class people participating in new, commercialised forms of leisure to a decline in political awareness within the working-class community.[15] This is to assume, as many contemporaries did, that the working classes were using these activities as a form of 'escape' and accepting, without question, the viewpoints presented to them. However, as Stephen G. Jones has perceptively noted, leisure activities are experienced in different ways by different social groups. It is thus wrong to assume that the working classes were passive consumers of the leisure product.[16] Indeed, despite contemporary observers' claims to the contrary, working-class consumers were not cultural dopes who lacked agency, and popular entertainment did more than show a mass of anodyne products that 'fed' middle-class ideology to them.

Unfortunately, many of the assumptions made by Leavis *et al.* have continued to dominate within the historiography of working-class leisure. This has much to do with the prominence given in the wider academic community to middle-class consumers. In fact, when it comes to matters of taste, a clear class bias has existed. Consider the work on the sociology of taste by perhaps the best known, and certainly most influential, writer in the field, Pierre Bourdieu. Bourdieu focuses on the 'fields of power' that operate within cultural production, circu-lation and consumption, and rightly argues that a homologous relationship exists between the producers of cultural texts and those who consume them.[17] However, because he also argues that cultural practices and preferences are based on educational level and social origin, he effectively denies working-class consumers their place within the cultural sphere.[18]

Bourdieu's influence within the academic community ensured that the taste preferences and consumption patterns of the working classes were frequently ignored by, or at least denied equal consideration from, subsequent academics. However, much recent theoretical work has concentrated on the role of working-class consumers, recognising that they too can command considerable cultural competence. There is a danger here, though, for a tendency towards hagiography. Simon Frith has argued that the majority of texts focusing on working-class taste have viewed 'every act of "popular" consumption [as] an excuse for celebration'.[19] Popular cultural forms are thus 'read for the positive or "transgressive" values the "popular" audience must have found there'.[20] As Frith adroitly notes, we should be aware that, like all consumers, 'popular' consumers' value judgments are never determined by the text. Indeed, popular taste is made up of various layers and strands, and these as often contradict orthodox assumptions of what constitutes working-class behavioural patterns as they do confirm them.

Any study of working-class taste, therefore, needs to account for the role of agency without resorting to sentiment or hagiography; and it should pay attention to the cultural form without insisting that its visual or literary structure is always the last determinant. However, it is here that academics have tended to divide into two separate schools: structuralists and culturalists. Structuralists, dominating the fields of visual and literary studies, aimed to reveal what meaning was supported by the text. Culturalists, primarily historians and sociologists, focused on the social function of the text.[21] Considered alone, neither approach helps to define a cultural commodity's meaning, nor explain why specific cultural commodities are chosen by the consumer. As John Storey noted: 'It is not enough to celebrate agency; nor is it enough to detail the structure(s) of power. We must always keep in mind the dialectical play between agency and structure, between production and consumption'.[22]

As a way out of this predicament, scholars 'turned' to the works of Antonio Gramsci, especially those which focused on the subject of hegemony. As Tony Bennett notes, cultural production and consumption were 'viewed as a force field of relations shaped, precisely, by these contradictory pressures and tendencies'.[23] This identification of the process of producing and consuming cultural goods as an active and mutually constitutive *relationship* holds the key to understanding the operation of agency, allowing us to discern what determinants influence the process. Unfortunately, many scholars handled the concept of hegemony too mechanically, suggesting that subordinate groups are dominated within the cultural sphere by their social superiors. George Szanto, for example, argued that: 'The full corpus of tastes ... are not part of democratic property but belong to the ruling class and its tradition'.[24]

Szanto appreciates the need for a close 'fit' between what producers offer and consumers desire (the 'comfort of old slippers'), but views the consumer as an observer, not a participant.[25] This is far from the case. Film producers and book publishers went to great lengths to ensure that their products remained popular (and thus profitable) with the mass consumer. They recognised that, as part of a reciprocal relationship, they had to tailor their products for their target audience, and acted accordingly, presenting their material in a manner that would be pleasurable for the consumer.

In fact, the main function of leisure, and this is something about which most academics have been grimly silent, is to generate pleasure. Pleasure should be seen as *the* overriding determinant in the producer/consumer relationship; the producer provided it, the consumer sought it. Any analysis of the social role of leisure needs to recognise the selectivity of audience taste, the complexities of audience creativity, and the cultural competence of the target audience. There are two fundamental issues at play here. The first concerns the question of choice. There was a huge range of entertainment of offer – competing leisure outlets such as radio, fiction, cinema and dance-halls – and people chose specific activities to perform particular social and cultural tasks; if they did not appeal to their target audience, they were hardly likely to be successful. The second issue involves patterns of representation. The determinants on these, such as constraints on artistic autonomy, were actually relatively minor. In addition, producers fashioned their products with the consumer in mind. Popular texts were popular, not because they attempted to promulgate a dominant ideology, but because they contained a reassuringly recognisable element. Indeed, Richard Hoggart has recalled how popular fiction in the 1930s had 'a felt sense of the texture of life' in the group for which it catered, and that publishers worked with a 'close knowledge of the lives and attitudes of their audience' and created in their texts 'the environment [which was] that of most readers'.[26] It is far more profitable, then, to view the relationship as one in which both producer *and* consumer were equally important, and to recognise that while the agency of both parties was continually negotiated, neither was ever wholly dominant.

Academic writing on cultural consumption has made an important contribution here. Daniel Miller, for example, views culture as a dynamic process which requires both production and consumption, both object and subject, and argues that neither should be 'privileged as prior, but rather seen as mutually constitutive'.[27] Ben Fine and Ellen Leopold argue likewise. Moreover, they believe that, because cultural commodities are socially constructed 'in their meaning [and] in the material practices by which they are produced, *distributed* and ultimately consumed' (emphasis added), patterns of provision should also be examined.[28] Indeed, it is only by understanding the conditions that influence a cultural commodity's production, distribution and consumption – what Fine and Leopold term 'the cultural context' – that we can begin to understand what social and cultural role it played, and thus begin to build a more representative map of consumers' taste preferences.[29]

Encouragingly, much recent theoretical work has been informed by the need to contextualise cultural activities. David Morley, for example, argues that 'the text cannot be considered in isolation from its historical conditions of production and consumption', and recognises that a text's meaning will be constructed according to the various discourses ('knowledge, prejudices, resistances') brought to bear on it by *both* producer *and* consumer.[30] Subsequently, he can argue that, while producers may have a 'preferred' reading for a text, it does not necessarily follow that a consumer will read it in the way intended. Consumers can read 'against the grain' as well as with it.[31] Morley's conception of the contextual expands its multiplicity further, for he stresses the need to take into consideration the context of participation. This attention to the *act* of participation is crucially important for understanding the consumption of all number of cultural goods. Why did a consumer of the 1930s choose to go to the cinema rather than visit the dance-hall or public house? Why did some choose to stay at home and read a book or magazine? What social forces came into play when these decisions were made? If we are to understand the nature of taste, the 'push' and 'pull' factors of consumption demand evaluation.

So, then, what do working-class consumers use cultural goods *for*? What are the *meanings* of the cultural commodity that has been chosen? What is it that is important about the form *and* function of the commodity being consumed? John Fiske's work on the issue of popularity is extremely useful here. Fiske recognises that, because all cultural activities operate within the same 'marketplace', we should not accept its popularity as given, but determine why it was popular. We should ascertain what other, but equivalent, goods were on offer, and also what different goods were made available; and we should examine what meanings, pleasures and social identification the cultural form offered.[32] Significantly, then, Fiske's approach provides a helpful rebuttal against the charge that consumers choose leisure products purely for escapist purposes. Too many critics of popular culture level this charge at the consumer when they should be addressing the issues of '*what* is escaped from, *why* escape is necessary, and *what* is escaped to'.[33] Moreover, because Fiske pays attention to the consumer's cultural competencies, and recognises the complexities of consumer creativity, he appreciates that displacements occur during the production/consumption process. The production, provision and consumption of cultural goods, then, is a process that involves various social agents, each with their own agenda, and it is only by recognising the influence these agents have, and discerning what determinants operate on them, that we can do justice to our subject's diversity and complexity.

John B. Thompson's 'tripartite approach' to analysing culture seems to be the most productive method to deploy here.[34] Thompson proposes dividing the subject into three separate, but closely interrelated, areas. He suggests that, firstly, we analyse the production and transmission of cultural texts by establishing how and under what constraints they are produced and distributed. Secondly, he proposes that we investigate, by using formal or discursive methods of analysis, how a text's message is constructed. Thirdly, he suggests that we examine how the text is received, interpreted and appropriated by the consumer. Thompson is aware that these processes are historically specific. In fact, this aspect binds his three-way approach.[35] Thompson's method is thus particularly useful for understanding the operation of agency in what is a complex and difficult subject.

This book will, therefore, chart three separate, but closely interrelated, histories. Chapters 1–3 'set the scene', focusing on the growth of working-class cinema-going and reading habits, exploring official attitudes towards them, and evaluating the attitudes of trade personnel. These chapters thus inform us of the processes *behind* the production and distribution of these cultural goods. To establish what happened to these products *after* they were made and distributed, I draw a series of maps of working-class taste in various locations across Britain. Chapters 4 and 5 establish national trends in working-class film and literature popularity. Chapters 6–8 look at the film and reading tastes in South Wales, Derby and Portsmouth. I distinguish between these taste-communities by assessing the popularity of certain films and novels, and analysing consumers' responses to them.[36] In fact, what has also been lacking in much of the recent historiography is a rich and nuanced account of the complexity of consumer response. I aim to fill this gap. I should point out, however, that I do not view taste as monolithic, and will not attempt to place a false homogeneity on working-class consumers. Perhaps I should, therefore, refer to the issue as one of working-class 'tastes' and not 'taste'.

Because the main area of research for this book is the nature of consumption, I end by analysing the *nature* of the material itself. This is done to an extent throughout the book, but space has been made in Chapter 9 for some *close* analysis of a few texts known to be popular with working-class consumers. This deploys the traditional methods of visual, literary and discourse analysis, rather than simple plot paraphrase. Due to word limitations, this analysis is brief, but I explore the cultural competence of working-class consumers by assessing what the producer *expected* them to know, and also what they took from their choice of leisure product.

Finally, I should say something about the geographical areas chosen for analysis. British society's experiences of the 1930s varied considerably from region to region. While one region experienced social turmoil, another stabilised. While one region prospered, another declined. Therefore, I have identified three distinct geographical locations – each facing different challenges – and assess the similarities and differences in working-class taste within them. South Wales was one of the regions hit hardest during the Depression; miners experienced high levels of unemployment and a sharp decline in wages.[37] Of course, the miners were a *specific* constituent of the working classes. Historians have identified areas of South Wales as 'little Moscows', witnessing growing political activism and militancy during this period.[38] The unique political culture of the South Wales coalfields certainly played a role in both the organisation of, and participation in, leisure activities in the region, and my examination of the tastes of miners (and their families) uncovers the effects these socio-economic difficulties had on the region's leisure participation.[39]

South Wales, then, was a region in which consumers experienced the worst effects of the Depression. The Midlands and South, by contrast, experienced relative prosperity during this period. Sidney Pollard has observed that a boom in new growth industries greatly benefited these regions.[40] Chapters 7 and 8 thus examine the film and reading habits of working-class consumers in two provincial towns located in these areas: Derby, located in the Midlands, and Portsmouth, located in the South. While both of these towns had their roots in industry – Derby was a manufacturing town with a diversified industrial structure; Portsmouth's principal employer was the Naval Dockyard – their socio-economic experiences varied considerably. While the South was certainly a region of economic prosperity, it fared less well than the Midlands. As H.W. Richardson has noted, it was the Midlands that 'reaped the fullest benefit' from the new industries.[41] Moreover, Portsmouth, as a naval town, fared less well than elsewhere in the South, despite attempts by local government officials to broaden the town's industrial base.[42] This was principally due to the 'declining demand' in shipbuilding in the period; both naval and commercial docks experienced contraction.[43] These structural differences affected each town's political denomination. Derby witnessed a significant swing to Labour in the 1930s; Portsmouth's support for the Party was well below the national average.[44] These structural differences had a bearing on the towns' consumption patterns, too.

The research methods of this book are revisionist. I have drawn from a wide range of archival material in each chapter. Official documents, popularity lists, trade papers, film fan magazines, cinema ledgers and library accession lists have been utilised to understand film and literary cultures in the period. However, part of the aim of this book will be to *speculate* on the reasons why texts were popular and consider the nature of the cultural tasks they performed, so I also take the imaginative leap from archival into interpretative work.

Notes

1 Q.D. Leavis, *Fiction and the Reading Public*, London, 1932, p. 27.
2 Cited in Margaret Dickinson and Sarah Street, *Cinema and State: The Film Industry and the Government 1927–84*, London, 1985, p. 1.
3 Charles Booth, *Life and Labour of the People in London*, First series 1–5, New York, 1969; Henry Mayhew, *London Street Life: Selections from the Writings of Henry Mayhew*, London, 1966.
4 J.B. Priestley, *English Journey*, Middlesex, 1934, pp. 281 and 379.
5 Ibid., pp. 387–388.
6 George Orwell, *The Road to Wigan Pier*, London, 1937, pp. 79 and 89.
7 Priestley, *English Journey*, p. 118.
8 Seebohm B. Rowntree, *Poverty and Progress: A Second Survey of York*, London, 1941, pp. 470–471.
9 Ibid., p. 472.
10 Leavis, *Fiction and the Reading Public*, pp. 185, 195 and 263.
11 Iain Wright, 'F.R. Leavis, the *Scrutiny* Movement and the Crisis', in Jon Clark, Margot Heinemann, David Margolies and Carole Snee, eds, *Culture and Crisis in Britain in the Thirties*, London, 1979, pp. 37–65; p. 38.
12 Priestley, *English Journey*, p. 102.
13 Orwell, *Road to Wigan Pier*, p. 137.
14 Wright, 'F.R. Leavis', p. 38.
15 See, for example, Gareth Stedman Jones, *Languages of Class*, Cambridge, 1983; Peter Stead, *Film and the Working Class: The Feature Film in British and American Society*, London, 1989; John Stevenson and Chris Cook, *Britain in the Depression: Society and Politics, 1929–1939*, second edition, London, 1994.
16 Stephen G. Jones, *Workers at Play: A Social and Economic History of Leisure, 1918–1939*, London, 1986, pp. 6–10. See also Peter N. Stearns, 'The Effort at Continuity in Working-Class Culture', *Journal of Modern History*, 52:4, 1980, pp. 626–655; Peter Miles and Malcolm Smith, *Cinema, Literature and Society: Elite and*

Mass Culture in Interwar Britain, London, 1987; Brad Beaven, *Leisure, Citizenship and Working-Class Men in Britain, 1850–1945*, Manchester, 2005.

17 See the editor's introduction to Pierre Bourdieu, *The Field of Cultural Production: Essays on Art and Literature*, London, 1993, p. 7.

18 Pierre Bourdieu, *Distinction: A Social Critique of the Judgement of Taste*, London, 1984, pp. 1–2 and 101.

19 Simon Frith, 'The Good, the Bad, and the Indifferent: Defending Popular Culture from the Populists', in John Storey, ed., *Cultural Theory and Popular Culture: A Reader*, second edition, London, 1998, pp. 570–586; p. 572.

20 Ibid., p. 573.

21 Tony Bennett, 'Popular Culture and the "Turn to Gramsci"', in Storey, ed., *Cultural Theory*, pp. 217–224; p. 218.

22 John Storey, *Cultural Consumption and Everyday Life*, second edition, London, 2003, p. 170.

23 Bennett, 'Popular Culture', p. 219.

24 George Szanto, *Narrative Taste and Social Perspectives: The Matter of Quality*, Basingstoke, 1987, p. 16.

25 Ibid., p. 155.

26 Richard Hoggart, *The Uses of Literacy: Aspects of Working-Class Life with Special Reference to Publications and Entertainments*, second edition, Harmondsworth, 1984, pp. 121–129.

27 Daniel Miller, *Material Culture and Mass Consumption*, Oxford, 1987, p. 18.

28 Ben Fine and Ellen Leopold, *The World of Consumption*, London, 1993, p. 15.

29 Ibid., pp. 15–16. Fine and Leopold closely follow the theory of culture offered by Clifford Geertz.

30 David Morley, 'Theories of Consumption in Media Studies', in Daniel Miller, ed., *Acknowledging Consumption: A Review of New Studies*, London, 1995, pp. 296–328; pp. 301–302.

31 Ibid., pp. 300–301. Morley is using Stuart Hall's 'encoding/decoding' model of communication.

32 John Fiske, 'The Popular Economy', in Storey, ed., *Cultural Theory*, pp. 504–521; pp. 505–506.

33 Ibid., p. 511.

34 John B. Thompson, *Ideology and Modern Culture: Critical Social Theory in the Era of Mass Communication*, London, 1990, pp. 303–313.

35 Ibid., p. 134.

36 There has been a growing interest among historians in recent years in the leisure habits of consumers in particular locations at particular times. The local case-studies in this book can thus be viewed alongside the work of, among others, Sue Harper, Julian Poole, John Sedgwick, Bert Hogenkamp, Stephen Ridgwell, Christopher Baggs and Jonathan Rose. For full references to these works see the Bibliography.

37 Stevenson and Cook, *Britain in the Depression*, pp. 67–68.

38 Ibid., pp. 156–157; Sean Glynn and John Oxborrow, *Interwar Britain: A Social and Economic Recovery*, London, 1976, p. 161.

39 For a history of the South Wales coalfields see Hywel Francis and David Smith, *The Fed: A History of the South Wales Miners in the Twentieth Century*, London, 1980.

40 Sidney Pollard, *The Development of the British Economy, 1914–1990*, fourth edition, London, 1992, p. 58.

41 H.W. Richardson, *Economic Recovery in Britain, 1932–9*, London, 1967, p. 284.

42 Colin Peter Walker, 'Municipal Enterprise: A Study of the Interwar Municipal Corporation of Portsmouth 1919–1939' (MA dissertation, University of Portsmouth, 2003), pp. 66–69.

43 Pollard, *Development of the British Economy*, p. 53; Derek H. Aldcroft, *The Inter-War Economy: Britain, 1919–1939*, London, 1970, p. 119.

44 Stevenson and Cook, *Britain in the Depression*, p. 279.

'The people's amusement': the growth in cinema-going and reading habits

Cinema-going was by far the most popular leisure activity in the 1930s. The most frequently used phrase regarding its popularity is taken from A.J.P. Taylor, who described cinema-going as 'the essential social habit of the age'.[1] Contemporary surveys attest to the cinema's immense popularity. In 1935, the *New Survey of London Life and Labour* declared that the cinema was 'easily the most important agency of popular entertainment,' describing it as 'the people's amusement'.[2] Simon Rowson's figures from the previous year lend weight to this claim. Rowson estimated that in 1934 the country's consumers made 963 million visits to the cinema and calculated that there was an average weekly attendance of eighteen and a half million cinema-goers to the halls across the country.[3] Sidney Bernstein's questionnaires, conducted in 1932, 1934 and 1937, also revealed that nearly fifty per cent of film-goers visited the cinema twice weekly; some made as many as seven visits a week.[4] Going to the cinema had thus become a mass leisure activity which attracted all social classes.

Of course, historians have long utilised these statistics to illustrate the all-pervading nature of the cinema-going habit during these years. We should not, though, use such quantitative material to make broad generalisations regarding society's consumption patterns in 1930s Britain. Recent historical research has raised questions over the ability of some members of society to participate in this form of mass commercial leisure. Andrew Davies has argued that access to the cinema could be 'structured by class, income, gender and age'.[5] Davies is right to raise these issues; a range of factors determined cinema-going patterns in the period. Indeed, one of J.P. Mayer's respondents recalled that her father was often unemployed and so could not afford to go to the cinema regularly.[6] To better understand the meaning of going to the cinema for consumers in the 1930s, then, we need to cast the net more widely. This chapter, therefore, provides a broad survey of the growth of the cinema-going

habit in the period, outlines the various reasons behind it, and assesses how different consumer groups could be attracted to this relatively new leisure form. Of course, as this book is a study of working-class taste, the appeal of the cinema to this social group will be the principal focus. We have established that cinema-going was the most popular leisure pursuit in the period; we now need ascertain why. Why did it take precedence over other leisure pursuits? What were the 'push' and 'pull' factors? What was it about the cinema-going experience that appealed to so many?

One transformation to the cinema-going experience which helped to attract consumers during this period was the conversion and enlargement of many small cinemas into new 'picture palaces'. In fact, while the number of cinemas had risen only slightly since the boom building period of the early 1920s, there were a greater number of these larger cinemas owned by the three large chains – Associated British Cinemas, Gaumont-British, and The Odeon; seating capacity thus rose significantly.[7] These lavish, plush and palatial buildings offered the film fan an entirely new type of cinema-going experience. Cinema's popularity cannot be attributed to this transformation alone, however. For while the number of 'picture palaces' certainly increased, many smaller cinemas remained. Rowson calculated that more than seventy per cent of the existing cinemas had fewer than one thousand seats, and more than fifty-two per cent of the total seating capacity could be found in these types of hall.[8] Therefore, while the growth of the 'picture palace' offered consumers more choice, other factors accounted for the cinema's growing popularity, especially among working-class consumers, who were less likely to visit this type of hall on a regular basis.

One important factor was the cost; cinema-going was a relatively inexpensive leisure activity. According to Rowson's survey, forty-three per cent of the entire cinema admissions in 1934 were for seats costing no more than 6d, and thirty-seven per cent for seats costing no more than 10d.[9] In the same year, one *Film Weekly* letter-writer claimed that cinema-going was 'an entertainment which is within reach of all. Even the man with only a few coppers in his pocket can have two or three hours' enjoyment and forget his worries for a time'.[10] Therefore, while the cinema attracted consumers with a range of incomes, the majority of cinema-goers were purchasing seats in either the smaller, and thus cheaper halls, or the lower-priced areas of the larger cinemas. While the cinema attracted all classes of citizen, then, it was the lower-middle and working classes who attended most often, and of these it was the latter who dominated in the smaller halls.

In fact, the social and demographic changes occasioned by the First World War had helped to create a new class of consumer, and it was from within the working classes where these 'new consumers' were principally drawn. Moreover, it was women, especially working-class women, who were regarded to be the main beneficiaries of these changes to society's consumption patterns.[11] Consequently, women were heavily targeted by those working in the film trade. For example, *The Thirty-Nine Steps* (1935) was marketed as a love story to attract female cinema-goers. The Gaumont-British film, adapted from John Buchan's novel, was a spy mystery which had an obvious appeal to the male cinema-goer, but it was given a feminine angle by the use of publicity material featuring the film's stars in affectionate embraces accompanied by slogans highlighting the couple's tempestuous relationship.[12] Unsurprisingly, the *New Survey of London* claimed that the films being produced had 'a real appeal to women'.[13] It is no coincidence that the survey also reported that girls and women accounted for seventy per cent of weekly cinema admissions.[14] Other contemporaries confirmed this gender disparity in cinema attendance. Frank Reynolds, art editor of *Punch* magazine, noted in his book on local cinema-going habits that women predominated in the five cinemas in the market town close to his village home.[15] Likewise, in an interview with a Mass-Observer, Sydney Cole, the manager of the Classic Cinema in Tooting, remarked, 'our business is kept by women'.[16]

This does not mean that men were not also attracted to the cinema. For many unmarried working-class men (and, of course, women) the cinema was an ideal place to take or encounter members of the opposite sex.[17] Many married men also accompanied their wives to the cinema. In a recollection of his life growing up in Salford, Robert Roberts commented on the emergence of this trend: 'Many women who had lived a kind of purdah since marriage (few respectable wives visited public houses) were to be noted now, escorted by their husbands to the "pictures"'.[18] On the whole, though, women were the cinema's most frequent patrons. Robert Roberts's comments on pub-going partly reveal why this was the case. 'Respectability' was a key determinant in attracting women to the cinema. Many working-class leisure pursuits, such as pub-going, were still something of a taboo for working-class women. The cinema was one of the first leisure activities deemed respectable enough for women to attend. It was partly because of its acceptance as a respectable pastime, therefore, that women, whether with their husbands, friends or alone, became the most frequent visitors to the cinema. The development of the matinée performance offers another reason for the cinema's growing popularity among women. Offering cheaper prices and greater flexibility, the matinée performance opened up a new leisure opportunity for women and became an additional factor in aiding the growth of the cinema-going habit among female consumers. Unsurprisingly, the *New Survey of London* reported that it was 'no uncommon sight to see women slipping into the cinema for an hour, after they have finished their shopping and before the children come home from school'.[19]

A number of other factors encouraged the growth of the cinema-going habit among working-class men and women. Pleasure, comfort and warmth are themes that regularly feature in contemporary records as enticements for both sexes. Three female respondents to Mass-Observation's 1938 questionnaire on the cinema commented on their cinema-going experiences thus:

Warm, cosy and happy.[20]

Pictures are a cheap as well as most entertaining occupation ... I can go and enjoy myself ... without feeling I am spending more than I can afford.[21]

The comfort and warmth of the Odeon is an aid to enjoying the film.[22]

In a similar vein, Frank Reynolds remarked that the cinemas in his locale 'flourish, being well patronised by an unsophisticated throng, who, after a tiring day, seek the sanctuary of the Picture Palace, which provides at least a place in which to sit down,' and 'has the great advantage of being warm in winter and cool in summer'.[23] George Orwell observed that unemployed men would visit the cinema for warmth and comfort. 'In Wigan a favourite refuge was the pictures, which are fantastically cheap there,' Orwell noted, adding: 'Even people on the verge of starvation will readily pay twopence to get out of the ghastly cold of a winter afternoon'.[24] William Woodruff has written about the cinema in an analogous manner and, recalling his poverty-stricken child-hood in Depression-era Blackburn, reminisces thus: 'Local cinemas advertised warmth not film. For threepence you could keep warm, be entertained, and forget the bleak world outside'.[25] In fact, Woodruff describes how he gained entrance to the cinema by handing the attendant 'two empty, clean two-pound jam jars'; this was hardly a prohibitive entrance fee, even for a child from an impoverished working-class family.[26] These remarks, then, establish cinema-going as a valued source of entertainment for the working classes, one which combined warmth, comfort, pleasure and low cost.

As the most popular leisure activity among the working classes, cinema-going inevitably played a major cultural role in their lives. Robert Roberts fondly remembers the cinema's cultural attractions for that social group. The cinema was 'the brightest lure of all,' Roberts contends; it 'burst like a vision into the underman's existence and … became both his chief source of enjoyment and one of the greatest factors in his cultural development'.[27] Mass-Observers wrote of the cinema's social and cultural importance in like manner. John Martin Jones, observing cinema-going habits in Bolton, found that the cinema had 'a profound effect on the everyday life of all social classes. It has affected their education, fashions, morality, leisure and their social attitudes'.[28] The *New Survey of London*, meanwhile, reported on the cinema's influence over the consumer's cultural life: 'At the time of writing, girls in all classes of society wear "Garbo" coats and wave their hair *à la* Norma Shearer or Lilian Harvey. It is impossible to measure the effect the films must have on the outlook and habits of the people'.[29]

It is noteworthy that these contemporaries allude principally to the social and cultural effects of the *films* being shown, not the environment in which they were exhibited. For, of course, the major factor determining the cinema-going habit was the exhibition of the films themselves. In fact, S.G. Rayment, editor of the film trade's key journal *Kinematograph Weekly*, argued that the comforts or appearance of a cinema were of no consequence; it was the films being shown that attracted the cinema-goer.[30] Those closer to the consumer argued likewise. '[Working-class patrons] are not concerned about the big kinemas or the luxury theatre,' wrote cinema manager E.B. Day, who ran the Vernon Picture House in Nottingham, adding: 'All they require is good entertainment, and so long as their favourite picture house is clean and comfortable, massive fronts and artistic interiors have little or no interest to them'.[31] These assertions are supported by Richard Carr's observation in 1937 that the 'shifting of audiences from cinema to cinema corresponds strikingly to the merits of the film showing'.[32] Therefore, while other factors lay behind the growth of the cinema-going habit, it was primarily the films that brought in the crowds. Going to the cinema was, as Annette Kuhn has rightly noted, more than a purely visual experience, but it was centred upon a visual experience nonetheless.[33] Ultimately, then, what was on the screen determined consumption.

Regardless of what attracted working-class consumers to the cinema in the first place, it was *both* aspects of the cinema-going experience – the films and the environment – that satisfied their social and cultural needs. Indeed, for many working-class consumers the practice of 'going to the pictures' brought a sense of camaraderie and belonging that may have otherwise been denied them.[34] Significantly, these aspects of the cinema-going experience acted as cultural signifiers for the working classes (and, indeed, any social group). What films cinema-goers went to see, and where they went to see them, was determined by, and helped to further determine, their social and cultural identity.

The class-specific nature of the cinema-going experience did not go unnoticed by contemporary observers. In 1937, a survey in *World Film News* divided the cinema audience into three 'taste' categories: working-class, mixed 'family' and middle-class.[35] *Kinematograph Weekly* regularly graded both the cinema audience and the type of films they consumed. Subsequent accounts have confirmed this compositional divide. Robert Roberts thus recalls that 'caste and culture forbade mixing' in the cinemas in his locale.[36] This is not to suggest that the different classes did not visit the same cinema; merely that they did not mix when they were there. Admittedly, it would have been unusual for middle-class patrons to frequent the smaller cinemas popular with the working classes (not only because of the halls' status, but because of the type of films being exhibited also), but the working classes did visit the larger, more palatial cinemas as and when they could afford it. Kuhn's research has shown that cinema-goers visited both luxurious cinemas and 'fleapits' depending on their cultural needs.[37] Working-class cinema-goers thus made conscious choices over which films to watch and what type of establishment to visit in which to consume them. Therefore, the various films on offer in any given location determined to a much greater extent the working classes' cinema-going habits. The working classes may have been seen by some contemporaries to be less cultured than other social groups, but they were just as discriminating in their tastes.

Indeed, while the film medium was undoubtedly popular with all classes in its infancy because of its novelty value, by the 1930s, with the advent of sound, it had become more sophisticated. Consequently, cinema-goers (and this includes *all* social groups) became more selective in their tastes. Film trade personnel certainly recognised this shift in the audience's cultural competences. 'Times have changed,' warned Portsmouth cinema manager Patrick Reed in 1939. 'The generation of to-day … has learned to take for granted the miracles of the past decade'.[38] Reed advised fellow managers not to 'sit back and take things easily,' and instructed them to: 'Go out and Fetch the Public into your Theatre'.[39] At the time of making these comments Reed was manager of the Odeon, a cinema serving a largely lower middle-class clientele, but between 1933 and 1936 he was an assistant, then manager, at the Commodore cinema in a less affluent area of the town.[40] Reed was thus highly aware of the tastes of lower-middle and working-class cinema-goers, and would have understood that many film fans were not always that discriminatory regarding the class of cinema they visited; they simply chose to visit whatever cinema was showing the film they wanted to see. Like so many people working in the film trade, then, Reed was acutely aware of the vagaries of consumer taste. More importantly, he also identified the need to use distinctive methods to attract cinema-goers to a particular film.

Being closer to the consumer than other contemporaries, cinema managers were adept at understanding their customers' wants. Indeed, one 'independent small-owner manager' explicitly pointed out in *Kinematograph Weekly* that it was people like himself who knew the tastes of the consumer better than any other:

> I consider I am closer to the public - my public - than any other people who are so much more articulate. Renters, producers, and the big chiefs of the circuits only know public likes and dislikes through the reports made and results attained by men in my position ... I should not be exaggerating if I said that the booker of films was always in advance of his public in matters of taste.[41]

Not surprisingly, *Kinematograph Weekly* kept abreast of the activities of the country's cinema managers. In fact, so keen was the editor of the trade paper to explore this aspect of the film trade that a regular feature detailed the techniques local managers employed when advertising a film. Portsmouth's Patrick Reed, who displayed considerable flair for film promotion, appeared regularly.[42] Naturally, most managers targeted as wide an audience as possible. Reed used a range of advertising techniques to attract film fans to the cinemas he managed; these incorporated tie-ins with local shops and businesses, handing out flyers to supporters at the local football stadium and workers at the town's dockyard and council offices, and posting handbills through the letterboxes of houses in the cinemas' vicinity. Nonetheless, it is possible to identify certain practices that reveal the class of cinema-goer being pursued. One Manchester cinema manager was clearly targeting working-class cinema-goers when, to promote the comedy *Hobson's Choice* (1931), he organised a competition for 'the best clog-dancer in several districts'; the winner opened the show.[43] Reed was similarly pursuing a specific class of clientele when, to promote the Hollywood romance *Beloved Enemy* (1936), he arranged for local restaurants to overprint menu cards with the words: 'After your meal here, you will enjoy Merle Oberon in 'Beloved Enemy' at the Odeon'.[44] Compare that to the promotion of British army reunion drama *Men of Yesterday* (1936), for which Reed arranged to have handbills delivered to ex-Servicemen's clubs, the naval barracks, the dockyard, Portsmouth football ground and from house to house.[45] It would be hard not to conclude that, for *Beloved Enemy*, Reed was trying to attract the middle and lower middle-class patron; while for *Men of Yesterday* a lower class of clientele was being pursued.

Similar practices of audience differentiation are evident in many of the film industry's advertising campaigns. Trade personnel showed a keen interest in the cinema audience's tastes, and had a clear idea of what type of film should appeal to sections of the cinema-going public. Film-producer Michael Balcon, for example, identified the value of film promotion and displayed an awareness of publicity matters.[46] How a particular film should be advertised was thus of major importance. How, then, did film-makers account for variances in audience taste? What methods were deployed when targeting the different classes?

To answer these questions we can turn to the myriad forms of publicity material available; they are an invaluable aid to understanding the methods used to attract consumers to particular films.[47] It is productive to examine material for films produced for various groups of cinema-goer. So, films have been divided into three categories – the highbrow, the popular, and the lowbrow.[48]

Pygmalion (1938) and *The Mikado* (1939) were both highbrow films with significant cultural status. Such was their cultural standing among the Establishment that they were selected by the British Council as 'specimen' films to exhibit abroad. Not surprisingly, the films' promoters advised exhibitors to take advantage of their cultural status to attract 'all people of intelligence and with appreciation of finer things'.[49] Posters advertising *Pygmalion* thus drew on Shaw's cultural capital; stills from the film were accompanied by sketches of the author. Posters for *The Mikado* similarly exploited the film's authorial status. A suggested display line ran thus: 'Sullivan's Music! Gilbert's Lyrics! Allied to that sheer splendour of spectacle that the screen alone can give.' *The Mikado* was also promoted as an art-form with a deep-rooted cultural reputation: 'First time in picture! The melodies you've loved all your life,' a poster exclaimed. Promoters for both films were thus playing on the cultural competences of the highbrow consumer in an attempt to attract them to the cinema.

However, film promoters were also aware of the need to attract as large an audience as possible if their films were to make a real commercial impact. Therefore, they suggested ways in which exhibitors could use their promotional material to attract 'the masses and the classes'. It was thus suggested that images of Leslie Howard, *Pygmalion*'s male lead, be employed to 'attract the average movie-goer'. *The Mikado*, meanwhile, was to be sold 'as an EVENT!' which was 'as new and different as "Snow White" ... the type of picture that comes but once or twice a year … and is enjoyed by audiences of *every type, every class, every age*'. To give *Pygmalion* a 'sure-fire appeal to the masses,' promoters recommended that exhibitors utilise its 'Cinderella motif'. Posters and theatre display-boards thus featured 'before and after' pictures along with catchlines such as 'Any girl can do it. You need a man and a trunkful of clothes'. The universal nature of *Pygmalion*'s subject-matter was also exploited to broaden its appeal. Suggested catchlines for the film ran thus:

> He was a professor of phonetics – she was a pupil of love.
>
> He gave her lessons in deportment – she gave him lessons in love.
>
> He made a lady out of her – she made a fool out of him.

Managers of cinemas serving the lower classes were offered this additional advice:

> [I]f Shaw's name is too 'arty' for your clientele, but you'd like to use his quota-tions, simply letter them alongside of scenes with Leslie Howard, Wendy Hiller and general production shots. The quotations will get many a smile and chuckle from the average movie-goer. They speak his own language.

One suggested line ran: 'The whole world is strewn with snares, traps, gins and pitfalls for the capture of men by women'. In such ways did promoters of highbrow fare attempt to lure the various groups of cinema-goer to see their films. The films' artistic and intellectual qualities were utilised to charm the 'classes', while strong visuals, humour and snappy, clear-cut messages about the films' subject-matter were used to bring in the 'masses'.

Films that promoters believed would be popular with the bulk of the cinema-going public needed no such distinctions in advertising practices. In fact, some, such as the Astaire-Rogers musicals *Swing Time* (1936) and *Top Hat* (1935), were considered to be highly popular 'star vehicles' needing limited 'push'. Nevertheless, even when a film was identified as a sure-fire success, promoters recognised the value of advertising in strengthening its appeal. The publicity material for *Swing Time* points out that while 'nothing succeeds like success … additional advertising and exploitation will reward you in your biggest money-spinner to date'. *Swing Time*'s promoters, then, while relying on cultural identification to bring in regular patrons, used advertising techniques to attract the occasional cinema-goer.

Predictably, bearing in mind the popularity of the films' stars, posters for *Swing Time* and *Top Hat* were dominated by images of Astaire and Rogers; the films' titles played second fiddle to the names of their stars. This is not to suggest that it was the stars alone that attracted the cinema-goer; far from it, in fact. For it was what Astaire and Rogers *represented* that was expected to draw in the crowds. Advertising posters may have been dominated by the duo's names and images, but it was their actions that were more important. They were dancing; they were having *fun*. Whether the images were sketchy caricatures of Astaire and Rogers on a poster, or a still from the film on a theatre display-board, the films' stars were always depicted in the same manner – smiling broadly and in motion. It was thus made clear what the films were about; the prospective audience were expected to know what they would be consuming; they were not expected to get it wrong. *Top Hat* and *Swing Time*, then, were about *pleasure*. It was the pleasure of watching Astaire and Rogers perform, and the joyful and comforting *experience* of going to watch one of their films that was being sold to the consumer. The films' tag lines promised to deliver this. 'Let yourself in for a wonderful time,' assured one poster for *Swing Time*; 'Get excited! Here they come!' and 'Come on over! America's favorite [sic] dancing stars are here in their gay, glad, glorious show! They're doing the "Piccolino",' declared posters for *Top Hat*. These popular films, then, while maybe not attracting the highbrow cinema-goer, were expected to have a very broad appeal, and it was an appeal that was centred upon the audience's awareness of the style of film on offer.

In fact, the *style* of these films was paramount to their success. This was clearly represented in the films' marketing strategies. Promoters were not only selling a film, they were selling a lifestyle, and it was a cultured, leisured lifestyle at that; one that was awash with elegance and sophistication. Consider some of the tie-ins associated with *Swing Time*. They included endorsing a wide range of consumer goods: shoes ('Swing Time Sandals'), drink ('Swing Time Cocktails'), beauty products (Max Factor cosmetics), music (Selfridges' musical department), food (ice-cream), clothing (evening dresses), and even quality furniture. Therefore, while the films' promoters were trying to gain a mass audience with the promise of pleasure, they were also trying to sell the films as quality entertainment that would appeal to the more cultured consumer. The type of merchandise being promoted, moreover, reveals that the audience for these films was expected to be comprised primarily of women who were, if not middle-class by origin, middlebrow in terms of attainment and taste.

Promoters of lowbrow features displayed no such pretensions regarding the type of consumer they expected to enjoy their films. Therefore, while *The Hawk* (1932) and *Way Out West* (1930) were similarly promoted as pleasurable features, they were certainly not offered as quality entertainment. Once more, advertising posters promoted the films' stars (Bill Haines for *Way Out West*; John Wayne for *The Hawk*); again, watching the films was sold as an experience. But it was an entirely different class of star and a completely different type of experience that were being promoted. Haines and Wayne were not portrayed as elegant, but unrefined; the viewing experience was not to be sophisticated, it was rough and ready. The style of language used in the films' tag lines and the aesthetic quality of the films' poster artwork made this quite clear. Observe some of the numerous suggested tag lines for Western comedy *Way Out West*:

Bold, Bad Bill Haines Goes 'Western' in a Riotous Rodeo of Roars, Romance and Red-blooded Action!

Where the fun begins - where laughs are laughs - where gals, guns and gags give bold, bad Bill Haines just the kind of picture his fans are yelling for.

William Haines out West, where men are men and cows are contented.

A rip-snorting comedy of the modern West.

Consider also one of *The Hawk*'s promotional slogans: 'filled with hard, rough riding and hairbreadth escapes'. Building on these linguistic impressions, posters for both films featured roughly-drawn images of the films' stars sitting atop a bucking bronco. The films' promotional material thus promised features with tempo, plenty of rough action, and, in the case of *Way Out West*, lots of humour. It was a particular type of entertainment for a particular type of cinema-goer. The films, and indeed their promotional material, were hardly likely to appeal to an audience with highbrow or middlebrow pretensions. They were, however, perfectly pitched to appeal to lowbrow cinema-goers who were expected to appreciate this type of film fare.

Of course, westerns were predominantly favoured by male cinema-goers. Promoters for *Way Out West* thus drew on the genre's cultural attraction to men and boys by using 'celebrated names' in the genre's history (Diamond Dick, Billy the Kid, Jesse James) 'to create teaser interest' among them. Nonetheless, promoters for both films were keen to attract a wider audience. Consequently, publicity material stressed that these films could also appeal to the female consumer. For example, cinema managers were informed that *The Hawk* could be 'aimed at the hearts of the women, for the plot carries a glowing romance'. *Way Out West*'s tag lines similarly guaranteed feminine appeal. 'He couldn't ride, shoot or rope – but when it came to the cowboys' gals he was a genuine "bad man",' asserted one; 'Whoopee Bill introduces sex appeal,' oozed another. Consumer tie-ins, which, predictably, were far more modest than those presented in the Astaire-Rogers campaigns, were also aimed at women. On one theatre display-board *Way Out West*'s female lead Leila Hyams offered 'tips on how to keep that schoolgirl figure'; and while there were no 'Max Factor' connections, one beauty product tie-in offered this salutary advice: 'Care of teeth important to women who keep youthful looks'. *Way Out West*'s promoters were also clearly aware that many of the film's patrons would be mothers accompanying their children to matinée performances; knowingly, they incorporated children's 'puzzles' promotions in their publicity material and advised cinema managers to place them in their foyers to 'help your matinée showings'.

In such ways, then, film distributors tried to tempt different classes (and sexes) of cinema-goer to the country's theatres to consume their products. While they, and indeed cinema managers, may have welcomed as wide an audience as possible, from the style and quality of materials used in their advertising campaigns, specific groups of cinema-goer were clearly being targeted. Class and gender distinctions were crucial in determining these patterns of advertising. However, film distributors and cinema managers were aware that the lower classes made up the bulk of the cinema-going public and targeted their products according to this social group's preferences. The wide-ranging nature of *Pygmalion*'s publicity material makes it abundantly clear that the film's promoters were hoping to convince this section of the cinema-going public that, despite the film's highbrow character, it was a feature they could enjoy.

Of course, film trade personnel right across the employment scale were keen to ensure that their films appealed to a wide audience-base. Film-producer Herbert Wilcox revealed in 1936 that when making a film he always 'set out to achieve two things – popular entertainment and star value ... for every class of exhibitor'.[50] Michael Balcon likewise acknowledged that the producer's 'judge is ultimately the man in the street. If the work he has been at such pains to accomplish does not please the public he will have failed'.[51] Whatever position they held in the film industry, then, trade personnel knew that they had to appeal to the mass of the cinema-going public if they were to be entirely successful (and thus financially secure). Predictably, many cultural critics bemoaned this situation. In 1932, leading theatre critic Hubert Griffith scathingly protested that 'the taste of the least educated [has] imposed itself on the taste of the most educated'.[52] Needless to say, Griffith's position is highly consistent with that of the aforementioned *Scrutiny* set. Regardless of the protestations of such cultural critics, film-makers continued to produce films that they hoped would be popular with the mass of the cinema-going public. This is not surprising; there was an economic necessity to do so. Cinema managers were similarly motivated; regardless of the type of theatre they managed, a packed house was a profitable one. Fiscal demands thus ensured that film trade personnel became highly responsive to the working-class consumer's demands. With such an acute awareness of that social group's tastes within the film trade, it is no surprise that going to the cinema became the most popular leisure activity among the working classes in the period.

For many working-class consumers, then, the cinema offered a new and exciting leisure experience. It was inexpensive, inviting and, most importantly, pleasurable. No wonder it became an integral part of that social group's cultural activities. However, there were a range of leisure activities on offer in the period; going to the cinema was just one of them. To better understand the social and cultural tasks cinema-going performed, we need to be aware of the various roles performed by other leisure pursuits and differentiate between them. That is why I have chosen to focus on two contrasting leisure activities: cinema-going and reading. What functions could reading perform that going to the cinema could not? Both offered contrasting experiences. Cinema-going was a communal activity, reading was a primarily solitary pastime; the cinema offered a visual and sound experience, reading offered a literary one. Nonetheless, there were many similarities in the production and consumption of these leisure forms. Fiction products dominated in both media; similar genres were popular with working-class consumers (although there were clear regional differences in taste). There was, then, more than a casual overlap between the cultural experiences both leisure activities offered.

Unsurprisingly, film and publishing trade personnel recognised the close links between the two industries; many attempted to consolidate them. In *The Publishers' Circular* in 1935, for example, Bryce MacNab called for 'Closer Co-operation Between Publishers and Film Producers'; he believed that a relationship between the two industries was 'increasingly important' because each was 'dependent upon the other for some of the most vital cogs in its machinery'.[53] Film-makers were, of course, drawing inspiration for their products from some of the publishing industry's most popular novels. Indeed, MacNab noted that out of a list of sixty-five best-selling novels, forty-six had been made into films.[54] The benefits for both industries were obvious. Film-makers, as MacNab perceptively noted, viewed popular novels as 'film material for which there is a ready-made audience'.[55] The publishing industry, meanwhile, expected there to be an increased interest in the novels that had been filmed.[56]

To no great surprise, personnel from each industry quickly exploited the opportunities the relationship presented. Film promoters regularly drew attention to the reputation of their films' authors. The example of Shaw's *Pygmalion* has already been given, but authors of lowbrow fare were similarly exploited. Edgar Wallace's popularity among the working classes was often used for film promotion, for example.[57] Public librarians were equally opportunistic. In 1931, Coventry's public libraries stocked bookmarks promoting *With Byrd at the South Pole* along with lists of books relative to the subject of Antarctic exploration.[58] Similarly, on the release of *Bulldog Drummond at Bay* (1937) the city's public libraries arranged special displays of H.C. "Sapper" McNeile's novels.[59] Film and book promoters also sought to exploit the advertising possibilities each medium offered. In *The Publishers' Circular* in 1930, B.H. Clough recommended using cinemas to advertise forthcoming books. 'Slogans, snappy, and carefully chosen, would make their appeal,' Clough wrote, adding (rather condescendingly), 'such ... would be the means of raising the uninterested and possibly lethargic public to the value and necessity of the great world of books'.[60] Popular magazines, meanwhile, frequently featured articles on the latest film releases and the cinema's most popular stars; some magazines, such as *Film Weekly*, *Picturegoer* and *Picture Show*, as their names suggest, focused exclusively on the film medium. A close alliance thus existed between the two trades during this period. Rather than compete with each other, many film and publishing trade personnel sought to bolster their products through cleverly considered marketing campaigns.

Significantly, members of each trade anticipated that consumers enjoying one leisure activity would take pleasure in the other. In 1934, *Kinematograph Weekly*'s editor declared that '*the reading public is the kinema-going public*'.[61] The manager of the Classic Cinema in Tooting concurred, telling a Mass-Observer that 'good readers make good cinema patrons'.[62] Publishing trade personnel were rather aloof regarding the cinema as a means of entertainment. Nonetheless, many were willing to co-operate with the film industry because they recognised the benefits to be gained from doing so. Of course, working-class consumers simply chose whatever activity answered their particular socio-economic and cultural needs. The two leisure products, then, while sharing many similarities, were chosen by consumers to perform specific social and cultural tasks. What role did reading play in the lives of working-class consumers? Of course, reading was not a new working-class leisure activity – it had much deeper cultural roots than the cinema – but during the 1930s it became far more popular with that social group. Indeed, by 1941, social observer Seebohm B. Rowntree could claim that: 'Among indoor activities reading figures far more prominently than it did at the beginning of the century'.[63]

The inter-war years witnessed a notable growth in the provision of reading material for the working classes, both in book and magazine form. The social and demographic changes that helped to create a market for the cinema also helped to generate a new market for popular fiction. Once more, it was the working classes, and principally working-class women, who were identified as the new consumers of popular fiction; they were thus targeted by both publishers and advertisers alike.[64] In fact, publishers were, as A.C. Hannay rightly noted, quick 'to adapt themselves to the needs of the day', producing fiction 'to meet a real and definite demand'.[65] There was a significant increase in the publication of books and magazines aimed specifically at a working-class readership. Low-priced editions of novels by authors known to be popular with working-class readers – Ethel M. Dell, Jeffery Farnol, Edgar Wallace – were made more readily available, while a number of new 'twopenny' magazines were introduced, such as *Red Star Weekly*, *Secrets*, and *Lucky Star*, that sought to attract the (female) working-class consumer.[66] Surveys in two contemporary publishing journals, *The Publishers' Circular* and *The Bookseller*, attest to this increase.[67] The working classes were thus offered a much wider range of reading material than had hitherto been the case.

It was during this period, moreover, when a transformation in the publishing industry's working practices altered considerably the nature of popular fiction. In an attempt to attract a wider reading public, authors were encouraged to write novels that could be read without the need for long, protracted reading spells, and to write fiction that could become part of a profitable series.[68] As one writer for Mass-Observation noted, 'a new kind of writing is called for, a way of writing that can be rapidly and easily absorbed and in which interest is maintained wherever you pick it up'.[69] Novels thus became shorter in length, while magazine stories were frequently serialised. D.C. Thomson's *Red Star Weekly*, for example, regularly contained stories which ran for many months, and was promoted by its editor as a magazine that had become 'famous for its long complete novelettes'.[70]

Publishers, like film trade personnel, also began to use modern, aggressive marketing techniques to advertise their wares. As one contemporary noted, the publisher 'now elaborately prepares the ground for any new book, plans a campaign for it, advertises much more largely, and vies with his competitors in the use of every legitimate means of publicity'.[71] This publicity took many forms. As mentioned, promotional material was displayed on cinema screens, but posters were also placed in cinema foyers and on public transport; newspapers and magazines, meanwhile, frequently carried bold and enticing features advertising the latest book releases.[72] *Red Star Weekly*, for example, regularly contained a section promoting novels that its readers were 'sure to enjoy'.[73] Publishers also used self-promotional techniques to publicise alternative magazines available from their publishing group. D.C. Thomson's magazines frequently carried advertisements for the firm's 'companion papers'. A typical edition of *Red Star Weekly* would contain features on magazines such as *Red Letter*, *Topical Times*, *Weekly Welcome*, and *Woman's Way*. At times, all the firm's 'women's' magazines would be featured in a single advertisement, thus targeting only one social group.[74] At others, a wider social demographic was targeted. One back-page spread in *Red Star Weekly* thus advertised its companion paper *Topical Times* as follows: 'An eight page summary of all the cup ties, written by experts who will size up every game in the big opening round. Also a real glossy photo of Bolton Wanderers'.[75] The male working-class reader was clearly being targeted here. Interestingly, while the latter paper's promoters would have known that *Red Star Weekly* was unlikely to have been read by the male consumer, they were obviously confident that, by placing the advert on the back page, it would have been highly visible to that social group as the paper was being read.

It was not content alone, but attention to aesthetic detail which became paramount in the marketing of any book or magazine. How these products were packaged featured prominently in the publishers' crusade to advertise them. According to G. Wren Howard, treasurer of the Publishers' Association and joint managing director of Jonathan Cape, publishers expended 'very considerable sums of money' on the presentation of their books in an attempt to draw the attention of the book-shop customer. Howard claimed that the novels' 'attractively designed' jackets served 'as enticing miniature posters'.[76] W.G. Taylor, president of the Publishers' Association and managing director of J.M. Dent and Sons, similarly noted that illustrated jackets on novels were 'part of the publisher's effort to attract attention to the book inside it'.[77] In 1935, S.L. Dennis confirmed this trend, writing in *The Publishers' Circular*: 'A book-jacket nowadays needs to be at once arresting, informative, decorative and protective. The order is significant ... The workaday overall has become an alluring kimono'.[78] Ronald F. Batty, the owner of a twopenny library, also confirmed the value of such attention to aesthetic detail when he stated that 'brightly coloured picture jackets are so valuable as an advertisement'.[79]

Publishers were thus using a variety of means to ensure they attracted a wider readership for their products. Books and magazines were being marketed like any other consumer product. Indeed, as early as 1930 a leading article in *The Publishers' Circular* had declared that:

> Books are a commodity ... there seems to be no valid reason why books should not be considered in the same way as any other article produced with the very definite object of attracting the notice of the public and with the ultimate aim of effecting sales.[80]

Predictably, not all those working in the publishing industry were appreciative of this trend towards commercialisation. Author Frank Swinnerton complained: 'I think what is the matter with our literature at the present time is excessive concern with either publicity or aesthetics'.[81] To no great surprise, more conservative cultural critics were equally dismissive of it. Q.D. Leavis argued that: 'The effect of the increasing control of Big Business ... is to destroy among the masses a desire to read anything which by the widest stretch could be included in the classification "literature"'.[82] Nevertheless, despite these theoretical objections, the mass-marketing of books and magazines continued. The provision of popular fiction had truly become an extensive commercial venture.

In addition, popular fiction became more accessible to the working-class consumer. The number of public libraries rose, the 'open access' system expanded, and the amount of books issued from the public libraries reached unprecedented levels.[83] As public library official Frederick J. Cowles wrote in 1932: 'All over the country we find a phenomenal increase in the use being made of public libraries'.[84] In fact, the number of people using public libraries grew year on year during the inter-war period, while the number of books issued increased dramatically – from 54.3 million in 1911 to a massive 247.3 million by 1939.[85] Public library usage had thus become widespread amongst the urban population. As Charles Nowell, chief librarian at Manchester Central Library, noted in 1935: 'Never before have the libraries of this country appealed to so many readers, never before has there been so comprehensive a selection of books placed at the disposal of all who care to use it'.[86]

We cannot attribute too much weight to these changes in public library provision with the growth of the working-class reading habit, however. Popular preconceptions of the public library among working-class consumers were often far from positive. William Woodruff remembered that his local public library possessed a harsh atmosphere ('the mousy librarian ... was usually hidden behind a glass partition. On the polished counter at which she sat stood a large unneeded "No Smoking" sign ... Other notices demanded "Silence"') and employed stern, unaccommodating staff ('The wise thing was to get a seat ... keep your head down, and ask for nothing').[87] Robert Roberts, meanwhile, captured perfectly the image of the public libraries which continued to dominate within working-class communities during our period:

> One branch library lay well beyond the confines of the village up two flights of stone steps. Its stock of about five hundred volumes - 'Fiction; Literature; Science; Art; Music' - stood bound in black beyond a broad high counter, save for a display in two glass 'turrets', one at each end of the bastion. Borrowers pointed through the window at the volume required.[88]

Admittedly, Roberts is recalling library usage before the 'open access' system was widely, if somewhat reluctantly, introduced. Nevertheless, these associations stuck firm, and the public library was invariably identified as an inaccessible 'castle', full of highbrow literature that was to be protected by 'turrets' and 'bastions'. Indeed, Mass-Observation's team of investigators observed that working-class men were particularly uneasy about using the public libraries because of their formalised protocol.[89]

It would be wrong to assume that the working classes shunned the public library completely. After all, public library usage *did* expand considerably during the 1930s, and it would be unwise to suggest that not one of these additional borrowers came from the working classes. Moreover, library authorities made various attempts to present the public library in a more popular light. In addition, a large number of popular novels appeared on public library accession lists during the period, which at least suggests they were responding to popular demand. It would be most surprising, therefore, if they had not achieved at least some success in attracting working-class readers. In fact, Mass-Observation's research points towards a growth in the appreciation of the public library within the working-class community, albeit a limited one. In an M-O door-to-door survey, conducted in a working-class area of Fulham in early 1940, one male respondent told Kathleen Box (a full-time investigator for M-O) that he considered public libraries to be 'better than the 2d ones', and criticised people who used twopenny libraries for thinking that 'they get better books by paying for them' because, he contended, 'you get better books at the public library'.[90] Similarly, when questioned about the quality of the public library service in Fulham, another male respondent replied that it was '[v]ery good', adding, '[t]he Central Library's exceptionally good'.[91]

So, *some* working-class readers were very happy with public library provision. But, on the whole, the public library's association with the 'mutual improvement' ethos of the nineteenth century, and the civic authorities' unwavering preference for highbrow literature (despite some concessions to consumer demand), ensured that many working-class readers remained sceptical regarding the services the public library could offer. For these consumers, it was the expansion of the commercial lending libraries that most encouraged their reading habits. Indeed, Robert Roberts has noted that while many working-class men exhibited a considerable aversion towards the idea of belonging to a public library, they were willing to obtain their reading material from either the local newsagent or the 'street barrow' libraries at the local market.[92] So popular was this type of establishment, in fact, that in 1933 W.J. Magenis claimed: 'The twopenny library is now to be found everywhere. Within the City of London there are over seventy'.[93] The secretary of the Commercial Libraries' Association, E.J. Olson, confirmed this trend in 1938 when he noted: 'In practically every town in England there is now a well run commercial library'.[94] Of course, the first commercial lending library had been introduced in the mid-nineteenth century (W.H. Smith opened its first book-stall in 1848), but it was only upon the introduction of a new generation of 'Pay-as-you-read', 'No Deposit', or 'tuppenny' lending libraries during the 1930s that working-class readers began to use them in any significant number.[95]

In fact, due to the success of the new generation of libraries in attracting working-class consumers, the established commercial lending libraries re-organised their own library departments by reducing lending charges and abolishing the deposit.[96] These shop-owners were clearly concerned about the strength of the competition from the new twopenny libraries; but they were also attempting to draw working-class readers to their own libraries. W.H. Smith, for example, alerted its newsagents of the need to be aware of the potential customer-base within the working-class community, or as one company official regarded them, 'the "Edgar Wallace type" of reader'.[97] A former manager of W.H. Smith's bookshop in Wolverhampton likewise discussed the economic gains to be made by attracting readers from lower social groups.[98] Despite these attempts, though, many working-class readers viewed the large commercial libraries with a certain uneasiness. As F.R. Richardson, chief librarian of the Boots' Booklovers Library, somewhat condescendingly noted, working-class readers 'would hesitate to enter one of the better-class bookshops or libraries because they would feel mentally and socially ill at ease in its unaccustomed atmosphere'.[99] While these remarks are rather unsavoury, they do reveal a truism: many working-class people chose to use twopenny libraries because they offered a comfortable, accommodating, and indeed, recognisable, environment in which to browse for reading material. Unlike cinema-going, then, where it mattered little which type of establishment was chosen to watch a film, the place where working-class consumers obtained their reading material mattered a great deal.

Because they were running commercial institutions, twopenny library managers and owners naturally paid close attention to the demands of the working-class consumer. The manageress of Ray Smith's Harlesden branch, for example, reported to a Mass-Observer that she chose for the library novels which were most in demand with her working-class customers; and these were the types of novel which 'one could put down and pick up without losing the thread of the story'.[100] Likewise, in his 1938 book *How to Run a Twopenny Library*, Ronald F. Batty advised potential book-shop owners to, '[e]stablish contact with customers, remember their particular likes and dislikes, [and] take a real interest in giving them personal attention on every possible occasion'.[101] As a businessman, Batty was keen to highlight the financial benefits of these small shop libraries. He believed that the addition of a lending library to a shop made sound commercial sense ('It is amazing the difference a shelf or two of brightly-coloured books can make to a shop').[102] However, he was also aware of the cultural role that reading played. 'Books mean comfort, leisure, ease,' Batty wrote, 'they call to mind the favourite chair, the favourite pipe and an hour before bedtime'.[103] Batty thus recognised that reading offered a welcome respite in many people's lives, and was conscious of the need to foster the right environment in which reading material could be obtained. Accordingly, he argued that the essential requirement of the book-shop owner was 'to make a stranger feel that your shop is a pleasant and friendly place'.[104] The fundamental ingredients for achieving this atmosphere were the library's appearance ('a very real help towards its success'), its range of books ('Every taste has to be catered for'), and the manner of its staff ('Whatever you do don't thrust your opinions down customers' throats').[105]

Batty was not alone in understanding that the twopenny library could act as an important hub of the community. Indeed, in her investigation of the reading habits of working-class girls in the mid-1940s, Pearl Jephcott identified these very attributes as helping to foster the twopenny libraries' appeal.[106] One question is particularly relevant; it ran thus: 'What is the appeal of these small "shop" libraries?', to which Jephcott's rejoinder was:

In the first place they are numerous and therefore more handy than the big library. They may also be open until 7 or 8 p.m. or at any of those convenient times the owner-served shop permits. They are in a homely setting and small enough not to present the alarming range of shelves that may well frighten off the unskilled reader. Dust-jackets are glued to the book covers and form a more brightly coloured clue to the contents than the sombre bindings used in many public libraries. Above all, the books are pre-selected to suit the tastes of the readers.[107]

In short, Jephcott found that twopenny libraries were advantageously situated, open at convenient hours, had a welcoming atmosphere, were attractively arranged, and encouraged and accommodated the avid and casual reader.

Mass-Observation's research uncovered similar benefits for working-class readers in the 1930s. One Mass-Observer noted that Ray Smith's Harlesden library was still open when the majority of working-class people finished work (and when public libraries were closed), and declared: 'It is here that the 2d library fulfils its function'.[108] The researcher described the library as a 'large double-fronted shop, painted scarlet, in busy working-class area; paper, book jackets in window ... Colourful book jackets are pinned to Board at entrance'.[109] When working-class readers were asked why they used twopenny libraries, some stated that they were not ratepayers, and thus could not use the public libraries.[110] Another believed her local twopenny library held 'a good selection for 2d a volume'.[111] Another declared that 'the books in the 2d library looked FRESHER' than their public library counterparts.[112] But the principal reason given by working-class respondents for using twopenny libraries was that they were 'much more of a social centre than any other type' of lending library.[113] In fact, as one Mass-Observer noted, while books were chosen relatively quickly (the average time taken was reported as five minutes), many working-class women spent a significant amount of time in conversation with both fellow library users and assistants.[114] Working-class men, too, often used their time in the local twopenny library for more than borrowing books. One, for example, asked (seemingly conscious of the Mass-Observer as a figure of authority): 'It's all right, is it? I sometimes have a bit of fun in there'.[115] Once again, then, we find that it was the twopenny libraries' accessibility (of both location and opening hours), their vivid appearance, and their pleasing ambience, that were the principal attractions for working-class readers.

So, twopenny libraries were much more than somewhere to borrow books; they were highly popular social centres as well. As such, they offered benefits that neither the public library, nor even the larger commercial lending libraries, could claim to offer completely. Working-class readers *did* use public libraries, but many preferred to borrow books from the more homely twopenny libraries. Indeed, Jephcott noted that while the girls she observed used public libraries as well as twopenny libraries, they regarded the former as 'merely a supplement, and an inferior one at that'.[116] The majority of those questioned in Mass-Observation's Fulham survey similarly preferred to borrow material from the twopenny library ('the library round the corner') rather than the public library.[117] It is also significant that the Fulham survey's questionnaire was structured so that if a respondent used a public library, no attempt was made to ascertain whether they used a twopenny library as well. The respondents' use of the twopenny libraries may have been even higher than M-O's findings suggest. Indeed, one male respondent actually informed Box that he had stopped using the public library 'since about Christmas' and had joined a twopenny library instead.[118] But this comment was merely an additional reply to Box's original question, and an unsolicited one at that.

One further point needs to be made. The majority of those questioned in the Fulham door-to-door survey said that they never used libraries, preferring to borrow books from friends and family members, or buying twopenny magazines from their local newsagent.[119] While this evidence must be treated with care (these respondents may have been trying to rid themselves of their door-step inquisitor), it does inform us that any analysis of the social role of the lending library provides only a partial picture of working-class reading habits. A fuller picture can be gained, however, by evaluating the *types* of literature that were consumed. Indeed, many of the respondents who told Box that they did not visit a library did express an opinion on what books or magazines, if any, they preferred to read.

These texts cannot be understood in a vacuum, however. They were born out of the society in which they were produced. They need to be understood in that context. Therefore, before I analyse the meaning of those texts found to be most popular with the working classes, I will provide an account of the determinants that influenced their production, starting with an assessment of the restrictions placed upon those working in the film and publishing trades by those with legislative power. Indeed, the popularity of the cinema and popular fiction caused a number of moral panics which were directly linked to the supposed negative impact on society these leisure forms had. Unsurprisingly, parts of the Establishment sought to influence the type of material being produced. However, these restrictions are only part of the story. Trade personnel had their own ideas about what constituted 'good' entertainment. Public taste was not only an issue that interested those in officialdom; trade personnel were also keen to understand it. Both attempted to improve it. The next chapter, then, assesses official attitudes towards both the cinema and popular fiction; Chapter 3 looks at trade attitudes towards them. Both chapters reveal contemporary attitudes towards working-class taste.

Notes

1 A.J.P. Taylor is cited in Jeffrey Richards, *The Age of the Dream Palace: Cinema and Society in Britain 1930–1939*, London, 1984, p. 11.

2 H.L. Llewellyn Smith, ed., *New Survey of London Life and Labour*, vol. 9, London, 1935, pp. 43 and 47.

3 Simon Rowson, 'A Statistical Survey of the Cinema Industry in Great Britain in 1934', *Journal of the Royal Statistical Society*, Vol. XCIX, Part 1, 1936, p. 115.

4 Bernstein's questionnaires are held at the British Film Institute Library, London.

5 Andrew Davies, *Leisure, Gender and Poverty. Working-Class Culture in Salford and Manchester: 1900–1939*, Milton Keynes, 1992, p. ix.

6 J.P. Mayer, *British Cinemas and their Audiences*, second edition, London, 1978, p. 105.

7 Rowson, 'Statistical Survey', p. 120; Llewellyn Smith, *New Survey of London*, pp. 44–45.

8 Rowson, 'Statistical Survey', p. 115.

9 'Discussion on Mr. Rowson's Paper', 1936, pp. 120–123. See also Simon Rowson, 'The Social and Political Aspects of Film', *British Kinematograph Society Paper*, 1939, p. 2.

10 *Film Weekly* (hereafter *FW*), 16 March 1934.

11 Peter Stead, *Film and the Working Class. The Feature Film in British and American Society*, London, 1989, p. 11.

12 The publicity material for this film is held at the British Film Institute.

13 Llewellyn Smith, *New Survey of London*, p. 44.

14 Ibid., p. 46.

15 Frank Reynolds, *Off to the Pictures*, London, 1937, p. 11.

16 Tom Harrisson Mass-Observation Archive, University of Sussex (hereafter M-OA): TC Cinema-Going Survey, 4/A, Interview with Sydney Cole, 22 November 1939.

17 William Woodruff, *Beyond Nab End*, London, 2003, pp. 26–27.

18 Robert Roberts, *The Classic Slum. Salford Life in the First Quarter of the Century*, Manchester, 1971, p. 175.

19 Llewellyn Smith, *New Survey of London*, p. 46.

20 These comments are published in Jeffrey Richards and Dorothy Sheridan, eds, *Mass-Observation at the Movies*, London, 1987. See Mary Ellen Stones, aged 74, p. 76.

21 Ibid., Margaret Ward, aged 19, p. 111.

22 Ibid., Mabel Melling, aged 25, p. 119.

23 Reynolds, *Off to the Pictures*, pp. 11 and 79.

24 Orwell, *Road to Wigan Pier*, p. 72.

25 William Woodruff, *The Road to Nab End: An Extraordinary Northern Childhood*, second edition, London, 2002, p. 387.

26 Ibid., p. 176

27 Roberts, *Classic Slum*, pp. 140–141.

28 Jones is quoted in Richards and Sheridan, eds, *Mass-Observation*, p. 21.

29 Llewellyn Smith, *New Survey of London*, p. 47.

30 *Kineweekly Year Book*, 1933, p. 12.

31 *Kinematograph Weekly* (hereafter *Kineweekly*), 9 January 1936.

32 *World Film News* (hereafter *WFN*), May 1937.

33 In fact, Kuhn argues that going to the cinema was 'less about particular films, or even films in general,' than about the *experiences* surrounding the activity. Annette Kuhn, 'Cinema-going in Britain in the 1930s. Report of a questionnaire survey', *Historical Journal of Film, Radio and Television*, 19:4, 1999, pp. 531–543; p. 539.

34 Kuhn, 'Cinema-going in Britain', pp. 535–536. See also Beaven, *Leisure, Citizenship and Working-Class Men*, pp. 208–213.

35 *WFN*, February 1937.

36 Roberts, *Classic Slum*, p. 140.

37 Kuhn, 'Cinema-going in Britain', p. 536.

38 *Kineweekly*, 12 January 1939.

39 Ibid.

40 Ibid., 29 October 1936.

41 Ibid., 25 July 1935.

42 Reed appeared twice in 1933 and 1934, once in 1935, twice in 1936, five times in 1937, six times in 1938 and three times in 1939. In 1938, he gained second place in a national 'showmanship' competition run by *Kineweekly*. See ibid., 13 October 1938.

43 Ibid., 3 December 1931.

44 Ibid., 8 April 1937.

45 Ibid., 18 February 1937.

46 Michael and Aileen Balcon Collection (hereafter MEB), housed in Special Collections at the British Film Institute Library. See file D/26, 1 May 1936.

47 All references to a film's publicity material have been taken from press books held at the British Film Institute. This is American promotional material, but Britain's trade personnel were expected to use it to promote films in Britain.

48 See *Kineweekly* in which films (and, indeed, cinema-goers) are routinely divided into the categories of 'highbrow', 'popular' and 'lowbrow'.

49 These comments were made apropos *Pygmalion*.

50 *Kineweekly*, 9 January 1936.

51 MEB/BFI B/47 (n.d).

52 Hubert Griffith, *The Nineteenth Century*, August 1932, vol. 112, pp. 190–200; p. 198.

53 *The Publishers' Circular* (hereafter *PC*), 7 September 1935. See also 16 May 1936.

54 Ibid., 7 September 1935.

55 Ibid., 16 May 1936.

56 See Ibid., 1 October 1932.

57 Wallace was referred to on a regular basis in *Kineweekly*. For example, his work was

discussed once in 1930, 1933, 1937, 1938 and 1939, and twice in 1931 and 1932 (the
year he died).

58 *Kineweekly*, 5 February 1931.

59 Ibid., 2 September 1937.

60 *PC*, 3 May 1930.

61 *Kineweekly*, 3 May 1934.

62 M-OA: TC Cinema-Going Survey 4/A, Interview with Sydney Cole, 22 November 1939.

63 Rowntree, *Poverty and Progress*, p. 376.

64 *PC*, 3 June 1933 and 7 October 1933; Joseph McAleer, *Popular Reading and Publishing in Britain, 1914–1950*, Oxford, 1992, pp. 53–54.

65 *The Bookseller* (hereafter *Bookseller*), 11 April 1934.

66 McAleer, *Popular Reading*, pp. 40–41. *Red Star Weekly*, *Secrets* and *Lucky Star* were introduced in 1929, 1932 and 1935 respectively.

67 See *Bookseller*, 1933–1939 and *PC*, 1930–1939.

68 *PC*, 24 October 1931.

69 M-OA: TC Reading Habits 1/A 'Reading Survey No 1 (October Directive)', October 1937.

70 For example, one 'cover story', *Jane Corder and the Shadow of the Red Barn*, ran from 4 January 1930 until 2 August 1930. For the editor's comments see, *Red Star Weekly* (hereafter *RSW*), 25 January 1930.

71 Frank Swinnerton, 'Authorship', in John Hampden, ed., *The Book World: A New Survey*, London, 1935, pp. 12–35; p. 14.

72 *PC*, 3 May 1930. See also Ronald F. Batty, *How to Run a Twopenny Library*, London, 1938, p. 52.

73 See, for example, *RSW*, 25 January 1930, in which Joan Daniel's *Two in a Tangle*, and Dorothy Vane's *The Satin Girl* were featured as 'Novels You are Sure to Enjoy'.

74 *RSW*, 5 April 1930.

75 Ibid., 4 January 1930.

76 G. Wren Howard, 'Book Production', in Hampden, ed., *Book World*, pp. 89–108; p. 108.

77 W.G. Taylor, 'Publishing', in Hampden, ed., *Book World*, pp. 49–88; p. 64.

78 *PC*, 9 February 1935.

79 Batty, *How to Run a Twopenny Library*, p. 38.

80 *PC*, 11 October 1930. In a later edition, however, a leading article argued, 'Books are not in the same category as soap, chocolates and cigarettes'. It was suggested that they should be marketed differently. Ibid., 22 April 1933.

81 Swinnerton, 'Authorship', p. 34.

82 Leavis, *Fiction and the Reading Public*, p. 17.

83 McAleer, *Popular Reading*, pp. 48–49.

84 *PC*, 17 February 1932. Cowles worked for the Swinton and Pendlebury Public Library service; his comments were first published in their bulletin.

85 John Stevenson, *British Society 1914–45*, second edition, London, 1990, p. 398.

86 Charles Nowell, 'The Public Library', in Hampden, ed., *Book World*, pp. 181–194; p. 194.

87 Woodruff, *Road to Nab End*, pp. 365–366. In contrast, the twopenny library he was 'allowed to plunder' is portrayed in glowing terms. See ibid., p. 315.

88 Roberts, *Classic Slum*, p. 132.

89 M-OA: TC Reading Habits 3/A 'Fulham Reading Survey', January 1940.

90 Ibid. The respondent was M.35.D.

91 Ibid., M.35.D.

92 Robert Roberts, *A Ragged Schooling: Growing Up in the Classic Slum*, Manchester, 1976, p. 94; Roberts, *Classic Slum*, p. 135.

93 *PC*, 3 June 1933.

94 *Bookseller*, 24 March 1938.

95 The first branch of this new generation of commercial lending libraries was opened by Ray Smith at Harlesden, London on June 1930. By the late 1930s their number had increased considerably. Smith claimed to be the 'original founder' of the '2d' library. See M-OA: TC Reading Habits 4/D '("Tupenny") 2d Libraries', June 1942.

96 McAleer, *Popular Reading*, p. 50.

97 Ibid., p. 58.

98 See *PC*, 28 February 1931.

99 F.R. Richardson, 'The Circulating Library', in Hampden, ed., *Book World*, pp. 195–202, p. 197.

100 M-OA: TC Reading Habits 1/D 'Directive Replies', November 1937–January 1938.

101 Batty, *How to Run a Twopenny Library*, p. 15.

102 Ibid., pp. 11–12.

103 Ibid.

104 Ibid., p. 15.

105 Ibid., p. 22 and p. 14.

106 Pearl Jephcott, *Rising Twenty: Notes on Some Ordinary Girls*, London, 1948.

107 Ibid., p. 114.

108 M-OA: TC Reading Habits 4/D '("Tupenny") 2d Libraries', June 1942.

109 Ibid.

110 Ibid.

111 M-OA: TC Reading Habits 3/A 'Fulham Reading Survey', January 1940.

112 M-OA: TC Reading Habits 4/D '("Tupenny") 2d Libraries', June 1942.

113 See M-OA: FR 1332 'Books and the Public: A Study of Buying, Borrowing, Keeping, Selecting, Remembering, Giving and Reading Books', July 1942.

114 Ibid.

115 M-OA: TC Reading Habits 4/D '("Tupenny") 2d Libraries', June 1942, M.35.D.

116 Jephcott, *Rising Twenty*, p. 112.

117 M-OA: TC 3/A. The respondent cited was M.50.D.

118 Ibid., M.25.D.

119 M-OA: TC Reading Habits 3/A 'Fulham Reading Survey', January 1940. Out of forty-nine people questioned, thirty-eight said that they did not belong to any type of lending library.

2

'Fouling civilisation'?: official attitudes towards popular film and literature

Film historians have noted that the state's relationship with the cinema has revolved around two main issues. The first is economic; the second, and arguably most important, is ideological.[1] As cinema audiences grew in the 1920s, it became evident to many within the Establishment and film industry that the most popular films with British audiences were those produced in America. Moreover, as film-producer Michael Balcon pointed out, the American film industry had an 'economic stranglehold' on the British film market because of its 'block' and 'blind' booking practices.[2] Unease was consequently expressed over the economic effects of this on the British film industry. One of the main objectives of those concerned, then, was to make the British film industry economically stable; protectionist measures were taken to buffer the industry against the dominance of the American market. The result was the 1927 Cinematograph Films Act, which was instrumental in aiding the expansion of British film production because it gave increased protection to Britain's film industry by demanding that a percentage of all films exhibited in Britain were British-made, thus limiting the ability for American films to dominate the market.

While this legislation did much to alleviate the situation, disquiet remained. In 1932, a Home Office report complained that the American film industry 'has important key theatres in the United Kingdom, and it imposes its products on the small theatres as well'.[3] This disquiet was principally generated by ideological concerns, however, for it was the type of film America was producing which caused the report's composer, Oswald H. Davis, most unease. Arguing that America 'sets the standard in English-speaking film production,' Davis lamented:

An inferior type of mind rules the American motion-picture industry ... For six half-days a week this mentality of turbid showmanship, operating through the screen by shoddy conceptions of art and a glossed materialism, saps the traditional culture and disposition of this country … Any movement to fight fairly the further propagation of debased cinema will have my support.[4]

Unsurprisingly, Davis's stance was typical of many in the Establishment. In a House of Lords debate earlier in the year, Lord Danesfort had remarked that 'the rank and file of our population would be far better instructed if … instead of seeing some somewhat perverted American films, they could see good films produced in the Dominions'.[5] Metropolitan Police magistrate J.A.R. Cairns spoke in a similar vein at a Religious Tract Society annual meeting in 1931, complaining that many American films 'give an exhibition of sex, making human love nauseating, disgusting and revolting'.[6] If that was not critical enough, Cairns added, with considerable venom: 'The people who are sending this stuff across the world are fouling civilisation. Hollywood will yet earn a distinction only to that of Gomorrah'.[7] These sentiments were not new. They had been expressed in a House of Lords debate on the Cinematograph Films Bill in 1927, during which Earl Russell had remarked, 'I can conceive nothing more horrible and nothing less valuable, from the point of view of either entertainment or of instruction, than these dreadful American cowboy films'.[8] These films, Russell believed, were loaded with 'mushy sentimentality' and included adventures which were 'entirely foreign to this country and to the spirit of this country'. Despite the implementation of the Films Act, then, anxiety about the ideological effects of the film product remained constant. In fact, it could be argued to have intensified. The comments made by Cairns, Davis and Lord Danesfort are certainly much stronger in tone than those of Lord Russell.

The phenomenal success of the cinema during the 1930s had been partly responsible for this increased anxiety. Like the cultural critics mentioned earlier, Establishment figures were blaming society's cinema-going habits for the cause of national decline and cultural debasement. Many American films were thought to be degrading and immoral. Indeed, Home Office officials corresponded with American producers over this very issue, and conveyed their unease over the body of American films made available to the British public.[9] The decade saw continued discussion on this matter within a number of government departments, despite the greater enforcement of the Production Code in America from 1934. Indeed, in 1938, with the expiry of the 1927 Films Act clearly causing much consternation, one Foreign Office official criticised the American government for continuing to 'look upon films as a purely commercial item … while we regard them partly, at least, as a cultural responsibility'.[10] It was assumed that the influence of these films would create the 'Americanisation' of British culture; a situation which, if left unchecked, could weaken the existing social structure. Branson and Heinemann have, indeed, argued that American domination of the 'screen dream-world' was a factor indirectly weakening respect for the Establishment's values among the working classes.[11]

The influence of American cinema may have been less expansive than these authors suggest, but the pre-eminent concern of many in the Establishment was whether the images shown on the cinema screen could have a palpable influence on its predominantly working-class audience. The aforementioned House of Lords debate on the 1927 Films Bill had, indeed, expressed concern over the matter. 'I think it is quite impossible to exaggerate the educational value and importance of the cinema in conveying ideas, especially to unlearned and simple people,' Lord Bishop remarked, concluding: 'The cinema is regarded by many as the university of the poor man'.[12] Of course, ideological concerns were not restricted to American films alone. There were a whole host of productions that were considered to be corrupting the cinema-going public. However, many Establishment figures held an overwhelming conviction that cinema audiences, especially working-class patrons, needed protecting from the images presented before them on the screen. It is thus predictable that when censoring the film product, stringent restrictions were routinely enforced.

The major censorship body in Britain during the 1930s was the British Board of Film Censors. Interestingly, while the BBFC was primarily a trade body (it was financed by film distributors who paid fees to have their films classified), its independence from the government was, as Julian Petley has rightly noted, 'more apparent than real'.[13] In fact, the Board had a somewhat vexed relationship with members of the cinema trade. An MoI official noted in 1939 that the Board viewed trade members as untrustworthy and, for this reason, advised against consulting them on matters of 'security' in the period leading up to the Second World War.[14] This is hardly a recipe for a harmonious working relationship between the two interested parties. However, despite these potential difficulties, the BBFC was highly respected by important figureheads in the cinema trade. In 1935, S.G. Rayment observed in *Kinematograph Weekly* that the Board had 'undoubtedly created a solid respect for itself; its decisions are acknowledged to be perfectly honest, and above all, the system works ... [It] carries on its rather delicate task with efficiency and success'.[15] In fact, Rayment had earlier chastised trade members for continuing to produce 'sordid' films despite the Rt. Hon. Edward Shortt's (the BBFC's president from 1929–1935) appeal for producers to avoid such subjects.[16] The BBFC thus held considerable sway in key quarters of the film industry.

The BBFC clearly operated a moral *and* political censorship; and it was one which focused primarily on issues concerning working-class society. Moreover, the Board, with much encouragement from both the government and many working in the cinema trade, was trying to influence the tastes of the consumer. Public taste was, indeed, one of *the* central issues troubling Establishment figures in the period; it was certainly a subject which gained much coverage. It is worth quoting at length from a 1932 Home Office report because it captures perfectly the underlying principles of those concerned with the matter:

> [T]he problem of the quality of films shown in the public resolves itself in two aspects. First there is censorship in the proper sense of the word: certain films must be prohibited and others must be pruned of their objectionable features. But there is also the wider question of the improvement of the general cultural level of the films produced, and the suppression of vulgarity and sentimentality that may be nearly as harmful as actual indecency and profanity ... Perhaps an improvement [...] can only come by a gradual education of public taste.[17]

As this passage reveals, while there was a concerted attempt to censor films that were deemed unacceptable for exhibition, a simultaneous effort was launched to raise public taste regarding the film product. In fact, for some, raising public taste was *the* most important issue. The Governor General of New Zealand, Lord Bledisloe stated that 'it is to public opinion, rather than censorship, that we must look for the positive influence which may bring about an improvement in the general standard of the film'; Bledisloe anticipated that pressure from the cinema-going public would force film-makers to improve the standard of their work.[18] A House of Commons deputation similarly pointed out that the 'cultural value of the film in the ordinary cinema' needed to be raised.[19] Clearly, the tastes of the majority of cinema-goers were routinely held in poor regard. Nowhere is this more evident than in a discussion of a paper submitted to the Renters' Society by Simon Rowson. Society member Charles Tennyson deprecatingly remarked that he was surprised 'the standard of the film was as high as it was considering the audience at which it aimed'.[20] Other members of the Society were more accommodating towards the mass audience. In fact, the Society's chairman, Professor Greenwood, was irritated by Tennyson's comments, and retorted: '"Uneducated" people received quite as much pleasure from fine books, pictures and music as their supposed superiors, when they were given the opportunity of reading, seeing and hearing masterpieces'.[21] But the message was clear: Greenwood believed that cinema-goers were simply not being offered the right type of film; 'when they were given the opportunity' are the key words here. Whether they blamed the cinema-going public, then, or the type of film being offered to them, public figures were certain of one thing: public taste needed to be improved.

Given the degree of interest in public taste, then, it is unsurprising that the cultural and educational benefits of the film medium were being examined throughout the period. In 1932, a Home Office report suggested that there was a need to 'investigate more fully the possibilities of the use of the cinema for education'; the report's compiler desired the 'promotion of educational and cultural films' to protect against 'the moral danger of darkness' lurking on the cinema-screen.[22] In the same year, a report of the commission on educational and cultural films, *The Film in National Life*, called for the film medium to be used as an educational tool.[23] While this interest was generated by anxiety about the effects of film on the whole of the cinema audience, there was significant unease about its effects on the young cinema-goer. Indeed, the need to both protect and educate this section of the audience gained much attention. In his 1935 book, *The Cinema in School*, W.H. George argued that the 'cultural aspect of the cinema demands urgent attention, especially in its relation to the young,' because children's tastes were 'being perverted by appeal to sensation and humour, to the exclusion of other appeals'.[24] In 1937, the parliamentary Secretary for Education, Kenneth Lindsay, claimed that the 'growing child should develop a taste for the good film – which is the same as the educational film'.[25]

It is interesting that the appreciation of the film medium among children produced similar anxiety levels to those generated by the film tastes of the working classes; evidently, the two social groups were seen as commensurate. Indeed, trade personnel certainly believed there were similarities between the tastes of these two groups. More to the point, though, this interest in the tastes of the young cinema-goer confirms that Establishment figures were trying to ensure that another generation of consumers was not lured by the same appeals; efforts were clearly being made by key figures in the Establishment to change the tastes of the mass consumer. Under consideration, then, was the use of the cinema as a cause for the good; it was anticipated that, as an educational and cultural tool, film could be used to stimulate good citizenship. As BBFC president Edward Shortt claimed, the film medium was 'an instrument to mould the minds of the young,' and thus a perfect channel to 'create great and good and noble citizens for the future'.[26]

Of course, these discussions were not concerned exclusively with feature films; documentary films and shorts were also part of the debate. Indeed, at times feature films rarely figured in official dialogue. In the late 1930s, for example, representatives of the British Council held a number of joint committee meetings with officials from the British Film Institute, Foreign Office, the Post Office, and the Department of Overseas Trade, to discuss the publicity of British films overseas; the only types of film mentioned with any regularity in the Committee's negotiations between 1936 and 1938 were industrial and documentary films.[27] However, from 1939, feature films were more frequently discussed; they were thought to be 'not so important as other types,' but it was agreed that it would be 'desirable to include at least a small number'.[28] It is tempting to suggest that fears of an impending war had encouraged these officials to use the feature film as a source of propaganda. Indeed, it is significant that the two 'specimens' chosen for exhibition in that year were *Pygmalion* and *The Mikado*. The former was selected because it was 'outstandingly national in character,' with a 'theme and scene essentially British'; the latter, because it had reached 'a new standard of technical perfection', and possessed 'an enchanting loveliness'.[29] Evidently, these organisations had identified the benefits of promoting good quality, highbrow feature films, which were either deeply national in character, or encapsulated the progressive qualities of the British film industry (and, therefore, the British nation as a whole). This deployment of feature films to promote a sense of 'British' national identity abroad was developed further later in the same year, when it was suggested that a list of feature films 'with an English background' be drawn up for exhibition at the New York World Fair.

Films of this nature were promoted by Establishment figures across the decade. Whether a film was aimed at a national or international audience, or indeed both, it was supposed to be edifying. This was an integral element for many of the organisations and institutions that figured prominently in trying to determine the type of film made available to cinema audiences. The role of the Historical Association is extremely important in this respect.[30] As its name suggests, the Association was principally concerned with historical films. It favoured historical accuracy, and, predictably, had a very negative attitude towards historical feature films. Key figures in the Association also viewed the majority of cinema-goers with some disdain. In a letter to *The Times* in 1936, Professor F.J.C. Hearnshaw, the Association's president from 1936 to 1938, made withering remarks about the type of film being produced and the tastes of the majority of cinema-goers.[31] In 1938, the Chairman of the Association's Films Enquiry Committee, G. Hankin, observed that working-class patrons had 'a limited background and vocabulary,' and required 'verisimilitude and local colour' in the historical films they chose to consume.[32] As Sue Harper has indicated, because the Association had close links with the government, its influence in the period was considerable.[33] However, as she has also pointed out, the Association's lofty stance had a less than positive effect on mass cinema-goers and those commercial producers who paid attention to their needs. In fact, as Harper argues, by condemning their tastes, the Association was merely confirming them, and simultaneously generating resentment towards the type of film which they were promoting.[34] We could thus argue that the Historical Association was out of touch with the needs of the mass cinema-goer, as indeed, were so many Establishment figures.

Time and again, then, Establishment figures walked out of step with mass taste. Driven by the desire to promote a culturally superior cinema, and thus protect the audience from the 'debasing' elements of popular film, those with legislative control repeatedly failed to understand why popular films were popular; they did not recognise the various cultural and socio-economic roles popular films fulfilled. This is no more in evidence than in a memorandum written in 1934 by Sir Cecil Levita, Chairman of the Cinematograph Advisory Committee. Established in 1931 at the request of the Home Office (as the Film Censorship Consultative Committee), the Committee acted as a link between the BBFC and local licensing authorities.[35] Its role was to assess the 'character of films shown to the public'.[36] As Levita's memorandum reveals, it looked upon the majority of films with considerable contempt. Levita began his memorandum with a call for 'the improvement of the entertainment provided at the commercial cinema', and continued by suggesting that Committee members,

> consider the film in its potentiality for what I will term spiritual content as one does consider a book. A library, especially a public library at which all classes of minds are catered for, does not, indeed could not, confine its literature to fiction, but the cinema, except for news-reels, in the main confines itself to fiction … Today it is commonplace to say that the public obtains what it requires. I do not believe this … Under the present system of large trusts owning cinemas throughout the country, the Manager of a chain house has no voice in the choice of films. He must shew [sic] what is sent to him. In smaller houses, individually owned, the licensee is too frequently a person of poor discrimination. [37]

While Levita is right to observe that the managers of the large chain cinemas had little control over the films they exhibited, he is wrong to suggest that the films they showed were forced upon their patrons. Consumption is a matter of *choice*; while the choice of films available *may* have been limited, cinema-goers made conscious choices about the films that were offered; *they* determined what they wanted to watch. After all, with so many cinemas operating in the period, the majority of cinema-goers had a large number of establishments, and therefore programmes, from which to choose. Moreover, contrary to Levita's beliefs, cinema audiences showed a preference for fiction films (as did most library users, who preferred fiction books to those of a more educational bent). In addition, even if, as Levita contends, the managers of the smaller cinemas were of poor discrimination, they were nonetheless adept at choosing the types of film *their* patrons wanted. If they did not, they would flounder; cinema-goers would simply choose another film at another local cinema.

The localised nature of taste was, indeed, recognised to be an issue of considerable significance. In 1933, a Home Office report on censorship suggested that officials allow for 'the exercise of local discretion which, in these matters of taste, is so important'.[38] In fact, the power held by local Watch Committees, and indeed, the Cinematograph Advisory Committee itself, is highly indicative of the need to allow for regional variations of taste. However, as Levita's comments plainly illustrate, despite paying close attention to the public's cinema-going preferences, Establishment figures repeatedly failed to understand the primacy of popular taste. Cinema managers underestimated it at their peril; predictably, they rarely did. Indeed, many kept abreast of their patrons' needs by producing questionnaires to ascertain what type of films they favoured. The cinema-goer thus played a crucial role in a reciprocal relationship; and it was a relationship in which the need to satisfy consumer demand dominated. Therefore, if we look at the reports drawn up by the Public Morality Council concerning the types of film being exhibited in cinemas 'in and near London', it is predictable that the most popular genres of the day dominated.[39] The Public Morality Council was an organisation which had a keen interest in the cinema, and, as its name suggests, was eager to promote 'clean' film entertainment. Despite being intimately linked with the Establishment – it sent reports to the Home Office expressing its views on the films its members examined – the Council was less critical of the cinema than would be expected. Tellingly, Council members used similar terminology to film trade personnel when describing the film product and public taste. Council members, then, were slightly more in tune with mass taste than other authority figures.

The cinema was not the only popular leisure pursuit the Council vetted. Society's reading habits also came under its watchful eye. As with its stance on the cinema, the Council's primary aim was to ensure that a 'decent standard' of literature was maintained.[40] In July 1932, the secretary of the Council, the Hon. Eleanor Plumer, wrote to one of the publishing trade's key papers to spell out the Council's underlying principles. 'The idea is to call attention to objectionable matter in books, plays and films,' Plumer noted, adding: 'As there is so much doubt about the interpretation of what is obscene, it is important that steps be taken to co-ordinate the views of the authorities responsible'.[41] Members of the Council examined novels which they believed failed to meet their exacting standards. Uppermost in their minds was the 'corrupting effects of bad books' on society's 'weaker' members.[42] George Moore's *A Story Teller's Holiday* was thus criticised because it could 'deprave and corrupt those whose minds are open to such immoral influences'.[43] Aldous Huxley's *Point Counterpoint* was similarly described as a 'degenerate and disgusting book' which 'could do untold harm' to the country's youth.[44] Even an expensively priced novel (and thus outside the purchasing ability of the working classes) such as *The Confessions of Aleister Crowley* was criticised because: 'Although the price is high, filth filters down'.[45] It was this outlook which ensured the Council's work had much in common with that of other governing bodies assessing the impact of this popular cultural form.

Along with the cinema, then, the popularity of reading within the working-class community generated considerable anxiety within the British establishment. Admittedly, because it was not a new leisure activity, reading did not generate as much consternation as those newer leisure practices; but heightened social tensions ensured that most cultural forms came under intense scrutiny, and reading was no exception. Concern was raised over the effects of popular fiction on not only the working-class reader, but on British society as a whole. As with the cinema, it was an anxiety which centred on, and was compounded by, the nature of the fiction being consumed. The Home Office, for example, expressed concern over various aspects of literature available for consumption by the working classes. The primary areas of concern related to issues of morality and cultural degeneration; appeals were regularly made urging publishers to curb the production of what was perceived to be 'indecent' or 'obscene' literature, or, if they failed to do so, face prosecution.[46] Significantly, while prosecutions were 'comparatively rare', due to the fear that doing so would only serve to advertise a book further (thus doing 'more harm than good'), there was greater judicial activity during our period because the Home Office felt that it had 'been forced to bring the question before the Courts owing to the growing audacity and shamelessness of books which publishers have been willing to publish'.[47]

Predictably, then, while the censorship of novels was comparatively limited, popular fiction did come under increased observation. It was this aspect which ensured that only certain types of fiction became widely available to the working-class consumer. The role of the Public Morality Council is of especial interest in this respect. Taken on its own, the work of the Council was rather limited. However, the Council's close working relationship with the Home Office ensured that its role was rather extensive. As with the cinema, the Council sent reports to the government body detailing its position on the literature its members had scrutinised. Measures were taken to ensure that the most 'doubtful' books were difficult to obtain.[48] Of course, the Home Office was reluctant to either censor literature, or prosecute publishers and authors. Nonetheless, it did have its own view on what constituted 'good' or 'bad' literature, and similarly desired to promote fiction that was 'not drawn by the lure of obscenity'.[49] Indeed, the Home Office encouraged authors to 'seek higher and more difficult appeals, through romance, invention, character study, and the spiritual imagination'; publishers were discouraged from publishing the type of novel which would 'create an unpleasant and unhealthy smell'.[50] The Home Office's desire, therefore, like that of the Council's, was to ensure that the literature provided was of a culturally educative value. Between them, the two bodies took measures to ensure that only certain types of fiction were widely distributed. This involved restricting the distribution of 'immoral' texts among the country's public libraries. The Council's report to the Home Office regarding Aldous Huxley's novel, for example, contained the request: 'I ask if in some way quietly you can get the Libraries to refuse it'.[51] In such covert ways, then, these governing bodies sought to ensure that 'bad' fiction was kept out of public reach; at the same time, they were heavily promoting 'good' fiction.

What, then, was deemed to be 'good' fiction? For an answer, we can turn to the library and book-shop accession lists drawn up by the British Council; these lists serve as an ideal index of the Establishment's preferred type of literature. The British Council was created by the Foreign Office, and its stance, unsurprisingly, was very conservative. In a list drawn up in 1936, it is the works of Byron, Chaucer, Dickens, Donne, Hardy, Joyce and Yeats which dominate.[52] Similarly, in a more expansive list compiled in 1940, featuring both books and magazines, it is once again the 'classics' – works by Conrad, Kipling and Waugh – that eclipse the number of all other book additions. The magazines made available were also of the 'better type'. These included *Women's Journal*, *Women's Magazine*, and *Picture Post*. Unsurprisingly, magazines aimed at a working-class readership did not feature on this list.[53] Despite claiming that its range of books was 'as wide as possible', then, the choice of fiction offered by the British Council was extremely limited in terms of cultural status.[54] The accession lists were slanted towards 'good' literature. The only 'cheaper editions' offered were those by Penguin Books, Florin Books, Everyman's Library, and such like; and these were middle-brow novels that were recognised as being culturally superior to the twopenny editions.

Significantly, the British Council had a close affiliation with the publishing trade. As *The Publishers' Circular* observed, 'ever since its formation the Council has enjoyed the generous co-operation of the publishers of books and of newspapers and periodicals'.[55] This co-operation took many forms. 'In addition to making a contribution to the funds of the Council,' the paper noted, 'the Publishers' Association have allowed the privilege of purchasing books, for presentation abroad, at trade prices, and on special terms when the books are required for reviews abroad'.[56] Not surprisingly, then, those working in the publishing trade were often also very conservative in terms of the types of book produced and made available to the reading public. Indeed, publishing trade personnel constantly debated the merits of the growth in the reading habit, particularly the tendency of the public to read more 'light' fiction. Indeed, the paper's discussions on the matter were frequently hot-tempered, especially when questioning the provision of fiction in the country's public libraries.

It is without doubt, then, the types of fiction made available to the working classes through the public library system that best illustrates what types of literature the British establishment preferred. Time and again, it is the 'better type' of fiction that dominates public library accession lists. Since many civic librarians concurred with the Establishment's position regarding what type of literature should be made available to the working classes, it is predictable that this is the case. Manchester's chief librarian, Charles Nowell, for example, noted that the public library's principal aim should be 'to maintain a healthy public interest in the novels and romances which are worth reading'.[57] In Peterborough, efforts were made to 'eliminate from the library the mere butterflies of fiction, the three volume novels here to-day and forgotten to-morrow'.[58] Librarian Ernest Baker believed that the ready supply of cheap fiction corrupted the tastes of working-class readers, and stated that 'if they have not enough energy left to read anything but trash, we should be doing them a real service if we could prevent them from reading at all'.[59] While there were some exceptions, there was a general distaste among librarians and library committees for the mass use of their facilities. This was driven, according to L.

Stanley Jast, librarian and president of the Library Association, by the belief that the working-class reading habit had 'swung almost entirely around amusements'.[60] Once again, then, we find cultural elites attempting to 'improve', the leisure activities of the working classes.

Of course, the growth of the public library system during the 1930s has long been regarded by historians as continuing the 'rational recreation' ethos of the nineteenth century. David Vincent has noted how library authorities had, since the public library's inception, advocated the purchasing of 'good' books in an attempt to 'better' the reading habits of the working classes.[61] Jonathan Rose has similarly noted how the aims of the civic authorities in this period were not dissimilar from the mutual improvement principles of nineteenth-century philanthropists.[62] Indeed, in 1927, the Kenyon Report – compiled by a committee of the Board of Education – identified the public library as 'an engine of great potentialities for national welfare'.[63] Many public librarians concurred. In Peterborough, for example, the public library was championed as a means of ensuring the working classes 'become more sober, more industrious and more prosperous'.[64] The way to achieve this, it was argued, was to stock books that 'would furnish ideas INTELLECTUAL, MORAL, RELIGIOUS, POLITICAL, AND ETHICAL'.[65] The public library movement's rationale, then, had changed little over time, and as Alistair Black has rightly pointed out, 'producing "good", passive citizens and contributing to the assets of the nation' were the aims which predominated.[66]

Undoubtedly, it was the belief that popular fiction could be used for the dissemination of political propaganda which was a very real concern for the British establishment in the 1930s. In fact, while middle-class observers, such as J.B. Priestley, believed that mass commercialised fiction was drawing the working classes away from the political arena, many of those in the British establishment believed the opposite to be true, and were highly concerned that popular fiction was drawing the working classes towards that arena. Indeed, many perceived a link between popular fiction and political radicalism. The British establishment thus did everything in its power to prevent the distribution of political propaganda, in whatever literary form it appeared. The Home Office, for example, made repeated calls to curb the spread of political literature, whether in leaflet, magazine, or book form.[67] In like manner, the Metropolitan Police sought to intercept literature that contained either Communist or Fascist propaganda.[68] Meanwhile, the Colonial Office drafted in extra staff to check the supply of literature from overseas ports that was deemed to be of a 'seditious and subversive' nature.[69]

Those working in the publishing industry similarly recognised the role that the written word could play in the dissemination of political propaganda. Some, such as publisher Victor Gollancz, who had set up the Left Book Club in the mid-1930s, saw the link between literature and politics as beneficial. 'It was political publishing that I thought about night and day,' Gollancz remarked, 'the passion to make people *see*'.[70] For others, the relationship was pernicious, and thus something to be disparaged. Frank Swinnerton, for example, was highly critical of fiction that was infused with a political theme. Indeed, he argued that it led to 'a confusion of fixed ideas in the world of books,' and thus made an impassioned appeal to his fellow authors for a return to fiction that was 'free of subservience to Continental political tyranny'.[71] Whatever stance was taken, though, the link between literature and radical politics had become a burning issue, and it was an issue which ensured greater constraints were placed on the distribution of popular fiction.

This is, in fact, borne out by the relatively small number of novels appearing in the country's public libraries which championed radical politics. Indeed, novels which were indoctrinated with Communist, Fascist, or socialist propaganda were frequently rejected by library committees.[72] Despite the supposed unwillingness within the British establishment to censor works of fiction, covert measures were employed to ensure that certain texts were kept out of public reach. In fact, one contemporary, William Munford, observed a marked growth in the number of libraries refusing to stock works of a political nature, and concluded that political censorship had become 'a thing to be reckoned with'.[73] In contrast, and to no great surprise, novels which *criticised* radical politics were permitted to be placed in the country's libraries. In Aberystwyth Borough Library, for example, the accession lists contain several works of fiction which criticised totalitarian regimes, of which the anti-Nazi adventure stories of Percy Westerman (*At Grips with the Swastika*) and Major Charles Gilson (*Out of the Nazi Clutch*) are but two.[74] These were the decisive elements when works of fiction were being evaluated by the country's public library committees. Like controversial films, novels that were imbued with a political theme were always liable to be excluded, unless they presented their subject-matter in a manner which invalidated any form of anti-Establishment propaganda.

The British establishment, then, had a vested interest in what type of fiction was made available to the working-class reader through the public library system, and it was not driven by a mere altruistic desire. In fact, steps taken by the various government bodies show that they viewed the public library with some scepticism. It was identified as both a danger and a benefit.

Indeed, Charles Nowell noted that many critics of the library movement were concerned about 'the risk of revolution that would surely follow this free circulation of books'.[75] While these misgivings were not new to our period, they did undergo intensification because of the heightened social tensions in the 1930s. The aforementioned steps were taken, therefore, to ensure that the libraries did not become hot-beds of political activity. Indeed, according to Alistair Black, the primary aim of the Establishment was to ensure that public libraries fulfilled a political role by 'dampening social unrest'.[76] Certainly, many contemporaries believed they could fulfil such a role. A journalist writing for the *Weekly Chronicle* in 1932, for example, noted that 'the institution was especially valuable in preventing, or minimising discontent'.[77] The public library, then, as Black rightly concludes, 'acted as an ideal instrument for conveying the socially calming messages that government and social elites wished to broadcast'.[78]

However, these libraries merely *acted* as conveyers of the messages that the authorities wanted to promote. This does not mean that they were used, or indeed the books borrowed from them were read, in the way that was desired. Working-class consumers used public libraries for a number of reasons, many of which would not have been approved of by library authorities. William Woodruff has outlined motives behind visiting the public library (and, indeed, the cinema) that had far more to do with socio-economic and political needs than those of a cultural nature. Woodruff noted that public libraries provided warmth ('Some of the unemployed workers just sat there with vacant, watery eyes daydreaming, killing time, glad to be off the cold streets'), and the opportunity to meet like-minded people (in Woodruff's case, communist activist Peter Shad, whom Woodruff met 'every Saturday morning in the library' to read the *Communist Manifesto*).[79] Therefore, while Black is right to highlight the important social and cultural role that these libraries and their contents were expected to fulfil, he is wrong to assume that they were successful in achieving such lofty objectives. Indeed, if this were the case, it would follow that the novels made available to the working classes, through *both* public and commercial libraries, functioned as mere tools of the Establishment. Not so.

The act of reading is a two-way exchange, popularity always prevails. In fact, if we turn again to the accession lists of Aberystwyth Borough Library, we find that the acquisition of so-called 'light' fiction was constant; novels written by the period's most popular authors – Dell, Farnol, Wallace – regularly feature.[80] This was fiction that was meant to be pleasurable; that was meant to be read *and* enjoyed; and it was this type of fiction which was preferred by the majority of working-class readers. The public library access-sion lists, then, are also fascinating documents of working-class taste because public library authorities, very much like publishers, could not afford to ignore the demands of the working-class reader, and thus, despite their many objec-tions, purchased for their libraries the type of fiction that the working classes wanted to read. Indeed, in Peterborough, the level of fiction books loaned out massively outnumbered borrowings of any other type of book, despite the culturally educative stance taken by library officials; librarians had no choice but to purchase large numbers of fiction stock to meet consumer demand.[81]

It bears repeating, then, that while popular fiction was undoubtedly chosen primarily for pleasure, it should not be dismissed as mere escapist entertain-ment; read, as Leavis (and indeed many historians) assumed, to while away a few hours, without making any demands on the mind of the reader. The working classes made conscious choices over what type of fiction they preferred, and it follows that they were using popular fiction to perform a variety of cultural roles. The cinema similarly performed a variety of social and cultural functions, and working-class cinema-goers likewise made mindful choices regarding which films they chose to see. To understand what these tasks were, it is necessary to analyse the nature of the working-class cinema-going and reading habits. We have identified what types of establishment working-class consumers chose to frequent to watch a film or borrow a book; what we need to ascertain now are the characteristics of the films and books they chose to consume. Before I move on to this area of discussion, however, I would like to turn to evaluate the attitudes of those working in the film and publishing trades regarding working-class taste. Were they any more approving of mass taste than Establishment figures?

Notes

1 Dickinson and Street, *Cinema and State*; Julian Petley, 'Cinema and State', in Charles Barr, ed., *All Our Yesterdays: 90 Years of British Cinema*, London, 1986, pp. 31–46.

2 Michael Balcon, *Michael Balcon Presents … A Lifetime of Films*, London, 1969, p. 13 and p. 28.

3 NA HO 45/15248: Sunday Opening of Cinemas; report by Oswald H. Davis dated 29 October 1932. All subsequent references to the NA indicate documents held at the National Archives, Kew.

4 Ibid.

5 *Hansard*, 5 series, LXXXIX, c. 292. House of Lords debate on the Importance of British Films, 4 May 1932.

6 See 'Perils of Popular Education', *PC*, 9 May 1931.

7 Ibid.

8 *Hansard*, 5 series, LXIX, c. 284. House of Lords debate on the Cinematograph Films Act, 28 November 1927.

9 NA HO 45/15206: Entertainments: Film Censorship in the United Kingdom, report dated 9 November 1931.

10 NA FO 371/21530: United States film industry: British film legislation, memo from Bevin, 10 January 1938.

11 Noreen Branson and Margot Heinemann, *Britain in the Nineteen Thirties*, London, 1971, p. 253.

12 *Hansard*, 5 series, LXIX, cc. 289–290. House of Lords debate on the Cinematograph Films Act, 28 November 1927.

13 Petley, 'Cinema and State', p. 41.

14 NA INF 1/178: Film Censorship, 14 April 1939, correspondence between Mr Woodburn and Mr Waterfield.

15 *Kinematograph Year Book*, 1935.

16 Ibid., 1932.

17 NA HO 45/15207: Entertainments: Film Censorship in the United Kingdom, 24 August 1932.

18 Ibid., correspondence between Lord Bledisloe and Herbert Samuel, 6 September 1932.

19 NA HO 45/15206: Entertainments: Film Censorship in the United Kingdom, House of Commons, Deputation from the Parliamentary Film Committee in regard to the censorship of films, 17 March 1932.

20 Rowson, 'Statistical Survey'; 'Discussion on Mr Rowson's Paper', 1936, p. 123.

21 Ibid., p. 128.

22 NA HO 45/15206: Entertainments: Film Censorship in the United Kingdom, 28 April 1932.

23 Commission on Educational and Cultural films, *The Film in National Life*, London, 1932, pp. 62–69.

24 W.H. George, *The Cinema in School*, London, 1935, p. 19.

25 NA ED 136/143, Educational Films, 26 July 1937. See also NA HO 45/15206: Entertainments: Film Censorship in the United Kingdom, 27 February 1932.

26 Quoted in Jeffrey Richards, 'British Film Censorship', in Robert Murphy, ed., *The British Cinema Book*, London, 1997, pp. 167–177; p. 169.

27 See, for example, NA BW 2/35: Joint Committee on Films: agenda, minutes and correspondence, 1936–38.

28 NA BW 2/31: Joint Committee on Films: agenda, minutes and correspondence, 31 January 1939.

29 Ibid., 9 March 1939.

30 For a comprehensive account of the role of the Historical Association see Sue Harper, *Picturing the Past: The Rise and Fall of the British Costume Film*, London, 1994, pp. 64–76.

31 Ibid., p. 65.

32 Hankin is cited in ibid., p. 66.
33 Ibid., p. 76.
34 Ibid., p. 181.
35 NA HO 45/15208: Film Censorship Consultative Committee, 1931–1933, 6 October 1931.
36 Ibid., 4 November 1931.
37 NA HO 45/24945: Entertainments: Film Censorship Consultative Committee reconstituted as Cinematograph Advisory Committee, memo dated 7 June 1934.
38 NA HO 45/15207: Entertainments: Film Censorship in the United Kingdom; Film Censorship in Scotland, 2 June 1933.
39 For a list of film genres see 'Reports on Programmes,' in NA HO 45/15206: Entertainments: Film Censorship in the United Kingdom, 9 November 1931.
40 NA HO 45/15139: Books and other Literature: questions on obscenity; memo on the work of the Public Morality Council.
41 *PC*, 30 July 1932.
42 NA HO 45/15139: Books and other Literature: questions on obscenity; memo on the work of the Public Morality Council.
43 Ibid., report dated 3 October 1929.
44 Ibid.
45 Ibid., report dated 5 October 1929.
46 NA HO 45/15139: Books and other Literature: questions on obscenity.
47 Ibid., HO memo on the position of the Home Office regarding 'obscene' or 'indecent' literature.
48 Ibid., memo on the work of the Public Morality Council.
49 Ibid., letter to the *Nation and Athenaeum*, dated 23 March 1929.
50 Ibid., letters to the *Nation and Athenaeum*, dated 23 March and 30 March 1929.
51 Ibid., report dated 3 October 1929.
52 NA BW 70/1: British Council: Books and Periodicals, 19 October 1936.
53 Ibid., 19 March 1940.
54 NA FO 395/641: British Council: its work abroad, 29 December 1938.
55 *PC*, 2 January 1937.
56 Ibid.
57 Nowell, 'The Public Library', p. 188.
58 Storage Box: 1905–1991, Peterborough Public Library Archive, Peterborough.
59 Baker is cited in Alistair Black, *The Public Library in Britain 1914–2000*, London, 2000, pp. 59–60.
60 Jast is quoted in ibid., p. 65.
61 David Vincent, 'Reading in the Working-Class Home', in J. K. Walton and J. Walvin, eds, *Leisure in Britain, 1780–1939*, Manchester, 1983, pp. 207–226; p. 213.
62 Jonathan Rose, *The Intellectual Life of the British Working Classes*, London, 2001, pp. 58–59.
63 Black, *Public Library*, pp. 54–56.
64 Storage Box: 1905–1991, Peterborough Public Library Archive, Peterborough.
65 Ibid. See folder 1880–1905, newspaper article (n.d.).

66 Black, *Public Library*, p. 59.
67 See, for example, NA HO 144/17832: Memo regarding the distribution of political literature.
68 See, for example, NA MEPO 2/3084: Distribution of Nazi literature in England.
69 NA CO 737/3: Memo concerning the censorship of seditious literature, 1937.
70 Victor Gollancz in cited in Betty Reid, 'The Left Book Club in the Thirties', in Jon Clark, Margot Heinemann, David Margolies and Carole Snee, eds, *Culture and Crisis in Britain in the Thirties*, London, 1979, pp. 193–207; p. 199.
71 Swinnerton, 'Authorship', pp. 18 and 34.
72 Black, *Public Library*, p. 64.
73 Ibid.
74 The Library Accessions Book for Fiction: Library Accession Register, Aberystwyth Borough Library, 1933–1939.
75 Nowell, 'Public Library', p. 182.
76 Black, *Public Library*, p. 59.
77 Ibid.
78 Black, *Public Library*, pp. 66–67.
79 Woodruff, *Road to Nab End*, pp. 365 and 369–370.
80 Library Accessions Book for Fiction.
81 Fiction borrowing accounted for nearly seventy per cent of all books borrowed. See Peterborough Public Library, Analysis of Stock, 1930–1939, Peterborough Public Library Archive, Peterborough. See also Accessions Register, vols. 1–3.

3

Trade attitudes towards audience taste

The film trade: *Kinematograph Weekly*

What were the attitudes of those working in the cinema trade towards working-class taste? To answer this question I shall turn to the cinema trade's most important journal in the period, *Kinematograph Weekly* (hereafter *Kineweekly*).[1] The value of this journal as a primary source cannot be overemphasised, for it provides unique access into the workings of the film industry. We gain intimate details of the role of those involved in the production, distribution, and exhibition of films, and an indication of the views of the cinema patrons themselves (albeit through the eyes of local cinema owners and managers). In addition, the journal provides access to the attitudes of those working in the trade regarding the restrictions placed upon them by various government bodies. Indeed, many of the period's key debates on film are played out within its pages. The educational role of film, its use for propaganda purposes, and the need for fuller control of the industry's output are referred to on a regular basis. *Kineweekly* thus functioned as both an arena for debate and a mouthpiece for the trade.

Interestingly, like the many government bodies dealing with the cinema trade, *Kineweekly*'s editorial board were often very conservative in their views regarding the role the cinema played in society.[2] Often the journal featured articles that questioned the morality of films and their effect on cinema audiences. In 1931, the journal reproduced the findings of a report compiled by the Committee of Church and Nation which observed: 'the kinema is exercising a baneful influence upon young lives, especially upon adolescents'.[3] Many films, the report noted, contained 'debased moral and spiritual values ... [and] suggestiveness', which it argued, 'stimulates an unhealthy sex curiosity, [and] opens the door to criminals'. Significantly, the report places the blame for the cinema's failings primarily on those films produced in America, thus alluding to the widespread concern over the Americanisation of British culture. The 'tone of many of the American films is deteriorating,' the report declared, adding, 'it is likely to deteriorate still more'. *Kineweekly* repeatedly features articles calling for greater control of the industry's output. In 1933, the president of the BBFC, the Rt. Hon. Edward Shortt, contributed to the journal's discussion of the issue, stating that 'the real future of this country, the future of its people or their children and grand-children depends on the way we regulate the kinema to-day'.[4] Shortt contributed again in 1934, stating, apropos his role as a film censor: 'My job in life is to try and prevent our morals being made worse than they naturally are. If I succeed in doing that, I have succeeded in doing a very great deal'.[5] Shortt was thus *using* the journal to call attention to, and ensure the wider dissemination of, *his* concerns about cinema's effect on society.

Not all of the journal's contributors were as critical of the cinema, however. In fact, some writers disapproved of the growing tendency towards a stricter censorship, especially one entailing the introduction of a national censorship body. In 1933 Eleanor Plumer noted: 'On the whole, the vast majority of kinemas provide programmes which are healthy and satisfactory, and which give legitimate recreation to a large number of people at a price they can afford to pay'.[6] It is perhaps surprising, given the nature of the Public Morality Council's role, to see Plumer taking such a tolerant stance. But this apparent broad-mindedness lay partly with the fact that the creation of a national censorship body would largely invalidate the Council's role. In addition, Plumer clearly saw the cinema as a means of ensuring that the population's leisure time was spent away from more lurid forms of entertainment. It is also highly likely that she is using an early injection model of media reception, viewing the cinema, in accord with many contemporaries, as a passive leisure pursuit, and as such, an ideal escape route to lead the 'masses' away from revolutionary politics and licentiousness.

Indeed, it is clear that cinema programmes were approved by the Council only so long as they were of a certain standard. Throughout our period the Council's members continued to vet the films being exhibited, and often lobbied for a better product. In 1937, they joined in a scheme with the Cinema Christian Council to 'work hand in hand in certain film matters'.[7] The Public Morality Council's members were obviously satisfied that their lobbying had produced the required results, for they remarked that they were 'pleased with exhibition of a raised standard'. The alliance with the Cinema Christian Council, however, illustrates that the Public Morality Council's members were determined not to rest on their laurels. For them, the cinema-going habit was a leisure activity that required constant vigilance, and the films the public went to see needed to be regularly scrutinised.

Bearing in mind this conservatism towards the film product, it follows that the educational value of film was frequently mooted within *Kineweekly*'s pages. In 1933, the journal reproduced a lengthy paper given by Sir Charles Cleland that discussed the cinema's use as 'Indirect Education'. It noted that:

> The masses of people who go to the picture house with no further thought than to be amused, unconsciously derive from it new ideas, new standards of value in life, and a new artistic outlook. The film also exercises an internationalising influence by giving them contact with other countries and civilisations. At every point the picture house unconsciously exerts an indirect educational influence upon its patrons.[8]

Cleland, the article noted, continued by calling for the newly established British Film Institute to 'exercise a guiding and stimulating influence, advising where called upon and classifying this huge output according to its educational and cultural usefulness'; he believed the basis of this project should centre on a 'tripartite partnership between education, the film Industry and the general public'.

Those with a civic responsibility were also keen to use *Kineweekly* to express their delight at the prospect of the cinema having an educational role. While opening a new Odeon in Leeds, the city's mayor Councillor Samuel Cartwright remarked that 'the development of the kinema Industry has been wonderful, and has helped Britain to become a much more sober nation'.[9] Cartwright continued: 'Once, it was said, schools and colleges were the guiding influence. The kinemas occupied that position nowadays'. Such was the importance of this role, Cartwright argued, that a 'tremendous onus' had been placed upon the cinema proprietor. Any cinema owner or manager reading *Kineweekly* had been warned: their role in society was a vital one.

Along with its educational potential, the cinema's capacity for promoting issues of national interest, both at home and abroad, was another topic that regularly featured in *Kineweekly*. In 1931, critic and Empire Marketing Board film-maker John Grierson noted that the cinema should be regarded as 'the greatest propaganda medium in the world'.[10] Similarly, in 1937, Ken Nyman, vice-president of the Cinematograph Exhibitors' Association (hereafter C.E.A.) wrote: 'Films were unique in connection with the country's propaganda and national activities'.[11] Such was the editorial board's belief in the importance of the cinema for propaganda purposes, that, in 1933, *Kineweekly* featured an extensive 'special overseas edition' which included a series of articles, such as

Robert J. Flaherty's 'The Film as Propaganda', that went to great lengths to promote British-made films abroad, primarily viewing them as a source of national propaganda.[12]

For many of the journal's contributors, then, the cinema was an ideal medium for promoting Britain to the nation and the rest of the world. For others, it offered an excellent means to promote social stability; a propensity which, while extremely important throughout the whole of the decade, became particularly meaningful at its close. Indeed, the period leading up to the Second World War, and of course, the years during which the conflict took place, witnessed a heightened interest in the use of the cinema both for propaganda purposes and alleviating social unease. It was an area of concern that was certainly recognised by *Kineweekly*'s editors, and the journal's discussions on the matter were frequent. In 1939, Richard R. Ford, of the Odeon Education Department, and author of the influential text *Children in the Cinema*, submitted an article praising the cinema's role in spreading national propaganda and assuaging audience anxieties concerning the conflict:

> There is no doubt that in an emergency the national importance of all kinemas would immediately increase ... not only for disseminating information, but in providing an antidote for worry and nervous strain. Indeed, the psychological value of the kinema in combating 'jitters' may well be its strongest claim to be regarded as a public servant.[13]

This theme was picked up again in a later issue, in which C.P. Metcalfe, a former President of the C.E.A., outlined the type of films that should be avoided when exhibiting to a war-weary public:

> In these times, when we have a part to play in preventing trouble laying heavily upon individual shoulders, the question of selection is more important than ever. Deep psychological themes, for instance, however well played, do more harm than good to an audience which yearns for the easiest form of relaxation.[14]

It is clear that Metcalfe also viewed the cinema as a vital component of the war effort. Indeed, he used *Kineweekly* as a channel to appeal to the Government to give those working in the film industry a greater role in war-time film production and exhibition.[15]

It is significant that both of these contributors allude to the cinema's importance as a leisure activity. Both Ford and Metcalfe acknowledge that the principal aim of the cinema should be to entertain, not educate; and both identify cinema-going as an ideal opportunity for the public to escape from their day-to-day worries. Indeed, while, like many of his contemporaries, Ford favoured the 'better' type of film, he conceded that: 'The primary business of the kinema is to entertain', and warned against cinema programmes being overtly didactic.[16] Ford and Metcalfe were thus highly aware of the cinema audience's tastes, and were using *Kineweekly* to offer advice to others working in the film industry, and, more importantly, to ensure that those calling for greater control of it were made aware that it was the people working in the industry itself who were closest to understanding the cinema-going public's tastes, and best left to run the industry with a minimum of outside interference. These were powerful arguments indeed when we remind ourselves that, due to the war, the Government was encroaching deeply into the running of the industry by creating organisations such as the Films Division of the Ministry of Information.

We can assume, therefore, that the editors of *Kineweekly* were keen not to offend those working in the film industry regarding their role in the provision of entertainment for the cinema-going public. They were eager to show that, as a trade paper, *Kineweekly*'s allegiance was with the cinema trade. Indeed, *throughout* the decade, and despite the highly moralistic leanings of some of their authors, most articles that debated the cinema's educational role, propaganda uses, or indeed film censorship, touched upon the issue of the cinema as a medium first and foremost concerned with entertainment. For example, Sir Charles Cleland noted that: 'Being primarily a vehicle for entertainment, it [the cinema] cannot be turned by teachers or educators into a medium of instruction without regard to its entertainment character'.[17] Therefore, while *Kineweekly* was being used by many (both within and outside the cinema trade) as a forum in which to debate the cinema's role in society, for *Kineweekly*'s editors, consumer pleasure was *the* dominant issue.

Nevertheless, editorial policy at *Kineweekly* appeared to be one which sought to influence the production and consumption of a specific type of film. Consumer pleasure was the dominant issue, but only certain pleasures were tolerated. Indeed, when discussing the cinema-going public's film tastes, the editors argued that the general public needed to be educated into wanting to see a better type of film. In 1935, an article discussing the work of the 'decency' campaign in America noted that 'the cause of wholesome entertainment was better served by the education of public taste while the producers worked to improve their films to meet the demand'.[18] We can assume that *Kineweekly*'s editorial board held views along these lines. Indeed, the reproduction of these debates surrounding the production and consumption of films in America appears to be an attempt by the editors to demonstrate to those working in the British film industry that 'clean and wholesome entertainment' could be profitable. In fact, the article concludes with an observation by Louis B. Mayer (a man whose reputation as part of the film production giant Metro-Goldwyn-Mayer would certainly have been noted by those who read the article) stating that 'fine clean pictures with the merit of entertainment now succeed [at the box-office]'. Consumer pleasure was once again alluded to, but this was tempered by the need to produce wholesome entertainment: 'The screen cannot replace schools and churches - but neither should it undo their fine work. Entertainment without offence is the solution'. Predictably, the two films recommended in the article for exhibition, American-produced adaptations of Charles Dickens's *David Copperfield* and *A Tale of Two Cities*, were both 'classics', and would have certainly featured on many highbrow critics' 'wish lists'.

These observations reveal that public taste, especially 'mass taste', was a burning issue for *Kineweekly*'s editors. In fact, analyses of public taste, many by prominent trade personnel, are a constant feature in the paper throughout the decade. In 1932, L'Estrange Fawcett, a one-time production manager at Gaumont, observed: 'There must be something in every film which appeals to the mass mind, or the producers would go out of business'.[19] The concluding part of this sentence reveals why Fawcett *et al.* were being so attentive; they were ever mindful of the need for films to be popular with mass audiences if they were to be profitable. Indeed, in 1937, S.W. Smith, managing director of British Lion, similarly declared: 'Entertainment for the masses [is the] only way to prosperity'.[20] Therefore, because *Kineweekly* was a trade paper, its editors were eager to address the issue of film popularity. A number of questionnaires on film taste were thus presented in, and analysed by, the paper. The most prolific contributor of these was cinema owner Sidney Bernstein. Bernstein conducted a series of surveys on public taste during the period; they reveal much about the tastes of the cinema-goer.[21] Producer Alexander Korda conducted a film questionnaire in 1935 on a range of issues, including audience taste and the appeal of films.[22] Local cinema managers also made regular forays into assessing their public's film tastes. The manager of the New Empire cinema in Ashton ran a competition, 'Testing Public Taste', in which cinema-goers won prizes if they completed a film questionnaire.[23]

What, then, does *Kineweekly* tell us about the issue of popular taste? What type of films did those 'in the know' believe would appeal to the 'mass mind'? It is worth returning to the findings of local cinema managers here, because, in 1935, one 'independent small-owner manager' represented perfectly the dominant attitudes of those working both in the cinema trade and for

Kineweekly regarding the issue of 'mass taste'. Describing the content of the films he believed answered to mass taste, the manager wrote: '*The cheapest and most obvious gags are the ones that get the laughs: the sloppier the sentimentality the more certain the tears*'.[24] In addition, he stated that 'more films "flop" because they are too good than because they are too bad', and concluded, with a certain element of snobbery: 'I think it is time somebody described bluntly how low the standard of culture is in the great mass of the population'. This cinema manager, then, clearly placed the working-class consumer in a lowly position within the cultural sphere.

Coincidently, the assumptions made by this cinema manager are very similar to those made in quasi-scientific studies of popular taste conducted in our own period. Popular taste has been habitually associated with poor taste; and popular culture is frequently disparaged as obvious, simple and passive. It is thus interesting, though perhaps not surprising, to note that those who predicted taste patterns in the 1930s frequently made these distinctions when choosing the films to be offered to working-class consumers. It is the notion of a film's need to be 'obvious' and highly coloured that is continually referred to when a film is chosen for the mass consumer by *Kineweekly's* review panel.

Each edition of *Kineweekly* featured a 'New Films at a Glance' section. This listed the films due for release, and an indication of the type of cinema-goer for whom the films were most suitable, or the category of cinema in which the films should be exhibited. The more detailed 'Reviews' section also included a brief discussion of the films' merits. For example, the American-produced *Dangerous Nan McGrew* was listed in the 'New Films at a Glance' section as a: 'Light booking for industrial halls'.[25] The review section described the film as a: 'Comedy burlesque,' which was 'well-mounted and is sufficiently humorous in an obvious manner to satisfy the masses. As a light offering this picture should please and satisfy in industrial areas'. Similarly, British comedy *The Hawleys of High Street* was listed as a: 'Good comedy booking for the masses', and was described thus:

> The dialogue is obvious, and the humour is artless, but good teamwork and timing enable the conventional, robust, knockabout situations to register and score the laughs ... The entertainment is designed with unerring skill for the consumption of the masses.[26]

It is crucial to recognise that *Kineweekly's* review panel's comments are shot through with notions of class identity. Compare these reviews to that of American-produced romance *Sweet Kitty Bellairs*: 'There is a charm and fragrance about the whole picture which makes it an acceptable offering for better class halls'.[27] This was a 'charm and fragrance' which, presumably, these predictors of taste believed the mass patron could not appreciate, nor indeed, comprehend. In fact, time and again, contempt for popular culture is expressed. A review for the British production *Josser Joins the Navy*, listed as a: 'Safe comedy booking for the masses', ran thus: 'broad gags, ripe innuendoes and breezy rough stuff ... This is not the fare for the better-class patrons, but the masses will no doubt find the picture to their liking, and it should do well in populous areas'.[28] Similarly, the review for *Under Eighteen*, listed as 'a picture mainly for the masses', noted:

> Sex element is there to provide popular sensationalism and box-office stimulus. Its extravagance in theme and presentation may not appeal to the intelligentsia, but the picture undoubtedly retains those qualities which make most direct appeal to the masses.[29]

Reviews along these lines are numerous. Ruritanian fantasy *Koenigsmark*, listed as a: 'Fair average spectacular entertainment for the masses', was identified as 'a proposition for the crowd rather than the discerning'.[30] Similarly, romantic drama *Sinner's Holiday* was the 'type of fare [which] is perhaps a little too strong to appeal to high-class audiences, but it should satisfy and entertain the masses'.[31] Military comedy *Kiss Me Sergeant* is listed as: 'Good light booking for popular audiences,' which: 'Although unlikely to appeal to the discriminating patron,' had 'all the qualities which can be depended upon to amuse and entertain the unsophisticated'.[32] These 'qualities' were the film's humour, which was described as 'broad and obvious'.

This notion of the mass consumer's lack of appreciation for, and understanding of, 'quality' films is made explicit in a review for the British-produced adaptation of Shakespeare's *As You Like It*. The film was listed as: 'Impeccable entertainment for intelligent audiences'. The film's review reveals why: 'To appreciate the film every word must be followed, and the task imposes too great a strain on the masses, the vast majority who insist upon talk being subservient to action'.[33] What is even more significant about this review, other than its very condescending tone, is its grading of the cinema audience. While the film was classified as an: 'Outstanding offering for the intelligentsia', it was also seen as a 'possible star booking for other than the industrial element'.

The majority of film reviews give an indication of the type or class of audience for whom the films were thought to be targeted. Indeed, some reviews even predicted in which geographical localities a film would succeed. *Dodging the Dole* was described as having: 'Lancashire written all over it'.[34] *It's a Grand Old World* was likewise identified as an: 'Attractive booking for the North and all industrial districts'.[35] Once again, then, we see a return to *Kineweekly*'s audience grading practices.

It is worth exploring this practice of grading the 'mass' cinema audience. *Kineweekly*'s review panel drew on a number of descriptive terms. Laurel and Hardy's comedy western *Way Out West* was described as a: 'Cast-iron comedy bet for the crowd'.[36] *The Fire Trap* was 'for popular and industrial audiences'.[37] *1,002nd Night* was expected 'to satisfy the modest demands of the small hall patron'.[38] Romantic drama *Cast Iron* was 'a picture for not too exacting patrons'.[39] The latter example reveals how low on the cultural register *Kineweekly*'s review panel placed the 'mass' consumer. Indeed, so low down were they thought to be, that, in many reviews, the films chosen for the 'masses' were considered as suitable only for one other type of cinema-goer: the child. *Arizona Legion* was thus 'a certainty for the masses and youngsters'.[40] *The Loser's End* was a: 'Very moderate second feature for industrial and juvenile audiences'.[41] Spy burlesque *Mr Stringfellow Says "No"* was classified as a: 'Sound two-feature programme booking for the masses, industrial audience and youngsters'.[42] Many examples of this likening of the mass cinema-goer with children are evident. 'Mass' cinema-goers were thus identified as possessing similar intellectual capabilities to a child, and it was no doubt assumed that they also held the same artistic appreciation of the movie experience.

According to *Kineweekly*, this appreciation was centred entirely on a few simple qualities. 'Obvious', 'broad', 'naïve', 'novelettish', 'slapstick', 'sentimental', 'punch', 'rough stuff': these were the characteristics that were judged to render a film successful with 'mass' audiences. For example, *I Spy* was 'a burlesque of the espionage theme, lavishly presented and broadly treated'; its humour was 'obvious and borders on the slapstick', and thus provided 'good, innocuous fun, skillfully tuned to the tastes of the masses'.[43] *The Wyoming Whirlwind* was a: 'Straightforward Western drama, with plenty of action and rousing fisticuffs'; its 'refreshing naiveté' made it 'a suitable supporting attraction for the masses'.[44] *A Perfect Weekend* contained 'gangsterdom … roughhouse humour and thrills,' and was deemed 'just the stuff to give the masses'.[45] *The Fire Trap* was quite simply 'crowded with popular interest'.[46] As the film's reviewer noted: 'Punch is what the masses demand, and here it is dressed to thrill'.

This, then, was *Kineweekly*'s attitude to 'mass' taste. The paper's influence was pivotal in predicting what types of film should be exhibited to specific cinema audiences. However, did exhibitors take note of *Kineweekly*'s advice and show the films that were recommended to them? Did cinema patrons actually go to see them? Do the box-office successes bear out *Kineweekly*'s recommendations?

The publishing trade: *The Publishers' Circular*

Like *Kineweekly*, the publishing industry's primary trade paper *The Publishers' Circular* functioned as both an arena for debate as well as a mouthpiece for the trade.[47] It is as informative and valuable as a primary source. Once again, we gain in-depth knowledge of the role of those working in the leisure trade regarding the production and distribution of a leisure product; we acquire a closer understanding of the relationship between leisure and the state; and we can begin to determine the attitudes of the trade towards working-class taste. Like *Kineweekly*, many of the period's key debates are played out within its pages; once again we gain access to the trade's attitudes towards outside interference. Unfortunately, *The Publishers' Circular* does not include a definitive list of new books with a prediction of their appropriate audiences. Nonetheless, we can gain an index of the paper's preferred books, and its attitudes towards the 'mass' consumer, through the content of the debates contained within its pages.

The Publishers' Circular contrasts sharply in tone to *Kineweekly*. It is significantly more conservative. Time and again, members of the trade are reproved by the editor E. Walton Marston if they display a too liberal attitude towards reading's social and cultural role. In 1931, for example, Frederick J. Cowles, chief librarian of Swinton and Pendlebury public library, printed an article in a library bulletin which displayed an acceptance of the growth in reading for 'entertainment and recreation only'. While Cowles agreed that 'as an institution the public library stands for the ideal of an educated public', he believed the librarian must always be responsive to consumer demand:

> Fiction is the favourite reading of to-day, and so it must be abundantly supplied
> … [We] have a duty to those ratepayers who desire entertainment and recreation
> only. Many a tired mill-girl finds her little hour of romance in a novel by Ethel
> M. Dell or Olive Wadsley. Many a weary miner lives for an evening in a thrilling
> world of adventure created by Edgar Wallace or Jackson Gregory. Who can say
> that the provision of such entertainment is not the function of a public library?[48]

Marston reprinted Cowles's article in *The Publishers' Circular*; his response to it was typically uncompromising:

> It is our experience that those who read fiction for 'entertainment and recreation'
> (it is difficult to suggest any other reason except possibly time-killing) are quite

content to go on doing so without any wish or desire for advancement to a higher literary plane … Many people consider the cinema a far more potent educational factor than the reading of hundreds of novels, but what a howl would go up from the cinema proprietors and shareholders at a proposal to launch a rate-supported public cinema. Unfortunately, those who handle the commodity of books are far too gentlemanly to howl.[49]

Of course, Marston is aggrieved that the growth in public library provision, and the policy of stocking fiction in free libraries, constituted a threat to the bookseller. But these comments also reveal a deep-seated contempt for the reading public who preferred 'light' fiction to novels of a 'higher literary plane'. In fact, Marston's stance on this is unequivocal. He believed that 'the publishing and bookselling trade must play an important part in preserving the mental and social well-being of the nation and so in furthering our progress to better times,' insisting that the act of reading 'be employed in a healthy and profitable way'.[50] *The Publishers' Circular* thus frequently features editorials that denounce those consumers whose idea of entertainment was to settle down and read purely for amusement, and those people in the trade who provided the type of material which satiated that public's needs.

Marston was not alone in his condemnation of both consumer and producer. In 1933, Edward Green, chief librarian of Halifax public libraries, observed: 'In recent years a vast army of new readers – the product of the elementary school – has been recruited from a lower mental strata, and the intelligent use of the printed page needs more encouragement and direction'.[51] A 1934 report of the Libraries Committee of the City of Westminster called for public libraries to be 'relieved of their obligation to cater for this particular taste of a portion of their readers [who prefer] low cultural equipment,' so that they were 'enabled to augment the provision of books of a higher class, of a greater claim to cultural or educational value'.[52] Consumer pleasure then, appears to be of little importance to Marston, or indeed, to many of *The Publishers' Circular*'s contributors. It is not surprising, given Marston's beliefs, to find a predominance of such views. What is notable, however, is that Marston, unlike the editors of *Kineweekly*, was in full control of his paper; there was no power struggle here.

Nevertheless, despite, or maybe because of, Marston's substantial editorial control, some people in the trade (especially those working closely with the 'mass' consumer) were stimulated by this high-handed approach to write in and defend their position. Indeed, Cowles's article, and Marston's response to it, generated much discussion in the paper, on both the role of the public library in particular, and the act of reading in general. Many contributors were supportive of Cowles's views; but these were typically drawn from those working in the same field. For example, Chesterfield librarian L.C. Jackson stated, 'The end to which all libraries are striving is the spreading of education, and education in its broadest sense'.[53] Significantly, Jackson also hinted that the consumer was able to derive various elements from a work of popular fiction: 'Many of the works of fiction published to-day, and articulated through the medium of the public library, suggest new ideas, fresh outlooks on life, to the reader'. Another supporter of Cowles, Arthur E. Gower, who was librarian and secretary in Grays, Essex, was even more liberal in his views, and extremely critical of Marston. 'The Editor of this journal … misses the whole point of public library service,' he snapped, adding, 'It is not what he wants the public to read, nor does it matter one iota what we librarians want the public to read … what they require must be the factor determining the issues'.[54] Moreover, Gower understood that 'Librarians are the servants of the public,' and claimed, 'I would wish no higher office'. His concluding remarks expressed his position most clearly, 'Pleasure in reading is the true function of all books'.

Marston was not to be moved by such liberal points of view, however. In fact, these demonstrations of tolerance only seemed to strengthen his resolve. In September 1932, he reiterated his and his paper's standpoint and claimed that its views were 'officially supported' by the Publishers' Association and the Associated Booksellers of Great Britain and Ireland.[55] The following month, he took up the issue again, writing:

> instead of directing, influencing or leading the public taste in reading towards books of an educational and uplifting character, the public library is in danger of becoming mechanized, a mere soulless organisation engaged in the squirrel-cage routine of exchanging one novel for another … The habitual novel reader in most cases is like the drug taker, who will go to any lengths to satisfy their craving.[56]

Many trade personnel, predictably drawn from outside the public library service, were similarly resolute. Indeed, the Cowles/Marston debate generated a flurry of activity among them, and letters that defended Marston's stance frequently appear.[57] Of course, as editor, Marston had control of what was included in the paper, but the sheer number of letters decrying the role of the public library and the reading of popular fiction that feature throughout the decade illustrates an unmistakable determination to make their views known. Moreover, Marston appears to have singled out Cowles as a figure for derision. He regularly reprinted Cowles's articles in the paper, and there is never a shortage of negative responses to them. In 1938, for example, a lengthy article written by Cowles, once again focusing on the continuing criticism of the public library service and the public's preference for 'light' reading, was roundly condemned. It is worth citing Cowles's comments at length because they display his unchanging acceptance of the public's preferences, and, more importantly, his recognition of the consumer as considerably more than a passive recipient of the leisure product:

> I have yet to discover any sane and reasonable argument against the circulation of fiction by public libraries ... The highbrow critics who assert that a reader cannot obtain anything of value from a light novel only display their own ignorance. Even the most sensational fiction often contains some out-of-the-way information which can be easily assimilated. The readers of light fiction obtain something more than actual facts and figures – they obtain either a mental opiate or a mental tonic. Both are badly needed in these days when so many of us have to live upon our nerves ... The educational functions of a public library are often overstressed. It is true that a library should be the cultural centre of the district it serves but, before it can become that, it must attract to itself all classes and conditions of readers.[58]

The many disapproving responses to this piece demonstrate that Marston's outlook, and indeed, that of the majority of those contributing to the paper, had remained equally unchanged.[59] Eric R. Stone, from Central Library, Fulham, thus remarked,

> I can see no reason why an institution whose function is primarily educational should endeavour, to the detriment of its own foremost obligations, to enter into vain competition with the cinema and twopenny libraries as a peddler of mental opiates ... I cannot agree ... that they should cater for the complete lack of taste reflected in 'A mystery and a love story please'. Let us remember that as librarians, it is our duty not to tamely accept and cater for lack of taste, but to rectify so sad a condition as speedily as we may.[60]

These comments illustrate that the strength of feeling against both the inclusion of fiction in the country's public libraries, and the continuing popularity of the same among the reading public, remained extremely static throughout the decade. Indeed, it was only at the decade's close when letters appeared which illustrated a more tolerant stance. Presumably, the stresses of war had caused a slight change of heart, for many contributors now championed the reading of 'light' fiction as an ideal form of escape from the war. Frank A. King thus wrote, 'Escape books are needed ... [a public] agitated by depressing home conditions will want to find a means of escape into the realms of gold'.[61] Cowles, always the opportunist, took this chance to promote his beliefs again and similarly observed, 'quantities of cheap fiction will be required ... The soldier will carry a book in his kit-bag, the civilian will keep books for his fireside ... We are a nation of readers, and the war is only going to increase the demand for books'.[62] For once, no-one disagreed with him.

On the whole, then, *The Publishers' Circular's* ethos closely resembled that of many of the period's leading cultural critics; Marston's beliefs blend well with what would now be identified as the Leavisite tradition. A brief glance through the pages of another important contemporary trade journal, *The Bookseller*, reveals that they were widespread within the publishing industry.[63] Thus, in a leading article in 1931, publisher Geoffrey Faber attacked the declining taste of the reading public and those who pandered to it: 'Literature is now in the hands of the mob ... Hence an ever-growing temptation to write for the herd, to publish for the herd, to buy and sell for the herd'.[64] In 1939, a regular contributor to *The Bookseller*, writing under the pseudonym Petrel, remarked,

> I have a low opinion of libraries. Their influence has been to the lowest level of literature and to make possible the production of a great mass of essentially demoralizing rubbish which does nothing whatever for the minds of its readers except to act as a pleasant narcotic and to deprive them of the necessity of making any mental effort whatever.[65]

Such were the views of those in the publishing trade regarding popular fiction and those who read it. A few trade personnel were complimentary towards it, but the majority of those contributing to the debate expressed their distaste in extremely withering tones. It was not only 'light' fiction that was being criticised, however. As many of the above contributors' remarks illustrate, the period's most popular leisure pursuits were coming under criticism from those working in the publishing trade. Indeed, anxiety about the popularity of the cinema is a recurring theme in both trade papers considered here. Certainly, Marston's comments exhibit contempt for the cinema trade and the people working in it. Petrel's views were far from complimentary either. Even contributors who thought that the cinema could be deployed as a useful advertising medium for the book had a lowly view of the cinema patrons' mental capacity. B.H. Clough, for example, promoted the use of the cinema 'as a means for co-operation and advertisement,' but stated: 'Unquestionably, the crowds that flock week after week to the cinema are not the type who would desire to possess a very beautiful edition of Shakespeare or "The Forsyth Saga", but there are books for every degree of intelligence'.[66] C. Clark Ramsay wrote in equally disparaging terms about the intellectual requirements of cinema and radio consumption:

Consideration of the printed page means nothing without the mental in addition to the visual or purely sensual appreciation. The radio is an entertainment of a purely sensual type, since mere sound can hold the 'interest' of the otherwise inactive mind. So, too, the flickering of celluloid shadows on a screen in 'thought-less' entertainment. But the printed word gives nothing without thought.[67]

Although Ramsay is far from dismissive about popular fiction, he clearly views many popular leisure pursuits as passive, not active. Once again, we see the 'mass' consumer being identified as a mere recipient of the leisure product, rather than an active agent with considerable cultural competence. It is this derogation of the nature of 'mass' cultural consumption, this dismissal of the 'mass' consumers' intellect, and indeed, of their cultural capital, which partly exposes the publishing trade's attitude regarding popular taste. It is the papers' discussions on the thorny issue of censorship which reveals them much further.

Marston made known *The Publishers' Circular*'s position on the censorship of books in 1930 when he stated in a leading article, knowingly entitled 'A Different Problem': 'Without some restraint, legal or moral, freedom would speedily degenerate into licence. There must be some limit, surely, some point where it becomes expedient to draw the line'.[68] Marston was unclear about the form that that censorship should take ('legal or moral'), but that there should be some form of control is something on which he was certain. What is inter-esting, though perhaps not surprising, is that this ambiguity extended into the paper's debates on the issue; the editorial power which Marston rigorously exercised in other matters was deployed with little effect here. For example, it would be predictable if moral guardians were presented in the paper to be wholly in favour of a censorship of books. Some were; in 1932, Eleanor Plumer demanded that the publishing trade fall in line with the cinema in regards to censorship. 'The idea is to call attention to objectionable matter in books, plays and films,' Plumer argued, adding: 'If you deal with one, you ought to deal with the three, is our argument'.[69] However, in contrast, Metropolitan Police magistrate J.A.R. Cairns, speaking at a Religious Tract Society annual meeting in 1931, had remarked, 'I do not believe in a censor. We have got to help to create a clean public opinion that will not tolerate things of this sort'.[70]

For Cairns, then, the public had to be educated into wanting to consume a better type of leisure product. Bearing in mind his lofty social position and the event at which his remarks were made, this could be a particularly surprising stance for Cairns to take. He identified the provision of certain types of fiction as problematic, so why did he not consider it best to tackle the problem at its source of production? Why did he look to the consumer and not the producer to solve his dilemma? It would be tempting to believe that Cairns is actually being rather pioneering, in that he is giving the consumer significant weight in the field of cultural relations. However, his comments most likely illustrate that he believed the consumer was primarily to blame for the state of popular fiction (and, indeed, all other popular leisure forms); producers were merely answering to the needs of an immoral public. While Cairns thus recognised that consumers had a role in the cultural field, he is not presenting it as a favourable one. This is a common theme running through many of the papers' discussions on censorship.

The ambiguity displayed by Marston, and underlined by the contrasting remarks of Plumer and Cairns, regarding the form which censorship should take, is particularly evident among publishing trade personnel. Some considered a legal censorship absolutely necessary. In 1935, Francis Hunt declared, 'Licence in literature is concomitant with moral decadence, and moral decadence with national decay ... A sane, reasonable censorship ensures a healthy minded nation'.[71] Others strongly disagreed. E.H. Baxter found the idea of an official censorship abhorrent, and responded to Hunt acidly:

> [W]hile there is some demand for a censorship, it must not be forgotten that such a thing usually has its own evils. An ignorant and narrow-minded censor brings contempt and scorn on his country; Art and Literature suffer ... The public generally resents any implication that its mentality is juvenile.[72]

A significant number of trade personnel called for the trade to regulate itself. In 1933, leading literary critic Desmond MacCarthy stated that he was 'against censorship by the State', but welcomed individual censorship by circulating libraries.[73] However, many others regarded self-censorship with as much, if not more, disdain as a state-led one. In a letter to the editor, Harold Forrester argued, 'Any form of censorship is bad ... but a voluntary censorship would be worse. Any book not submitted for consideration would be suspect'.[74] He used the control of the country's film industry to detail his concerns:

> the film censorship was a device of the producers to safeguard themselves from persecution by over-zealous Watch Committees. It has resulted in, on the one hand, a low standard of production in which inanity abounds and, on the other, a sailing near, if not an actual crossing of, the line of indecency ... This is the state of affairs in the film world, and we must not have it in books.[75]

Regardless of whether we agree with Forrester's portrayal of the film industry's output, censorship could have varying effects on it, and it is this which generated most interest within the publishing trade. Indeed, publishing trade personnel were certainly looking towards the example of film censorship to make their decisions.[76]

Like *Kineweekly*, then, *The Publishers' Circular*'s position on censorship was far from clear-cut; censorship was undoubtedly a highly contested issue which triggered a wide variety of responses. As one letter writer astutely observed: 'The matter of any kind of censorship is full of difficulty'.[77] Those working for and contributing to *The Bookseller* had similarly conflicting beliefs.[78] Despite this, it was generally believed within the publishing trade that the public needed protecting from the 'evils' to be found in much popular fiction. Indeed, after many years of debate which had seen little resolution, there was consensus within the publishing trade on this matter in 1936. In *The Publishers' Circular* one contributor claimed, 'Indecency and sexual immorality have become so common … some sort of censorship [is] so flagrantly necessary that even the Trade can see that it is; the best thing that we can do is to agree among ourselves which form is the best for it'.[79] Even popular novelist Ethel Boileau believed that there should be a curb on political, immoral and overtly sexual novels because it could cause 'a considerable alteration in human values and standards of conduct'.[80] *The Bookseller*'s J.L. Dobson concurred: 'It is the general atmosphere of loose morals and farmyard partnerships prevailing in fiction that offends good taste and disregards public decency'.[81]

Between 1930 and 1936, then, the publishing trade's discussions on censorship were frequent. They reached a peak in 1936, but ended that same year after a rapprochement between the conflicting parties. They were raised again in 1939 when, due to the war, censorship once more became a burning issue. Significantly, though, the only mention of censorship was made concerning 'technical' books; no-one appeared to be concerned about fiction. Without a doubt, this stance was influenced by the belief that the public needed to be distracted from the pressures of war.[82]

Of course, what has become evident from this discussion of censorship is that the publishing trade had an extremely poor opinion of public taste. There was clearly a consensus among trade personnel and moral guardians which concluded that while fiction may have declined, public taste had slipped much further. Therefore, while it was generally believed that censorship, whether state-led or self-regulated, would have a detrimental effect on the publishing profession, it was understood that its effect on public taste could be extremely beneficial. The publishing trade's attitude towards censorship may have been highly ambiguous, but its stance on public taste was not. Indeed, the majority of contributors to *The Publishers' Circular* and *The Bookseller* allude to the need to improve it. 'If there is a public which demands lustful and blasphemous literature, the only remedy I can see is to raise the standard of public taste,' argued a letter writer in *The Publishers' Circular*.[83] Bookseller Charles Young likewise asserted in *The Bookseller*, 'We should influence good taste, which needs stimulating, for sometimes the standards of good taste are partly obscured'.[84] Like those who contributed to *Kineweekly*'s debates on censorship, then, it was not always the nature of the product on offer that came under most criticism, but the public's consumption of it.

Predictably, then, and like *Kineweekly*, *The Publishers' Circular* questioned the nature of public taste, including the tastes of the working classes, throughout the decade. In 1933, the paper reported that steps were being taken to gauge the reading tastes of 'various occupational groups, including farm and industrial workers, clerical workers, housewives, seamen and others'.[85] In the same year, there was an attempt to establish the popularity of 'the Classics' among contemporary readers.[86] In 1938, Frederick J. Cowles produced a questionnaire for public library users asking why they had chosen certain books.[87] Of course, these investigations were conducted for analogous reasons to those carried out by members of the film trade. Publishing trade personnel were attempting to gain an impression of the public mood, both with an eye to sales (or in the case of Cowles, to assess library issues), and to establish the level of public taste. As Herbert N. Cassoon fittingly remarked in 1935: 'In order to know the people of our day, we must have a look at the books they are reading'.[88] What were the findings of these investigations?

By far the most notable element to be found in *The Publishers' Circular*'s assessment of public taste, and one which stimulated much interest from a range of trade personnel, referred to its varied and unpredictable nature. In 1933, for example, publisher Cecil Palmer remarked, 'It cannot be too greatly emphasised that the reading public is not a homogenous whole. It is a heterogeneous mass'.[89] In the paper's analysis of the year's publications in 1935 it was observed that readers had 'an endless diversity of interests and tastes,' and thus 'demands an ever-increasing supply of an ever-increasing *variety* of books'.[90] In 1937, popular author Dorothy Sayers referred to the rapidly changing tastes of the reading public, declaring, 'all of us have got to do our best to find out somehow what are the greater wants, and to supply them'.[91] Frederick J. Cowles did likewise in 1939, and described the period as an 'age of speed' in which 'literature may not be lasting, but it suits the mood of the moment. Little is permanent'.[92] In such a highly volatile environment, Cowles argued, the public library should not only 'represent every age, but it must be always up to date. It must cater, as wisely as it can, for the tastes of the period'.

While recognising diversity, not all contributors particularly welcomed it. Palmer, in fact, while relatively amenable in his opinions at the start of the decade, was less positive near its close, scathingly remarking: 'Trying to earn a living by writing to please the reading public is not a bed of roses. It is, at best, a couch of thorns. Popular authors especially are victims of the reading public's fickleness of heart and capriciousness of mind'.[93] These are harsh words, indeed, but perhaps Palmer had fallen out of step with the public mood. In fact, is it possible that his anger had been stirred by resentment that his publications had never corresponded with the most popular genres of the day? The fact that Palmer is discussing the irresistible draw of detective fiction on contemporary readers in this article, not particularly the type of fiction he had in mind when he confidently wrote in 1933, 'He who reads the penny "blood and thunder" to-day is more likely to develop a love for Robert Louis Stevenson tomorrow', suggests that it is.[94] This is, in fact, the main difference between *The Publisher's Circular* and *Kineweekly*; in their never-ending quest to improve public taste, the publishing trade paper's contributors repeatedly failed in their attempt to second-guess the public's mood; those at *Kineweekly* rarely made that mistake.

What becomes most evident from *The Publishers' Circular*'s analyses of public taste, therefore, is the overriding conviction among publishing trade personnel that it was their *duty* to improve it. Many of these investigations expose a desire on behalf of their architects to improve society's reading habits. In 1934, public librarian Edward Green was pleased to observe that his survey had revealed that children regularly borrowed 'classics' such as *Lorna Doone*, *Robin Hood* and *Robinson Crusoe*, leading him to gush: 'The reading of young people in Halifax is distinctly gratifying, and a definite contribution to cultural advancement'.[95] Even the liberal Cowles was delighted to report that the results of his 1938 questionnaire revealed that 'in every case, the books named were outstanding works of fiction'.[96]

While these librarians may have been trying to bolster support for the inclusion of fiction in public libraries, they also saw the institution as one which ought to encourage improved reading habits. Librarians working outside of the public library environment had the same conviction. In an article which offered advice on how to set up a factory library, R. Rose Price, welfare supervisor and librarian at Rego Clothiers, declared, 'The workers of this country taken as a whole are still unaccustomed to devoting their leisure to serious reading,' and thus warned potential librarians to be more assiduous when choosing books for inclusion: 'we need not sink to the ranks of the "penny dreadfuls" or the sickly sentimentality of some of the cheap novels obtainable'.[97] Price remained aware of the risks of being overtly didactic ('Never let the cultivation of the love of knowledge cause our efforts to appear patronizing'), but nonetheless believed that factory libraries should 'lead [readers] on from mere entertainment to wider interests and the love of fine literature for its own sake'. Price's article was published in 1939; the views of those contributing to and working for the paper regarding public taste had remained unchanged throughout the decade.

Given *The Publishers' Circular*'s dogmatic stance on the function of reading, it is predictable to find examples like these, but there are very few instances where the new reading public's preferences are defended, so these beliefs were extremely widespread. Indeed, if we turn to the pages of *The Bookseller* we find that a very similar picture is painted. Furthermore, of the few instances in which the public's tastes are defended in *The Publishers' Circular*, most are couched with a moralising fervour. In 1936, V. Phillips acknowledged that, 'The "right" type of book is as difficult to define as is the "right" type of anything,' but nonetheless concluded: 'In broad lines, however, it should cater for an active mind'.[98] Some contributors appeared to be less condescending. In a report, the London Public Library Service stated that its aims were to bring 'all classes of people into contact with all classes of books,' because: 'The assumption that "popular" reading is inferior reading is plain nonsense'.[99] But the very ethos of the public library was built upon improving public taste.

These, then, are the views of those working in the publishing trade regarding *public* taste. To further understand the trade's attitudes towards *working-class* taste we shall turn to that most popular of locations from which the mass reading public chose to borrow fiction – the twopenny library – and examine *The Publishers' Circular*'s stance towards it. What did the paper have to say about the working classes' favourite book-borrowing haunts?

As can be expected, *The Publishers' Circular*'s opinion of twopenny libraries was far from favourable. In fact, time and again, the paper featured articles by various trade personnel criticising both the libraries themselves and the public's appreciation of them. While the paper's editor occasionally led the vanguard, his contributions were more often a response to the growing number of articles and letters by trade personnel who had written to the paper to air their views on what they perceived to be a growing menace. The publishing trade's criticism of twopenny libraries was based upon a number of factors, but financial imperatives directed much of the debate. With book borrowing increasing, trade personnel feared a reduction in the number of readers actually buying books. One letter writer thus witheringly described the twopenny library as a 'canker' threatening the 'legitimate' bookseller.[100] In addition, the twopenny library owner's ability to circumvent trade legislation was also criticised. Marston, for example, considered twopenny libraries 'unfair competition' because they were 'exempted from the provisos of the Shops Acts in the matter of hours of business'.[101] Unsurprisingly, schemes were mooted on how best to regulate their activities and simultaneously reduce the bond between the twopenny library and the mass reading public.[102]

Financial considerations aside, trade personnel also criticised both the category of fiction available in twopenny libraries and the type of reader who frequented them. In 1932, W.J. Magenis complained that, 'The poorer classes in the suburbs, country town, villages and hamlets get their reading either for nothing or for the minimum cost of 2d a week. They are not too particular as to what they read so long as the book is interesting'.[103] Elaborating on this the following year, Magenis observed that the most popular novels were those 'which required no introspective effort to read'.[104] The mass reading public's principal desire, Magenis sniped, was to read 'books that "got off the mark at once," like Wallace, Oppenheim and Le Queux'. In 1934, a report of the Westminster Libraries Committee likewise declared that twopenny libraries supplied books which satisfied the demands of 'readers of low cultural equipment'.[105] An independent library proprietor similarly stated in 1938 that twopenny library users 'deal with a book not on its individual merits but as so many pages of mass dope'.[106] Predictably, these views were echoed in *The Bookseller*.[107]

In such ways, then, were the reading habits of the lowest social groups subjected to critical opprobrium. Indeed, this analysis has revealed how low down the cultural sphere publishing trade personnel placed working-class readers. Popular taste is repeatedly lambasted, as were those institutions, such as the public and twopenny libraries, that the working classes chose to frequent to borrow reading material. Indeed, these libraries, especially the latter, were blamed for both the decline in reading standards and the rise of the poorer class of fiction. Of course, popular fiction continued to be produced and consumed in ever-growing quantities throughout the decade, many trade personnel must, then, have been more positive towards it, but these papers routinely identified popular fiction as the poor cousin of highbrow literature. It is here where we can see similarities between these publishing trade papers and the film trade's equivalent. The types of product that attracted the 'mass' consumer were habitually disparaged in both *The Publishers' Circular* and *Kineweekly*. The latter may have been less conservative, and, therefore, more responsive to popular taste and consumer pleasure, but the improvement ethos nonetheless existed. The fact that popular texts continued to be produced, however, is evidence that many trade personnel were not as naïve as to bow to the pressure put upon them by their trade representatives, and it is to the work of these people to which we shall now turn.

Notes

1 A fuller analysis of *Kinematograph Weekly*'s attitudes is made in my article. See Robert James, '*Kinematograph Weekly* in the 1930s: Trade Attitudes Towards Audience Taste', *Journal of British Cinema and Television*, 3:2, 2007, pp. 229–243.

2 S.G. Rayment was editor, John Dunbar was managing editor, and A.L. Carter was associate editor.

3 *Kineweekly*, 21 May 1931.

4 Ibid., 1 June 1933.

5 Ibid., 1 March 1934.

6 Ibid., 18 May 1933.

7 Ibid., 4 February 1937.

8 Ibid., 29 June 1933.

9 Ibid., 1 October 1936.

10 Ibid., 22 October 1931.

11 Ibid., 22 April 1937.

12 Ibid., 14 September 1933.

13 Ibid., 7 September 1939.

14 Ibid., 11 January 1940.

15 Ibid.

16 Ibid., 7 September 1939.

17 Ibid., 29 June 1933.

18 Ibid., 16 May 1935.

19 Ibid., 14 January 1932.

20 Ibid., 14 January 1937.

21 Ibid. See 10 December 1931, 14 April 1932 and 7 January 1937.

22 Ibid., 15 August 1935.

23 Ibid., 26 September 1935.

24 Ibid., 25 July 1935.

25 Ibid., 7 August 1930.

26 Ibid., 1 June 1933.

27 Ibid., 25 September 1930.

28 Ibid., 24 March 1932.

29 Ibid., 14 January 1932.

30 Ibid., 23 January 1936.

31 Ibid., 11 December 1930.

32 Ibid., 14 August 1930.

33 Ibid., 10 September 1936.

34 Ibid., 2 July 1936.

35 Ibid., 21 January 1937.

36 Ibid., 6 May 1937.

37 Ibid., 9 April 1936.

38 Ibid., 1 February 1934.

39 Ibid., 8 January 1931.

40 Ibid., 9 March 1939.

41 Ibid., 6 February 1936.

42 Ibid., 8 April 1937.

43 Ibid., 17 August 1933.

44 Ibid., 4 May 1933.

45 Ibid., 29 November 1934.

46 Ibid., 9 April 1936.

47 *The Publishers' Circular* was, from 1932–1939, the 'official journal of the Publishers' Association and the Association of Booksellers of Great Britain and Ireland.' See *PC*, 24 September 1932.

48 *PC*, 18 April 1931.

49 Ibid.

50 Ibid., 31 December 1932.

51 Ibid., 3 June 1933.

52 Ibid., 17 February 1934.

53 Ibid., 25 April 1931.

54 Ibid., 26 March 1932.

55 Ibid., 24 September 1932.

56 Ibid., 1 October 1932.

57 See, for example, letter from Lionel W. Jones, ibid., 27 June 1931. See also 'Borrowing versus Buying', ibid., 29 August 1931.

58 Ibid., 19 March 1938. Cowles was responding to a series of letters that had appeared in editions of the paper over a three-week period. See 'Public Libraries as Buyers of Fiction; Conflicting Views', ibid., 5 March 1932; 12 March 1932; and 19 March 1932.

59 Ibid., 26 March 1938.

60 Ibid. See also letter from Barbara R. Kyle, a Senior Assistant of Fulham Public Libraries.

61 Ibid., 9 December 1939.

62 Ibid., 28 October 1939.

63 *The Bookseller* was edited by Edmond Segrave.

64 *Bookseller*, 3 April 1931.

65 Ibid., 6 July 1939.

66 Ibid., 3 May 1930.

67 *PC*, 3 October 1936.

68 Ibid., 17 May 1930.
69 Ibid., 30 July 1932.
70 Ibid., 9 May 1931.
71 Ibid., 27 July 1935.
72 Ibid., 3 August 1935.
73 Ibid., 14 January 1933.
74 Ibid., 17 August 1935.
75 Ibid.
76 This is similarly evident in *The Bookseller*. See article by Max Kenyon, 4 March 1936.
77 See letter from Charles C. Darton. *PC*, 22 February 1936.
78 See Max Kenyon's 'Against Censorship', *Bookseller*, 5 February 1936; and articles by both Kenyon and Dobson, 4 March 1936.
79 *PC*, 7 March 1936.
80 Ibid., 12 December 1936.
81 *Bookseller*, 4 March 1936.
82 See leading article 'Censorship of Books; Publishers and the Press Bureau'. *PC*, 23 December 1939.
83 See letter from Edith M. Frost. Ibid., 29 February 1936.
84 *Bookseller*, 24 April 1931.
85 *PC*, 15 April 1933.
86 Ibid., 21 January 1933.
87 Ibid., 2 July 1938.
88 Ibid., 28 December 1935.
89 Ibid., 26 August 1933.
90 Ibid., 28 December 1935.
91 Ibid., 12 June 1937.
92 Ibid., 5 August 1939.
93 Ibid., 7 May 1938.
94 Ibid., 26 August 1933.
95 Ibid., 20 October 1934.
96 Ibid., 2 July 1938. Cowles and his assistant Neil Bell handed out over 300 question-naires; 110 were returned.
97 Ibid., 21 January 1939.
98 *PC*, 5 September 1936.
99 Ibid., 28 January 1939.
100 See letter from R. Borras, ibid., 1 July 1933.
101 Ibid., 10 August 1935.
102 Ibid. See also 17 February and 10 November 1934.
103 Ibid., 20 August 1932.
104 Ibid., 3 June 1933.
105 *PC*, 17 February 1934.
106 Ibid., 6 August 1939.
107 See letter from Francis B. Gabbutt. *Bookseller*, 18 April 1934. See also 18 March 1936 and 6 July 1939.

4

'What made you put that rubbish on?': national trends in film popularity

Broader patterns of popularity

Before *Kineweekly* began publishing its list of 'Box-Office Winners' in 1936, reliable evidence on film popularity is rather limited. However, film fan magazines do provide a number of indicators. *Film Weekly* and *Picturegoer*, the two major film fan magazines, conducted a number of film popularity surveys throughout the decade. From the late 1920s, *Film Weekly*, which sought to attract a more literate readership than *Picturegoer*, asked its readers to vote for their favourite British film; the results were published in its annual British film poll.[1] As David Sutton has observed, comedy films fared extremely well in these polls, especially during the early part of the decade.[2] In 1930, 1931 and 1932, for example, comedy films topped the polls (Aldwych farce *Rookery Nook* [1930], naval comedy *The Middle Watch* [1930], and romantic comedy *Sunshine Susie* [1931], respectively).[3] Comedy films also featured heavily as runners-up. Many of these films were based on popular stage plays, and featured a number of well-known stage actors.[4] Audience recognition and, indeed, satisfaction was thus virtually assured. It is no surprise, then, that *Film Weekly* claimed that comedy had triumphed at the box-office.[5]

While comedy films were undoubtedly popular with *Film Weekly*'s readers, other film genres also fared extremely well. Dramatic films were very well represented. *Rookery Nook* may have topped the poll in 1930, but *Atlantic* (1929), described by the magazine as a 'thrilling drama of the sinking of a great liner,' came second, and *White Cargo* (1930) – 'A tense drama' – came third.[6] In 1931, second place went to a hard-hitting drama about a crippled girl, *The Outsider* (1931), and one of the film's stars, Harold Huth, was given the 'best performance' award by the magazine's readers for his role as the girl's unorthodox practitioner. Similarly, in 1932, Korda's romantic comedy *Service for Ladies* (1931) may have been placed second, and *Jack's the Boy* (1932), starring Jack

Hulbert and Cicely Courtneidge, fourth, but the romantic dramas *Michael and Mary* (1931), *The Faithful Heart* (1932), and *Hindle Wakes* (1931) came third, fifth and sixth respectively.[7] The 'best performance' award for 1932, meanwhile, was given to Emlyn Williams for his role in the Edgar Wallace thriller *The Frightened Lady* (1932). *Film Weekly*'s readers were thus equally content to watch, and vote for, more challenging British film fare along with the comedy staples.

Of course, American-produced films held more appeal with the majority of the cinema-going public than those films produced in Britain, so the results of these surveys rather skew the evidence regarding audience taste. Indeed, in another survey carried out by the magazine in 1930 to establish which films held 'the widest appeal' for the country's cinema-goers, only two British films – *Atlantic* and *Rookery Nook* – are present.[8] The remaining eleven 'screen successes of 1930' are all high-gloss, high-budget American productions. Moreover, it is not comedy, but musical films that dominate the list. Five musicals are present – *The Desert Song* (1929), *Gold Diggers of Broadway* (1929), *The Love Parade* (1929), *Rio Rita* (1929), and *Sunny Side Up* (1929). The remaining films on the list are the dramas *Bulldog Drummond* (1929), *Raffles* (1930), and *The Big House* (1930), western *Romance of the Rio Grande* (1929), historical adventure *The Four Feathers* (1929), and comedy drama *High Society Blues* (1930).

When conducting this survey, *Film Weekly* consulted 'proprietors of leading cinemas throughout the country and other film experts whose business is to study the ever changing tastes of the film-going public'.[9] The results, they believed, could 'be regarded as an accurate reflection of the hard cash judgment of the box-office, [that] most ruthless and most unerring of all film critics'.[10] This survey, then, reveals that cinema audiences in 1930 favoured American films over British productions and musicals over any other type of film. Significantly, though, *Film Weekly* also noted that cinema proprietors had identified 'marked changes in film fashions' during the course of the year. The range of musical films on the list was, they claimed, the result of a keen interest in this type of film during the first few months of the year only. Apparently, their appeal diminished as the year progressed, and 'open-air romances' did well in the summer months. These were, in turn, superseded by 'laughter-making films' and 'detective stories which appeal to the spectator's intelligence' at the year's close. Proprietors also reported that there had been a 'steadily increasing demand for British films' as the year progressed. Such reports reveal the often quite extreme fluctuations in audience tastes. They also demonstrate how difficult it is to judge a film's popularity through film surveys alone.

Despite their inadequacies, these film surveys do reveal that Britain's cinema-goers were highly adventurous in their film tastes. *Film Weekly*'s editor acknowledged this, approvingly noting: 'That the types of film favoured at different theatres and districts varied widely is evidence of the critical judgment of filmgoers. It also shows that the cinema to-day is capable of providing entertainment for every class of the community'.[11] Not surprisingly, then, the results of *Film Weekly*'s surveys correspond closely with other surveys carried out in the period. In 1933, for example, *Film Weekly* published a list of the year's 'principal picture successes'.[12] Out of the eleven films listed, six appear in at least one other contemporary film survey. Dramatic tear-jerker *Smilin' Through* (1932) not only featured as one of *Film Weekly*'s 'principal picture successes', it also appeared in *Picturegoer*'s 'Award of Merit' – for Norma Shearer's dual roles as ghost and young lover, and Leslie Howard's performance as a grieving and lonely recluse.[13] Korda's historical epic *The Private Life of Henry VIII* (1933) likewise featured as one of the year's 'principal picture successes', gained recognition from *Picturegoer*'s readers for Charles Laughton's performance, and achieved second place in the 'Very Good' film category of Bernstein's Questionnaire.[14]

Such was the widespread popularity of some films, moreover, that they featured in all of the abovementioned film surveys. War melodrama *I Was a Spy* (1933) not only appeared in *Film Weekly*'s list of 'principal picture successes', it was also placed in Bernstein's 'Very Good' film category, *and* won accolades from *Picturegoer*'s readers for Madeleine Carroll and Conrad Veidt's sterling acting performances.[15] The film also topped *Film Weekly*'s annual British film poll; Carroll and Veidt also gained first and second place respectively in the magazine's 'performance' category.[16] Historical spectacular *Cavalcade* (1933), meanwhile, one of the major film successes of the decade, not only topped Bernstein's 'Very Good' film category for that year, it also led the list of *Film Weekly*'s 'principal picture successes'.[17] Its leading stars were highly placed in *Picturegoer*'s 'Award of merit' – Clive Brook was awarded first place in the 'actors' category; Diana Wynyard came second in the 'actresses' category.[18] *Cavalcade*'s extraordinary popularity is confirmed by its exhibition patterns. In Sedgwick's statistical analysis, *Cavalcade* heads the list of films released in 1933, and is given a POPSTAT rating of 92.89 – the highest index of any film in the years Sedgwick's investigation covers.[19] In addition, Harper has shown that *Cavalcade* was the second biggest 'runaway hit' at the Regent in the decade, attracting 31,824 patrons in September 1933.[20]

These films, then, were answering to the tastes of the majority of Britain's cinema-goers. They included elements that guaranteed popular success. One determining factor was, of course, the attraction of the stars that appeared in them. Indeed, all the performers that featured in the abovementioned films appeared in a number of popularity lists across these years. Tom Walls and Ralph Lynn, who starred in *Rookery Nook*, were among the 'Most popular [male] film stars' in Bernstein's 1932 Questionnaire report.[21] Ronald Colman, who played lead roles in *Bulldog Drummond* and *Raffles*, topped Bernstein's list in that year and was one of the 'Best liked' stars in the *Daily Express* film census.[22] In 1930, Maurice Chevalier was chosen by *Film Weekly*'s readers as the film world's most popular star.[23] In addition, he was listed as one of a number of the magazine's 'Class A attractions' in 1931.[24] The list included, among many others, Ronald Colman, Ralph Lynn and Tom Walls. The close correlation between film popularity and the popularity of particular film stars is, in fact, startling, and it is a trend that continues throughout the decade.

Time and again, then, the films that appear in these surveys featured the cinema audience's favourite stars. Of course, there are exceptions. Hertha Thiele earned a place in *Picturegoer*'s 'Award of Merit' in 1932 for her emotionally charged performance in the German-produced drama *Mädchen in Uniform* (1931).[25] Neither Thiele nor the film appeared in any other popularity list. The film's inclusion on *Picturegoer*'s list undoubtedly has much to do with the manner in which the 'Award of Merit' was chosen. The award was presented to film stars whose acting performance had most appealed to the magazine's readers. It is, however, hard to envisage any of the magazine's readers voting for a star they disliked just because they performed well.[26] Indeed, it is highly unlikely that they would have chosen to see the film in the first place. In this sense, then, *Picturegoer*'s 'Award of Merit' dealt with issues of both film *and* film star popularity. And the choice of stars, and the film performances for which they were nominated, are consistent with other film surveys which were based solely on a film's success or a performer's popularity. The only minor difference is that films with a strong dramatic content tend to dominate. In 1932, for example, the top three films in both 'actor' and 'actress' categories were all 'serious' films. But this variation has more to do with the nature of the award than public taste.

So, contemporary surveys reveal that a core body of films were answering to the tastes of the majority of the nation's cinema-goers. Sedgwick's POPSTAT findings confirm this trend.[27] Of the top ten POPSTAT films in 1932, for example, five were mentioned in at least one contemporary survey. Nineteen additional films in POPSTAT's top 100 films of 1932 also appear in the film polls consulted here. POPSTAT's results for 1937 provide the most interesting reading, however. *Every* film in the top ten appears in at least one of the contemporary film popularity surveys consulted. In fact, out of the top twenty films, nineteen appear elsewhere, and out of the top 100 films, fifty-one are mentioned in contemporary surveys. This has, no doubt, much to do with the more systematic recording of box-office successes by *Kineweekly* in that year, but the close correlation between the films listed in POPSTAT and those mentioned in contemporary surveys does help to confirm the effectiveness of Sedgwick's method of establishing a film's relative popularity. The author's STARSTAT index, which lists the top 100 stars between 1932 and 1937, further contributes to our understanding of the audience's relationship with cinema culture.[28]

Of course, what Sedgwick's POPSTAT index cannot tell us, or indeed the majority of the contemporary sources employed thus far, is to which *class* of cinema-goer these films were appealing. *Film Weekly* and *Picturegoer* sought to attract an upper-working and lower-middle class readership.[29] Therefore, if they were attracting their target audience, it would have been these classes of consumer that were reading, and voting in, these fan magazines, so the results of their many surveys can only represent the tastes of these social groups. *Kineweekly's* findings were based on box-office takings, and while this does not remove working-class consumers from the equation, by the same token it does not exclude other social classes either. Korda's Questionnaire appeared in a number of national newspapers and would likewise have attracted responses from a wide-class readership. Sedgwick's findings, meanwhile, are based upon the booking patterns of metropolitan and leading provincial cinemas listed in *Kineweekly*; his results can, therefore, only reveal the tastes of the patrons of these undoubtedly classier cinemas. The results of these surveys cannot, then, be isolated to any particular social class. Nonetheless, they can be said to reveal the tastes of the *mass* of the cinema-going public, and in that sense they do also say something about the tastes of working-class cinema-goers.

Sidney Bernstein collection

There is more class-specific material available, however. While Bernstein's finalised reports summarise information gleaned from the patrons of a number of the Granada chain's cinemas, the pre-report material divides the data by the audience's sex, age and, most importantly for my purpose, 'class'.[30] Researchers graded cinemas according to the area in which they were sited, and the types of cinema-goer that patronised them.[31] In 1932, the 'working-class theatres' were the East Ham Rialto, Edmonton Empire, Plumstead Kinema, Shrewsbury King's and West Ham Kinema, with an average seating capacity of 1,210. The 'middle-class' cinemas were the Enfield Rialto, Leytonstone Rialto, Shrewsbury Empire, Tooting Granada, Walthamstow Granada and Willesden Empire, and averaged 1,919 seats. Shrewsbury's two cinemas were not included in Bernstein's 1934 survey; the Maidstone Granada (working-class) and Watford Regal (middle-class) were new additions. The segmented results are very illuminating. Unless we are vigilant, though, results might be skewed by the ratio of middle-class to working-class votes.[32]

Bernstein's pre-report material reveals that there is some correlation between the tastes of the middle and working classes. In 1932, Ronald Colman and Norma Shearer were the favourite stars of both classes, and religious spectacular *Ben-Hur* (1925), starring Ramon Novarro and Francis X. Bushman, was the 'all-time' favourite film overall. In 1934, George Arliss and Clark Gable were liked equally by both classes, and Marie Dressler and Norma Shearer were the top two female stars. But there are also differences in taste. In 1932, only two of the eighteen male stars listed have equal standing (Colman and Novarro). The remainder differ in rank by between one and eight places. Working-class audiences favoured Charles Farrell and Jack Holt, while middle-class audiences preferred George Bancroft and Gary Cooper. The contrasting screen personae of these stars undoubtedly explain their differing appeal. Farrell featured in sentimental melodrama *The Man Who Came Back*, musical *Delicious* and romantic drama *Merely Mary Ann* (all 1931). In each of these films Farrell is the heroic figure who comes to the rescue of a damsel in distress (in each case Janet Gaynor). Jack Holt, who played lead roles in buddy melodrama *The Last Parade* and disaster spectacular *Dirigible* (both 1931), is a robust hero with a tender side. The Prince Charming/Cinderella theme clearly played well with Granada's working-class cinema-goers.

The tastes of the chain's middle-class patrons could not have been more different. George Bancroft's success reveals that this section of the audience liked their male screen personalities to be socially and financially successful with a domineering personality: Bancroft played a ruthless shipbuilder in *Rich Man's Folly* and a hard-nosed and heartless newspaper editor in *The Dark Page* (both 1931). *The Dark Page* also starred Kay Francis as Bancroft's down-trodden but unfaithful wife, and Clive Brook as her lover. As Brook was placed very highly by middle- and working-class cinema-goers, his role as the underdog clearly attracted widespread sympathy. Gary Cooper, meanwhile, consistently played tough men who were weakened by strong women. In romantic drama

His Woman (1931) he is a Caribbean freighter who falls for the charms of a stowaway (Claudette Colbert). In sophisticated gangland melodrama *City Streets* (1931) he is a shooting gallery showman who gets drawn into mob life by a gangster's daughter (Sylvia Sidney). And in comedy romance *I Take This Woman* (1931) he plays a cowboy who embarks in a disastrous marriage with New York socialite (Carole Lombard). These films allow their female characters great latitude, but there is always repositioning at the films' end. Audiences are thus allowed to contemplate, for a time at least, a world without social and gender constraints. It is no surprise they found favour primarily with a middle-class clientele strictly bound by social etiquette. Perhaps surprisingly, though, Colbert, Sidney and Lombard did not feature in Bernstein's favourite female star category. It would appear that their characters' social antics were too risqué for middle-class audiences to warrant a vote in a popularity survey.

There were, in fact, very few class distinctions regarding audience taste in female stars in 1932. Of the twelve actresses listed, seven are equally placed, with only Joan Crawford ranking significantly higher with working-class audiences, and Jeanette MacDonald more strongly favoured by middle-class cinema-goers. In 1934, however, there were considerable differences between the stars' rankings. Only two stars share equal popularity (Greta Garbo and Cicely Courtneidge). Interestingly, Joan Crawford's popularity now rested predominantly with youngish, female middle-class audiences. This shift in taste reflected a swing in Crawford's screen persona. In 1931, when she was ranked highly by working-class audiences, she played strong, often erring, female leads (in gangster thriller *Dance, Fools, Dance*, romantic drama *Laughing Sinners*, and melodramas *This Modern Age* and *Possessed*). In 1933, when she was favoured by middle-class audiences, she was gentility personified (in musical romance *Dancing Lady* and romantic drama *Today We Live*).

As in 1931, then, these working-class audiences favoured female stars who played strong, independent women: Janet Gaynor as a rebellious princess in *Adorable* (1933), Jessie Matthews as a spirited entertainer in *The Good Companions* (1933), Jean Harlow as a hard-boiled dame in *Hold Your Man* (1933), and the indomitable Gracie Fields in *This Week of Grace* (1933). Without a doubt, these stars' performances encouraged the (female) audience's sense of self, so it is no surprise that they were popular with them. But, with the exception of Gaynor, they also attracted a healthy number of votes from working-class men. Because the highest number of votes for all four stars was among the 'less than twenty-one' age group, their appeal lay primarily among young male and female cinema-goers who clearly liked their women to have a bit of spirit.

There is more consistency between the rankings of male stars in 1934. Of the nineteen actors listed, five were liked equally by Granada's middle- and working-class audiences (George Arliss, Clark Gable, Charles Laughton, Leslie Howard and Jack Holt). Interestingly, though, Jack Holt's popularity with working-class audiences had fallen dramatically since 1932. His style of macho eloquence was now being provided by another star – Clark Gable, who ranked second. As regards taste distinctions, Granada's working-class audiences favoured Warner Baxter, Jack Buchanan and Herbert Marshall, while its middle-class audiences preferred Fredric March and Robert Montgomery. Montgomery starred in a series of 'society' films during 1933, and his screen personae ranged from ruthless press agent (*Made on Broadway*) to narcissistic mother's boy (*Another Language*). It is not surprising working-class audiences failed to fall for his charms. March, meanwhile, played a tortured air-ace in *The Eagle and the Hawk*, a beleaguered lover in *Design for Living*, and a commoner wooed by a Princess (Claudette Colbert) in *Tonight is Ours*. In a sense, then, he duplicated the model of Gary Cooper (whom he starred alongside in *Design for Living*) as the vulnerable male. These working-class audiences wanted their men to be strong, but fair, and their women to be spirited, not domineering. Indeed, Baxter's popularity surely rested on his role as the sanguine and just Broadway director who allows Ruby Keeler's feisty chorus girl the chance of stardom in *Forty-Second Street* (1933).

If we turn to film popularity, we find that class differences in taste are even more marked. There are two resources available here. One is a list, drawn up in Bernstein's 1932 Questionnaire, of the audiences' 'all-time' favourite films; the other is an 'Attendances Sheet' that lists the attendance figures for some of the films the chain exhibited in 1931. What taste distinctions can be detected?

Of the twenty-two films listed in the 'all-time' favourites' category, only one, *Ben-Hur*, shares equal ranking between Granada's middle and working-class audiences. The remainder differ in rank from between one and thirteen places. The most notable difference in film popularity in this category concerns the sentimental drama *Over the Hill*. The film was ranked sixth by working-class audiences, but nineteenth by middle-class cinema-goers. Two versions of the film had been produced by the time this survey took place – one silent (1920), one 'talkie' (1931) – and while it is not clear which film is being referred to, both contain the same narrative drive. Adapted from the poems *Over the Hill to the Poorhouse* and *Over the Hill from the Poorhouse* by Will Carleton, the films explore the plight of an aged mother who ends up in a poorhouse after being abandoned by her large and relatively successful family, but who is then rescued by her wayward son. Dealing with the loss of kinship, social humiliation and, finally, redemption, this was a social conscience tale that was more likely to appeal to working-class audiences who were able to identify with the principal character's plight.

Indeed, the chain's working-class audiences were inclined to favour films with a social conscience, but only so long as they were relevant to their own experiences. They liked Charlie Chaplin's melodramatic sentimentality in *The Kid* (1921), but were less enamoured with his efforts in *The Gold Rush* (1925) and *Shoulder Arms* (1918). While none of these films' settings were that pleasing, it would seem that the locations of the latter two were either less identifiable or less appealing for this taste-community. *The Kid* was set in a slum area, and was thus readily identifiable, but *The Gold Rush* was set in the Yukon – a location alien to these consumers, and *Shoulder Arms* was set in the trenches of First World War France, which undoubtedly held painful associations. Indeed, they liked *Broken Blossoms* (1919), D.W. Griffith's bleak adaptation of Thomas Burke's novel, *Limehouse Nights*. They also liked his Civil War epic *Birth of a Nation* (1915). However, Griffith's account of a seduced and shamed country girl, *Way Down East* (1920), and his French Revolution epic, *Orphans of the Storm* (1921), went down less well with these working-class audiences. In fact, the French Revolutionary theme did not appeal at all to these patrons, for *Scaramouche* (1923) fared very badly indeed. Other costume dramas did better. *Ben-Hur*, of course, topped the poll, and its blend of piety and adventure, mixed with rousing action sequences, went down well. Rudolph Valentino's first major film *The Four Horsemen of the Apocalypse* (1921) also did well, and *The Hunchback of Notre Dame* (1923) was runner-up to *Ben-Hur*. Significantly, *Hunchback* was less favourably received by Granada's middle-class patrons. This is perhaps predictable when we bear in mind that the film champions marginal groups, celebrates popular cultural forms, and presents the state's representatives as social pariahs. It is, of course, perfectly clear why Granada's working-class cinema-goers appreciated it.

Interestingly, these working-class consumers also displayed a willingness to embrace the experimental, for *Vaudeville*[33] and *Metropolis* (1927) were both respectably placed. Of course, the popularity of *Metropolis* also had much to do with its depiction of the miners' city in the bowels of the earth. The least popular film with Granada's working-class patrons was, in fact, one of the most commercial: the romantic drama *Smilin' Through* (1922). The 1932 version of this film, starring Leslie Howard, Fredric March and Norma Shearer, attracted significant acclaim from the readers of *Film Weekly* and *Picturegoer*, but the working-class section of Granada's audiences were not charmed by the silent version. No, these working-class cinema-goers wanted their dramatic films to offer something to which they could relate, and they could hardly identify with this film's lead characters – Wyndham Standing as a wealthy man with a large estate and Norma Talmadge as his intended bride.

Bernstein's attendances register lists fifty films exhibited in the chain's cinemas in 1931. Some films, such as slapstick comedy *Reducing* (1931), were shown at most, although not all, of the cinemas included in the 1931 survey. Others, such as the musical drama *The Blue Angel* (1930), had very limited appeal, and were only shown at one cinema. The most successful film at each of the chain's 'working-class' cinemas were Chaplin's sentimental comedy *City Lights* (1931), romantic drama *Born to Love* (1931), farce *Canaries Sometimes Sing* (1930), *Reducing* (1931), and the musical comedy *Whoopee!* (1930). These films were also screened at the chain's 'middle-class' cinemas, so they were expected to appeal to both sections of the audience. Nonetheless, because they were extremely successful at 'working-class' cinemas, they were obviously answering to the tastes of that section of the audience.

Chaplin cemented his appeal with Granada's working-class patrons in the 1920s, so it is not surprising to see *City Lights* playing well. Once again, Chaplin explores the plight of the disenfranchised, and employs humour to soften his particular brand of social critique. The masking effects of comedy undoubtedly helped the film gain widespread appeal, because it also did well at Granada's 'middle-class' cinemas. We can, however, identify geographical and gender distinctions in taste. *City Lights* gained more votes from male than female cinema-goers. Of the 'working-class' cinemas, *City Lights* drew its biggest audience at the Edmonton Empire, but attracted fewer cinema-goers to the West Ham Kinema, and significantly less to the East Ham Rialto.

In fact, patrons at the East Ham Rialto preferred a different type of comedy altogether, for the most popular film there was *Reducing*, which featured Marie Dressler as the proprietor of a beauty salon and reducing parlour. Dressler had appeared earlier in the year in *Min and Bill*, but while this atmospherically photographed tale of two down-at-heel slum residents was one of the year's most popular films, it fared less well here. The poor showing for *Min and Bill*, and the success of *Reducing*, suggests that this working-class audience wanted their humour to take them away from an identifiable world, and transport them in to an imaginary one. *Reducing*'s success also had much to do with its *type* of humour: slapstick. Slapstick comedy did extremely well at the East Ham Rialto. Laurel and Hardy's *Jail Birds* (1931), Ernie Lotinga's *PC Josser* (1930), and Wheeler and Woolsey's *Hook, Line and Sinker* (1930) all drew respectable audience numbers. Significantly, apart from *Reducing*, none of these films were shown at the Edmonton Empire; they also only managed to attract a few of that cinema's 'wandering public'.[34] There are, then, clear *inter*-class taste distinctions. Gender distinctions are, again, apparent. Dressler was renowned for playing strong, independent women, and her role in *Reducing* was no different. Not surprisingly, the film was preferred by female cinema-goers.

Reducing drew a respectable crowd to the West Ham Kinema, but the most successful film here, especially with female cinema-goers, was the romantic drama *Born to Love*. This is the only non-comedic film that outperforms all others at a 'working-class' cinema. Featuring Constance Bennett (who was popular with Granada's working-class audiences) as a nurse who bears the child of a soldier, *Born to Love* offers a candid and challenging depiction of pre-marital sexuality and romantic fulfilment. At a time when female working-class consumers were awarded greater social freedoms, it is not surprising that this type of fare went down well with them. Indeed, musical comedy *Whoopee!*, a film that accords much narrative space to rancher's daughter Sally Morgan (Eleanor Hunt) as she willingly flouts social and gender conventions, was the most popular film at Plumstead's 'working-class' cinema. The film's musical exuberance and highly comedic bearing allows the audience easy access into Morgan's world of the frivolous and carefree, and one can just imagine Plumstead's female customers leaving the cinema singing, with a glint in their eyes, the film's popular theme tune 'Making Whoopee'.

Significantly, and quite unlike the aforementioned *City Streets*, *His Woman*, and *I Take This Woman*, there is no moral repositioning at the end of *Whoopee!* and *Born to Love*. These women *get what they want*. It is perhaps predictable, then, that both of these films were only shown at one other 'working-class' cinema (the Edmonton Empire, where they also attracted large audience numbers). It is tempting to suggest that the Secretary of the Film Society, Miss J.M. Harvey, who was responsible for the selection of films at Bernstein's cinemas, was troubled by the effects these films could have on the chain's 'impressionable' working-class patrons.[35] The fact that *Born to Love* also assuages any anxiety working-class audiences may have felt regarding their social position by portraying upper-class life as staid and emotionally detached, would only have aggravated her consternation.

Crucially, none of these films were produced in Britain. Only one British film outperforms all others at a 'working-class' cinema (the Shrewsbury King's), and that was the Tom Walls comedy vehicle *Canaries Sometimes Sing*. Based

on Frederick Lonsdale's play, *Canaries Sometimes Sing* employs the same narrative and textural formulae that were used in all of Walls's screen farces. These
films present a parody of class behaviour, where self-interest and social status
outweigh tolerance and mutual support. They embrace class separateness, not
consensus. Interestingly, *Canaries* was only shown at one other 'working-class'
cinema (Plumstead); Harvey may have been concerned about the effects of
this film on working-class audiences too. However, the film attracted only a
limited number of patrons from other 'working-class' cinemas. Some part of
the working-class audience must, then, have been discomfited by its radical
interpretation of society. Indeed, the chain's middle-class patrons tended to
prefer Walls's type of humour. Middle-class cinema-goers could, of course,
laugh along with these films knowing that they were secure in their class
position. The chain's working-class patrons, knowing they were not, usually
preferred films that reassured them.

Indeed, the least successful film shown at Granada's 'working-class' cinemas
was Howard Hawks's crime thriller *The Criminal Code* (1931). It was only
shown at one 'working-class' cinema (again the Shrewsbury King's), achieved
the lowest attendance figures at that cinema, and attracted very few of the
chain's working-class 'wandering public'. It could, quite simply, be that these
cinema-goers did not like crime films, for no other crime film was shown,
unless we include Laurel and Hardy's *Jail Birds*, which is hardly representative of the genre. But the film's handling of its subject matter must also have
lessened its appeal. Set in a penitentiary and focusing on the incarceration and
rehabilitation of Robert Graham (Phillips Holmes), *The Criminal Code* criti-
cises the individual for any failings that may befall them. It is hardly surprising
to find working-class audiences failing to appreciate a film that did little to
relieve their anxieties about their place in the world.

No, these audiences wanted to see films that encouraged their sense of
self; films that provided reassurance about their place in society. As such,
these audiences' film tastes say much about their hopes and aspirations, about
their attitude towards society, and about their feelings towards their position
within it. In fact, the dominance of American-produced films is in itself highly
significant. While they were favoured by many working-class consumers
because of their high-gloss production values and narrative speed, American
films were also, as Marcia Landy has rightly noted, often heavily critical of
'entrenched wealth and privilege,' and more willing than British-produced
films to 'pose radical social alternatives to oppression'.[36] It is not surprising
that these working-class cinema-goers, experiencing significant social changes

and suffering the effects of the Depression, would turn towards such film fare for entertainment.

Bernstein's pre-report material thus provides detailed information about the tastes of particular sections of the cinema-going public. It reveals that there were similarities in taste between middle- and working-class cinema-goers, but that there were also significant taste differences. Not only that, but there were inter-class taste differences that were structured along the lines of age, gender, and locality.

Mass-Observation Archive

Mass-Observation's survey of cinema-going habits in Bolton in 1937–1938 allows unrivalled access to the views expressed by cinema audiences.[37] As part of their investigation, M-O researchers handed out questionnaires to the patrons of three cinemas – the Odeon, the Crompton and the Palladium. The latter, as Richards and Sheridan have observed, was a down-market cinema that drew audiences primarily from the working-class city-centre area.[38] The responses to these questionnaires provide valuable information on the tastes of a small group of working-class cinema-goers.

Researchers also interviewed the Palladium's manager, Mr Gregson, along with the manager of the Embassy, another down-market cinema that attracted a similar clientele.[39] It is worth citing the comments of the Embassy's manager, Mr Hull, at length because he makes some very interesting remarks about the cinematic tastes of his largely working-class clientele, and, in doing so, reveals something of his attitude towards his customers:

> If I get an exceptional picture like *Rosalie*, its seventh run in Bolton, we always do well. 500 people were at the opening matinée of that film out of 600 seats. That's not bad for a seventh run. I've seen people out at the front say 'Oh, we'll go and see this again.' They won't go only once, but two and even three times to a good musical. Musical pictures in Lancashire go the best for any. Mystery pictures are nowhere. Give them anything they have to think about and they're lost. I ran *Firefly*, 8th run, 50 per cent increase. *Maytime*, 8th run, 50 per cent increase, same as with *Rosalie*, about 10 per cent increase … But bad musicals don't go. They flop dead. Cheap American or British musicals are no good. Mystery pictures don't go in Lancashire. You can cut them out. The finest mystery picture in the world I can't run it 3rd run. Another thing they like is old melodrama, especially in the cheap seats. They love it when the villain comes in and say 'Aha, fair maiden, so you've gone that way.' Spectacular films are another that go well. Anything spectacular. Like *Hurricane*. There was nothing in it except studio effects, but it went very well. A clever film will not go. I had a very good picture, *The Divorce*

of Lady X. Couldn't run it 2nd run. *Bluebeard's Eighth Wife* was another. Third run was no good. I've had good pictures in here and they've come out and said, 'What made you put that rubbish on?' I've even had them come out and say, 'How much did they pay you to put that on?' That was after *Bluebeard's Eighth Wife*. They don't want hidden humour. They're working all day, and they come up here at night all dressed up like dandies. They think they're on top of the Earth, you've got to make them think that they are. If there's anything crude they like it. Think it's a smasher. Look at *Escape from Devil's Isle*. We were packed out, yet it was the crudest thing going. You could see everything coming.[40]

Despite Hull's condescending tone, he does display a healthy respect towards his customers' cinematic needs. He recognises that, in order to stay in business, he has to book the types of film they wanted to see. He may have *wished* that his customers held more sophisticated tastes; he could *not* afford to ignore them. In this sense, then, Hull's remarks further underline the importance of the consumer in the production/consumption process. If the Embassy's patrons were not willing to pay to see a certain type of film – and they were not afraid to express an opinion when a film did not please them – Hull could not afford to keep booking them. Despite his dismay, Hull sang the tune of his paymasters, and his stance was very much in line with many of his contemporaries. Indeed, one Scottish cinema manager summed up succinctly the mantra that all cinema managers must surely have followed: 'they who live to please, must please to live'.[41]

As well as alerting us to the intricacies of the cinema manager's relationship with his customers, Hull's comments also reveal much about the consumer's enjoyment of the whole cinema-going experience. Part of the pleasure gained from going to the cinema was, of course, the opportunity it afforded to leave behind the working environment and indulge in the delights on the screen – whether that be a mother leaving the family home to enjoy a matinée performance of *Rosalie* (1937), or a couple of 'dandies' escaping the grind of the factory to take pleasure in an evening performance of *The Hurricane* (1937). But Hull's remarks reveal that there was more to it than this. The act of cinema-going helped his customers *believe they were somebody*. They were 'dandies' who were 'on top of the Earth', and Hull had to ensure that their self-belief was not dented. Just as the Regent's lower middle-class patrons gained pleasure from being seen at the most expensive cinema in Portsmouth, the Embassy's homely environment appeared to offer its working-class patrons a *sense of belonging*. Of course, the Regent's exalted status partly explains why its aspirational patrons wanted to be seen there, but the Embassy's patrons clearly liked to share in the camaraderie that being at the cinema afforded. The act of cinema-going made these working-class consumers feel good about themselves; it gave them confidence in their class position.

Not surprisingly, then, the Embassy's patrons wanted to see films that bolstered that feeling; like the Granada chain's working-class patrons, they wanted reassurance about their self-identity. It is understandable that *Bluebeard's Eighth Wife* and *The Divorce of Lady X* (both 1938) fared so badly. *Bluebeard's Eighth Wife* features Claudette Colbert as an impoverished French aristocrat who marries for money. Despite possessing a humorous narrative that centres on Colbert's attempts to punish her much-married suitor (Gary Cooper) for his philandering ways, a primarily working-class audience would hardly fall for the charms of a down-at-heel lady and a millionaire with a fondness for a harem. *The Divorce of Lady X*, meanwhile, focuses on the budding romance between a nobleman's daughter (Merle Oberon) and a barrister (Laurence Olivier). This was hardly the stuff that would appeal to the Embassy's patrons. No, like Bernstein's working-class patrons, this audience wanted films that encouraged *their* sense of self, and it was that type of film that played well here.

Take the spectacular dramas *Escape from Devil's Isle* (1935) and *The Hurricane*. Both films champion the underdog. Norman Foster (*Escape from Devil's Isle*) and Jon Hall (*The Hurricane*) play innocent convicts who manage to escape their incarceration. Both men are symbols of resistance to oppression and injustice. These are not tales of individual endeavour, however. There are larger forces at work to assist them. *The Hurricane's* violent storm, which aids Terangi's (Hall) escape from prison, functions as a tool to punish the authorities for their corrupt behaviour (epitomised in Raymond Massey's malevolent governor). In *Escape from Devil's Isle*, Johanna Harrington's (Florence Rice) love for Dion (Foster) overrides, and effectively replaces, the affection she felt for former sweetheart Dario (Victor Jury) and her father (Stanley Andrews). Crucially, Harrington's father and Dario were (guilty) captives who had escaped with Dion. Her father pays for his crime with his life, and Dario returns to prison. Both are thus punished for their guilt. It is Dion's integrity that saves him and love is his reward. These films thus carry strong moral messages; they warn against individual transgression and institutional corruption. Significantly, though, it is the latter that is shown to be the social pollutant. It is not surprising they went down well at the Embassy.

Interestingly, neither *The Hurricane* nor *Escape from Devil's Isle* appeared on any contemporary popularity lists. Nor do they feature in Sedgwick's POPSTAT index. Their appeal must have been far from widespread. While this may have something to do with the films' lack of star values, it does illustrate that distinctions exist between *popular* and *working-class* taste. Because, of course, the films that featured in popularity lists answered to the tastes of middle- *and* working-class audiences (and the class fractions in between). These two films did not appear because they failed to attract such a broad audience.

Of course, as Hull observed, it was musical films that played best at the Embassy. The three musicals he mentions – *The Firefly*, *Maytime* and *Rosalie* (all 1937) – were lush, high-gloss, expensive American productions. All of these films featured popular star pairings. They were all expected to perform well at the box-office. Of course, musical films have habitually been branded as tonics, containing little or no social relevance, and providing 'escapist' entertainment only. Certainly, we can hardly argue that the Embassy's patrons chose them for their educational value. But it would be wrong to dismiss them out of hand. Indeed, despite being post-Code, these films are sensual, florid and exotic, and give great latitude to their female characters. We have strong, independent women playing with notions of identity: Jeanette MacDonald in *The Firefly* as a Spanish dancer who seduces French officers in the Napoleonic wars in order to obtain secret information; Eleanor Powell in *Rosalie* as an incognito Balkan princess. And we have talented, successful romantics: MacDonald as a highly regarded opera star in *Maytime*. The films' sets are richly decorated, and the women's costumes are flowing and sexual. There is, then, narrative and textural balance. Female cinema-goers (these films were undoubtedly favoured by the Embassy's female patrons; *Rosalie* was shown at a matinée performance after all) were thus expected to gain considerable encouragement from their characters' excesses.

Crucially, though, these excesses occur abroad (*Rosalie*), in an earlier period (*Maytime*), or both in the past and overseas (*The Firefly*). The films' framing devices thus place these passionate females at a safe distance; their excesses cannot pollute polite society. In addition, the women are always recuperated, either by fidelity or death. However, while these films may not have foregrounded issues of female sexuality and pleasure in the same way as the aforementioned pre-Code films *Born to Love* or *Whoopee!*, they still gave audiences access to adventures in which feminine identities were tried and tested. They played with the flexibility of identity; it is shown to be fluid, not fixed. Moreover, it is presented as a *constructed* quality, not a natural one. The distances of time and place permit this. The Embassy's patrons certainly seemed to appreciate, and indeed require, this distancing technique, for *The Divorce of Lady X*, which also dealt with the issue of female masquerade, but contained no distancing element, did not appeal. Of course, *Divorce* was a romantic comedy, not a musical film. It also featured less well-known actors, and was produced in Britain. These elements may have lessened its appeal. But one thing is certain; the Embassy's female cinema-goers took great pleasure in watching a film that took them away from a known world in which they were doubtless undervalued and inhibited, and replaced it with a mysterious and exotic one in which women were appreciated and granted considerable freedom.

Significantly, all of the films that performed well at the Embassy were lavish, fast-paced, Hollywood spectaculars. American-produced films were expected to appeal to Britain's working-class cinema-goers. They did. In fact, when the Palladium's respondents were questioned about their film preferences, around seventy-five per cent said they preferred American films. As the following comments reveal, the foremost reason given for choosing American films over the British product was the lack of action in the latter:

> I don't like many British films owing to there not being sufficient action, and the actors are not acting their part properly.[42]

> I like American films best because they have more action and humour than our British films. Our own films are too dry.[43]

> The Reason why I like American films is because British Pictures are too slow in their actions. They want to put more pep into their Acting.[44]

> In American pictures you get more action and more crime and they hold your interest to the end. In British pictures they seem very slow and gradually lose interest.[45]

> In my opinion the American productions are far ahead of the English, there is something snappy and altogether definitely conclusive about an American film, while most English films are slow and absolutely vague and lacking in interest.[46]

> American films are far better than English films. The English films have good actors and no action. Americans have both.[47]

Of course, 'seventy-five per cent' does not make a whole, so there were exceptions. One particularly patriotic male cinema-goer expressed a preference for British films, and called for 'more British Navy in Action and what the British Army do' in his film fare.[48] One female cinema-goer preferred British films, believing them to be 'more solid,' but admitted that they were 'not as colourful as American films'.[49] But these types of comment were few and far between, and the majority of respondents preferred the American product. Indeed, one respondent quite tellingly noted that, 'One often hears the remark, "It's a British Picture, let's go elsewhere"'.[50]

This preference for American films cut across gender lines, but the remarks of the Palladium's patrons reveal some taste differences between the sexes regarding film type. Men, on the whole, preferred crime films, and westerns were far down the list of female preferences. However, there is a striking parity when it comes to musical romances; both sexes gave these a high ranking. Drama and tragedy and historical films were also well placed by the Palladium's male and female patrons. Both sexes displayed a real dislike for society comedies, and, somewhat surprisingly, shared a loathing for slapstick comedies. Interestingly, though, when asked what they wanted to see more of in films, both sexes ranked 'more humour' first and 'more action' second.[51] The current crop of comedy films was clearly providing the wrong kind of humour for some respondents. Perhaps predictably, men displayed a hatred for love stories, but this type of film was also placed low down the list of female preferences. There are, then, differences in taste between these Bolton cinema-goers and Bernstein's metropolitan and provincial patrons. Crime films were a particular dislike of Bernstein's working-class patrons, while slapstick comedies were sure favourites in at least one 'working-class' cinema. However, there is a time difference of at least six years between the two surveys. Perhaps we are witnessing a more widespread shift in working-class taste.

As well as ranking film types and making general comments on their film preferences, many of the Palladium's patrons also discussed their favourite films and film stars. The film that attracted most comment from the Palladium's patrons was the high-gloss, high-budget, star-packed Metro-Goldwyn-Mayer production *San Francisco* (1936). Two male and six female patrons discussed the merits of this film. One young male cinema-goer admired its realism ('the likeness of the earthquake and scenery'); one female patron praised its 'good singing [and] action'.[52] But two female patrons commented on the importance of the film's meaning. One simply observed that the film 'had good meaning,' but another elaborated further: 'I enjoyed that picture because it showed that death and destruction destroyed that city through its vice and wickedness. It also showed how a bad man retrieved his character through a good woman'.[53] *San Francisco* thus held qualities that provided comfort and reassurance for working-class audiences: the corrupt will always be punished, but there is always the chance of redemption for wayward souls.

Significantly, while *San Francisco* carried a strong moral message, it did so without being overtly didactic, and thus running the risk of alienating working-class audiences. Other films which handled their subject matter in a similar manner also drew repeated comment from the Palladium's patrons.

Historical military adventures *The Charge of the Light Brigade* (1936), *The Lives of a Bengal Lancer* (1935) and *Mutiny on the Bounty* (1935), for example, attracted significant interest from these respondents.[54] Each film extolled the virtues of duty and deference, but only so long as the system in which they operated was just. Crime dramas *They Gave Him a Gun* and *You Only Live Once* (both 1937), which gained similar attention, warned against indulging in criminal activity, *but* sympathetically portrayed individuals who, through circumstance and bad luck, were driven towards a life of crime.[55] According to one respondent, they conveyed 'a very good meaning and ... are also good all round entertainment'.[56] In musical romance *Rose Marie* (1936) justice prevails, but the film is an unmistakable celebration of female independence. Not surprisingly, it drew repeated comment from these patrons.[57] No comedy films received more than one mention; but the films' stars did. The most popular comedy stars with these respondents' were, somewhat surprisingly given the overall low ranking of slapstick comedy, Laurel and Hardy, the Marx Brothers and George Formby.[58] The Marx Brothers' *The Cocoanuts* (1929), *Monkey Business* (1931) and *A Day at the Races* (1936) were also singled out for particular attention.[59] Despite the genre's poor standing, then, some section of this audience appreciated this type of film fare. The attraction of all these comedy stars undoubtedly had much to do with their screen characters' ability to triumph over adversity. Their films not only amused working-class audiences, they comforted them too.

These were the films, then, that most appealed to this taste-community. Some may have warned against transgressing social boundaries, but they all offered to comfort and soothe working-class audiences. In fact, some, such as *A Day at the Races* and *A Night at the Opera*, actively sought to give them confidence in their class position.

Audience response

We have established what types of film the Palladium's patrons preferred. What, though, were the reasons given by the respondents for choosing these particular types of film? At a basic level, of course, films simply provided entertainment, cultural nourishment, and a distraction from the daily routine. A range of respondents thus discussed their cinema-going habits in these terms:

> Western pictures are very interesting because they are something out of the ordinary. By that, I mean the things we see in western pictures are not seen in everyday life. Such as horse-riding, the buildings, the scenery.[60]

I like Western films, because there is plenty of excitement, action, killing. When you have spent a dull dreary day in the spinning room you want to see some open air life as you usually get in Western films.[61]

When one has finished his or her's Labours at Home, or work it acts like a Tonic when one sees a film like *San Francisco* or *The Street Singer*. The picture shown this week, *Thirteenth Chair*, held one in suspense all through, and was very interesting.[62]

For myself I like a good musical comedy, because it helps you to forget every-thing, and makes you feel you are really enjoying yourself. I also like a good gangster film, that also holds you and takes you right out of yourself.[63]

But look a little closer at these remarks, and it becomes clear that these cinema-goers chose particular films to perform specific social and cultural functions. The first two respondents, both young men, reveal a desire to use the western genre as a means to encounter an untamed and, undoubtedly, more masculine environment. Older men and women, as the final two respondents indicate, sought a different, more wide-ranging, type of film fare to answer their cultural needs. But all these respondents have one thing in common. They chose films that made them *feel good about themselves*. Films thus provided a gauge against which these consumers could gain a sense of proportion.

In addition to that, of course, films provided an emotional release. They offered cinema-goers the chance to vent a whole range of emotions. This aspect of the cinema-going experience is alluded to by the above respondents; it is made explicit by another:

A good, clean comedy is worth any-one's money, if it is only to banish the blues. A good laugh, a cry and a little breath taking, in films suits me down to the ground.[64]

We are reminded of this use of the cinema by a number of respondents to M-O's 1950s cinema-going survey. Of course, the time-span of this survey ensures much of the material is of little use here; but some respondents do refer back to the 1930s. One housewife recalled, 'I was very young and enjoyed my tears a good deal. In my youth I enjoyed anything which gave me great emotional upheaval. It was a safety valve which I could let loose and enjoy'.[65] Among the films that triggered these emotions were *Ben-Hur*, *Broken Blossoms* and *Smilin' Through*. The 'stiff upper lip' mentality may have obtained in their daily lives, but for many respondents the cinema environment was a place in which they could set free their inhibitions without fear of censure.

For many respondents, then, going to the cinema was a way of coming to terms with their own lives; it was a coping mechanism. As one 1930s respondent explained:

> When going to the cinema we go to be entertained and amused, and I think there is enough crime and tragedy in the world without seeing it on a screen … People flock to hear a good singer in a picture and surely beautiful music is one of the best remedies to make us forget our troubles.[66]

Such comments often lead to accusations of escapism. But these consumers were making cultural choices; they were choosing which films most answered their cultural needs. Not surprisingly, films were frequently identified by respondents as vehicles from which they could *learn something*; films could teach them about the ways of the world:

> I go to the pictures mostly to be able to study the possibility of being taught what I am unable to afford 'i.e.', the ways and most of all the actions of certain characters of the past and present film stars. I also go because in my opinion the Pictures are the cheapest possible way of education and they give you the feeling that you are human beings after all.[67]

> Royalty, Aristocracy, beautiful people, and beautiful things help us to compare the 'other side' of Life. They give us something to realize and often make youth ambitious, which is the spirit of the British Race … Love stories, Drama and tragedy have their lessons and Pathos of life.[68]

> I attend the cinema regularly as an amusement and also as an inspiration to my mentality. It is interesting to see people living ordinary lives such as you or I, also the screen reveals the lives of people we do not come into contact with. The network of humanity is a very interesting study.[69]

Education, a sense of purpose, self belief, encouragement: these were some of the reasons provided by respondents for the cinema's appeal. For many more, films also acted as a moral compass. The observations apropos *San Francisco* allude to that film's ability to allow audiences to negotiate a path between acceptable and improper behaviour. Other films functioned in like manner. 'The thing I like about crime pictures,' noted one young female respondent, 'is that they show people however good they do the crime they nearly always make one slip which goes against them more so than if they were told on. It also ought to teach people the lesson that "crime does not pay"'.[70] Films that taught lessons were tolerated, then, but only so long as they entertained.

It is significant that the films that most answered the respondents' cultural needs removed them from a known world into an unknown one. These cinema-goers appreciated gaining access to an unfamiliar world in which insecurities about their social status were addressed and, ultimately, resolved. Not all respondents wanted their film fare to transport them away from the realities of their daily life. One young female respondent complained:

> I have never seen a leading woman yet who looks real. Perfect teeth, perfect
> flawless skin, spider-like eyelashes and a perfectly set, West end coiffure even first
> thing in a morning. I want more films of people like us who live and breathe, not
> beautiful statues or tailored dummies.[71]

But this was a lone voice in the crowd. The majority of the Palladium's patrons
preferred films that dealt with their anxieties at a symbolic level. For them,
cinema-going was a leisure activity which helped them obtain knowledge
about the world around them, it was a means to gain new experiences, it
provided an escape route from a drab and constrained environment to one of
freedom and unknown riches, it provided an emotional release, and it offered
to give them confidence in their class position.

Smaller, fugitive types of evidence confirm these trends among working-
class audiences. J.P. Mayer's 1948 book, *British Cinemas and their Audiences*,
which reproduces the 'Motion Picture Autobiographies' of more than a
hundred cinema-goers, offers a similar perspective on the meaning of cinema
for the working classes in our period.[72] On the lessons that could be learned
from films in the 1930s one respondent wrote:

> Films taught all the things I should like to associate with life. Crime does not
> pay, the wrong-doer getting his just deserts; kindness pays; love-thy-neighbour;
> plumping for the 'small' man, 'flaying' the rich; making the best of life; 'true'
> love wins in marriage; decency; the mild and honest man triumphing over the
> immoral, unscrupulous one; all the ideals worthy of life, which we would all
> like to see.[73]

On the films' emotional effects, a miner's daughter recalled that she 'would
cheer and boo energetically and my boy cousin would jump up and down
with excitement when the hero chased the villain at the end of the film and
handed him over to the Law'.[74] A sense of justice pervades these comments.
This also obtains for the remarks of a railwayman's daughter, who observed,
apropos westerns, 'in these film stories the strong protected the weak, jeering
villains were given good hidings, and noble deeds were done in defence of the
weak and helpless'.[75] Such films provided solace, and, for this cinema-goer at
least, protection (in the form of the screen world's 'tough guys', who held an
allure that could not be matched by men in the 'real' world).[76] In fact, the
'real' world held little appeal for this young cinema-goer. For her, as indeed
for many working-class cinema-goers, films provided access to a liberal and
exotic world; one that was far removed from the harshness of reality.[77] And,
like them, she sought to find in this fantasy world solutions to help her cope
with the realities of her own existence.

This use of the cinema is also captured in William Woodruff's recollection of life in Depression-era Blackburn. 'Her idea of heaven,' he wrote of the daughter of the family with whom he was residing,

> was to go to the Troxy on Commercial Road on Saturday nights with some bloke who was prepared to stuff her with chocolate, ice cream and oranges. For those few hours she lived the life of the screen. When she came home she'd dance about the living room taking off the stars she'd seen. The Troxy was where we all went to dream. It relieved us of the drabness of our surroundings. In other people's hopes, loves and hates, we saw ourselves.[78]

This, then, was the function of the cinema for many of the country's working-class consumers. It is no wonder they flocked to it in droves.

Notes

1   Initially, the magazine provided a list of films from which to choose. The practice ended in the late 1930s.
2   David Sutton, *A Chorus of Raspberries: British Film Comedy 1929–1939*, Exeter, 2000, pp. 96–97.
3   *FW*, 16 May 1931; 29 April 1932; 26 May 1932.
4   Sutton, *Chorus of Raspberries*, p. 97.
5   *FW*, 16 May 1931.
6   Ibid.
7   Ibid., 26 May 1933.
8   Ibid., 27 December 1930.
9   Ibid.
10 The magazine provided a caveat, admitting that while some films may have 'triumphed' in some locations, they may have 'failed badly' elsewhere.
11 Ibid.
12 Ibid., 29 December 1933.
13 *Picturegoer*, 28 April 1934.
14 *FW*, 29 December 1933; *Picturegoer*, 15 June 1935; Bernstein Questionnaire, 1934.
15 *FW*, 29 December 1933; Bernstein Questionnaire, 1934; *Picturegoer*, 28 April 1934.
16 *FW*, 4 May 1934.
17 Bernstein Questionnaire, 1934; *FW*, 29 December 1933.
18 *Picturegoer*, 28 April 1934.
19 John Sedgwick, *Popular Filmgoing in 1930s Britain: A Choice of Pleasures*, Exeter, 2000, pp. 264 and 274.
20 Sue Harper, 'A Lower Middle-Class Taste-Community in the 1930s: Admissions Figures at the Regent Cinema, Portsmouth, UK', *Historical Journal of Film, Radio and Television*, 24:4, 2004, pp. 565–587; p. 581.
21 The findings of the questionnaire are partly reproduced in *Picturegoer*, 4 June 1932.
22 Paul Holt, 'Census Tells What Film Stars Britain Prefers', *Daily Express*, 14 November 1933. Holt was the paper's film critic.

23   *FW*, 6 December 1930.

24   Ibid., 21 November 1931.

25   *Picturegoer*, 24 February 1934.

26   In fact, in 1934, and in response to the readers propensity to nominate 'their favourite star with a list of all the pictures in which they had ever appeared,' *Picturegoer*'s editor felt obliged to stress that the 'Award of Merit is *not* a popularity contest. Its aim is the acknowledgment and honouring of acting performances that gave us pleasure and contributed to screen art'. Ibid.

27   All references to the following discussion of the POPSTAT rankings can be found in Sedgwick, *Popular Filmgoing*, pp. 262–276.

28   Ibid., pp. 189–191 and 196–198.

29   Mark Glancy, 'Temporary American Citizens? British Audiences, Hollywood Films and the Threat of Americanization in the 1920s', *Historical Journal of Film, Radio and Television*, 26:4, 2006, pp. 461–484.

30   This pre-report material is only available for the 1932 and 1934 Questionnaires, Sidney L. Bernstein Collection (hereafter SLB), held in Special Collections, British Film Institute, London.

31   Cinemas were divided between 'poor', 'petty-bourgeois', 'county + petit-bourgeois', 'county + poor' and 'county + poor + rural', SLB. See Llewellyn Smith, *New Survey of London*, for confirmation of class fractions in the areas investigated by Bernstein.

32   See Gerben Bakker, 'Building Knowledge about the Consumer: The Emergence of Market Research in the Motion Picture Industry', *Business History*, 45:1, 2003, pp. 101–127; p. 110. Bakker argues that Clark Gable 'was liked nearly twice as much by women than by men, and most by women below 21 and richer customers'.

33   Three films had been made by 1931 that shared this title. Two were American-produced animated films (released 1924 and 1931), the other was a German film (also known as *Varieté* [1925]). It is impossible to be sure which of these films is being referred to, but they were all innovative and experimental.

34   The term 'wandering public' was used by Bernstein's report compilers. It referred to the practice of patrons from one cinema visiting an alternative cinema to watch a particular film.

35   Comments on 1932 Questionnaire, SLB.

36   Marcia Landy, *British Genres. Cinema and Society, 1930–1960*, Princeton, 1991, p. 433.

37   The results of this survey are reproduced in Richards and Sheridan, eds, *Mass-Observation*, pp. 21–136.

38   Ibid., pp. 32–33.

39   Ibid., pp. 27–31.

40   Ibid., pp. 29–30.

41   *Kineweekly*, 8 August 1935.

42   Richards and Sheridan, eds, *Mass-Observation*, William Turnock, aged 18.

43   Ibid., James Hutchinson, aged 18.

44   Ibid., p. 52, Mr A. Wiggans, aged 60.

45   Ibid., p. 57, Mary Ann Sixsmith, aged 27.

46   Ibid., Mrs Phyllis Cann, aged 30.

47 Ibid., p. 58, Mrs B. Smith, aged 46.

48 Ibid., p. 47, W. Rimmer, aged 21.

49 Ibid., p. 57, Mrs Nellie Barber, aged 31.

50 Ibid., p. 46, James A. Walsh, aged 50.

51 Ibid., p. 38.

52 Ibid., p. 44, George Nicholson, aged 15; p. 54, Miss Ida Heyes, aged 15.

53 Ibid., p. 57, Mrs Nellie Barber, aged 31; p. 54, Beatrice Hamer, aged 13. The other respondents to comment on *San Francisco* were George Fletcher, aged 42, ibid., p. 51; Miss Hettie McDerby, aged 14, ibid., p. 54; Miss Annie Hill, aged 23, ibid., p. 56; and Emily McKenna, aged 23, ibid., p. 56.

54 See comments by John McMunn, aged 18, ibid., p. 46; Thomas Weatherall, aged 19, ibid., p. 47; Leo Greenhalgh, aged 25, ibid., p. 49; Edgar F. Andrews, aged 32; ibid., p. 50; and Emily McKenna, aged 23, ibid., p. 56.

55 See observations of William Manning, aged 14, ibid., p. 43; Fred Grundy, aged 23, ibid., p. 48; and Emily McKenna, aged 23, ibid., p. 56.

56 Ibid., p. 48, Fred Grundy, aged 23.

57 Two male respondents praised the film. See ibid., p. 46, John McMunn, aged 18, and p. 47, Thomas Weatherall, aged 19.

58 See comments by Walter Chadwick, aged 14, ibid., p. 43; William Turnock, aged 18, ibid., p. 46; Thomas Weatherall, aged 19, ibid., p. 47; Albert Hill, aged 25, ibid., p. 49; Leslie Emms, aged 30, ibid., p. 51; Kathleen Doherty, aged 14, ibid., p. 54; and Annie Hill, aged 23, ibid., p. 56.

59 See Leslie Emms, aged 30, ibid., p. 51 and Annie Hill, aged 23, ibid., p. 56.

60 Ibid., p. 45, Walter Rollinson, aged 18.

61 Ibid., p. 47, Thomas Weatherall, aged 19.

62 Ibid., p. 51, George Fletcher, aged 42.

63 Ibid., p. 58, Emily Freeman, aged 48.

64 Ibid., p. 56, Miss Josephine Hawkins, aged 23.

65 Sue Harper and Vincent Porter, 'Moved to Tears: Weeping in the Cinema in Post-war Britain', *Screen*, 37:2, 1996, pp. 152–173, p. 156.

66 Richards and Sheridan, eds, *Mass-Observation*, p. 57, Mrs J. Holding, aged 24.

67 Ibid., p. 49, John Thomas Longden, aged 27.

68 Ibid., p. 52, James Hope, aged 57.

69 Ibid., p. 57, Mrs Phyllis Cann, aged 30.

70 Ibid., p. 55, Ethel Rollinson, aged 15.

71 Ibid., pp. 55–56, Ivy Williams, aged 18.

72 Mayer, *British Cinemas*.

73 Ibid., p. 139.

74 Ibid., p. 65.

75 Ibid., p. 27.

76 Ibid., pp. 27–28.

77 Ibid., p. 27.

78 Woodruff, *Beyond Nab End*, pp. 26–27.

5

'The appearance is an added incentive': national trends in literature popularity

Fiction popularity

The most comprehensive list of the working classes' favourite authors is provided by twopenny library owner, Ronald F. Batty. In an appendix to his 1938 book *How to Run a Twopenny Library*, Batty produced a 'Short Check List of the Most Popular Twopenny Library Authors'.[1] The list is divided into eight categories: 'Adventure', 'Air and War Stories', 'Detective and Mystery', 'Humorous', 'Love and Romance', 'Modern Novels', 'Novels' and 'Western'. According to Batty, the authors included in these lists represented 'the "high spots" in stock selection, the authors whose books never fail you'. Of the eight categories, 'Novels' is by far the largest with seventy-eight authors named, including Ursula Bloom, Ethel Boileau, Gilbert Frankau and Lady Eleanor Smith. 'Detective and Mystery' and 'Love and Romance' each feature sixty-seven authors, including, in the former category, Gilbert Collins, A.E.W. Mason and Dorothy L. Sayers, and in the latter, Ruby M. Ayres, Simon Dare and Jeffery Farnol. The 'Western' category is well populated, with forty-three authors, including Buck Billings, Jackson Gregory and Zane Grey. The 'Adventure' category features twenty-five authors, including Baroness Orczy, 'Sapper' and Edgar Wallace. Some authors appear in more than one category. Jeffery Farnol, for example, appears in both 'Love and Romance' and 'Adventure' categories. Ian Hay and Dornford Yates, meanwhile, each crop up in three genre categories. Bearing in mind the popularity of film comedy, it is perhaps surprising that the least populated category is 'Humorous'. It featured only twelve authors. Unlike, say, the romance genre, which did well in both written and visual form, comedy fared much better in the latter. In fact, at least three of the authors in the 'Humorous' category – Jerome K. Jerome, Ben Travers and P.G. Wodehouse – had their works adapted into highly successful feature films.

Batty does not explain why he placed authors in specific or multiple categories. But most works of fiction were expected to hold a gender-specific appeal. Indeed, Batty recommended that library owners divide stock into 'novels and love stories, etc' and 'detective stories, westerns, etc'.[2] So, the authors placed in Batty's 'Love and Romance', 'Novels' and 'Modern Novels' categories were expected to appeal to women, while those placed in the 'Air and War Stories', 'Detective and Mystery' and 'Western' categories were understood to hold a more masculine appeal. Significantly, then, the authors that appeared in multiple categories must have produced work that was expected to appeal to both sexes. Batty's recommended stock ratio is thus significant. He believed that 'at least fifty per cent., probably more, of the former [novels and love stories] will be needed. The average library contains from fifty to seventy per cent. novels, from thirty to fifty per cent. thrillers and westerns'.[3] Batty thus expected more women than men to visit or borrow books from a twopenny library.

While Batty's stock recommendations point towards a gender imbalance in working-class reading habits, the findings of his publishing industry contemporaries reveal other variations in reading trends between the sexes. Although less comprehensive in scope, the *Library Association Record* and *The Bookseller* also compiled lists of the most popular authors at twopenny libraries (in 1933 and 1935 respectively).[4] As with Batty's lists, authors of romantic fiction dominate. Of the sixteen authors listed by the *Library Association Record*, seven featured in Batty's 'Love and Romance' category. Of the thirty-six authors on *The Bookseller*'s list, seventeen appear in that category. The ratio of authors per category is misleading, however. For the most popular author overall is not, as one might expect, a romantic novelist, but thriller writer Edgar Wallace. In fact, while the total sum of romantic fiction titles available in the two libraries surveyed came to seven hundred and seventy-three, Wallace alone had an impressive two hundred and one titles available. Moreover, if we classify adventure, detective and western fiction as primarily male reading preserves, the number of titles available to men is extensive.[5] The range of authors stocked by these two libraries, therefore, bears little relation to the number of their titles available. The most revealing aspect about these figures, then, is that they point towards a conservatism in the reading habits of working-class men. Whereas working-class women tended to cast the net widely and read fiction from a range of authors, men appeared to stick to a relatively small number of their favourite writers.

Along with identifying gender differences in the working classes' reading habits, these lists also provide evidence of the ebb and flow of author popularity among them. As we have seen, Wallace's popularity continued throughout the decade, despite the lack of new material following his death in 1932. But Marie Corelli, who featured in the 1933 and 1935 surveys, does not appear among Batty's recommendations. Charles Garvice, Nat Gould, H. Rider Haggard and F.E. Mills Young, meanwhile, all featured in *The Bookseller*'s 1935 survey. They do not appear in the *Library Association Record*'s list; nor do they feature in Batty's lists. No authors from Batty's 'Air and War Stories' and 'Modern Novels' categories appear in either of the two earlier lists. Exactly why these fluctuations in popularity occur is difficult to determine. Are we witnessing generational shifts in taste? Did Corelli's popularity wane as the decade progressed? Does the mid-decade popularity of Garvice *et al.* signal a rapid rise and then decline in their fortunes? Were Batty's writers just starting their path to ascendancy? Maybe; but it is more likely that we are observing *geographical* distinctions in taste. For, of course, Batty could only recommend authors based upon *his* experiences in book-lending; the lists provided by the *Library Association Record* and *The Bookseller* likewise represent only the tastes of the customers of the twopenny libraries they surveyed. The absences from these lists, therefore, probably reflect differences in taste from one twopenny library to another. Indeed, after the death of Ethel M. Dell in 1939, *The Times* referred to Garvice and Gould, along with Dell and Wallace, as 'the most popular novelists in the English-speaking world', thereby providing evidence of their continued popularity throughout the period.[6]

If we look more closely at the lists of the *Library Association Record* and *The Bookseller*, it is possible to identify the types of fiction preferred by those readers using each of the two libraries surveyed. The customers of the library examined by T.E. Callender in 1933 (for the *Library Association Record*) appear to have been very eclectic in their tastes. While authors of romantic fiction dominated, with Warwick Deeping, Margaret Peterson and Joan Sutherland all placed high on the list, all of the authors in the top five wrote different types of fiction. Edgar Wallace topped the list, Deeping was placed second, detective writer E.P. Oppenheim was third, comedy writer P.G. Wodehouse was fourth, and western writer A.G. Hales was placed fifth. It is interesting to see Wodehouse placed highly, because comedy was under-represented in Batty's lists of recommendations. Wodehouse's popularity probably had much to do with the release of the filmed version of his novel *Summer Lightning* in the year the survey took place. In fact, the growing trend for turning literary works into films helped to increase the popularity of many authors. It is thus not surprising to see Wallace placed at the top of the list, because his body of work was something of a cinema staple in the period. Between 1925 and 1939 over fifty of his stories were made into films.[7] Most of these were produced in Britain by British Lion or other small British production companies, but a number of films, including *The Menace* (1932), *Before Dawn* (1933) and *Mystery Liner* (1934), were produced in America. Two other authors in Callender's top five also had films based on their work released in the year the survey took place. The American-produced *The Midnight Club*, starring Clive Brook and George Raft, was based on Oppenheim's novel of the same name; Deeping's *Sorrell and Son* was filmed by Herbert Wilcox for the British production company British and Dominions. While these films were released after Callender had conducted his survey, pre-release promotional material would have made readers aware of the links between the novel and forthcoming film.

We must not place too much credit on the film industry for the success of these authors, however. Many of them had established their popularity with the reading public long before any of their stories were adapted for the cinema. Indeed, Richmal Crompton, who was the only other author of humorous fiction on Callender's list, did not have any of her stories filmed until 1939, when ABPC released *Just William*. Crompton also appeared on *The Bookseller*'s list of popular authors and was recommended by Batty, so her popularity with working-class readers preceded, and probably influenced, the interest shown in her work by the film trade. In addition, many films based on the work of these authors failed to perform as well with working-class cinema-goers. The films were certainly popular with them, but only a few featured among their favourites. The popularity of these authors, then, was based more on their status as masters and mistresses of the type of fiction working-class consumers desired. In fact, Batty candidly referred to the somewhat transient nature of a book's popularity after it had been filmed. 'Tie ups,' he argued, 'will result in a strong but only temporary demand for the advertised title'.[8] Certainly, the filmed versions of a novel would have helped raise interest, but these authors were successful in their own right. They had become popular, and remained so, because they were responding to the demands of the *reading* public.

Not surprisingly, then, all of the authors that featured in Callender's list also appeared in *The Bookseller*'s list, drawn up by Garfield Howe in 1935. Howe's list contains twenty additional authors, so it would seem that the customers of the library he surveyed had highly adventurous reading habits. However, if we look closely at the range of authors available, and especially their ranking, we find that these readers were, in fact, slightly *less* adventurous. Wallace again topped the list, reflecting his continuing popularity, but of the other four authors in the top five, two wrote detective fiction (J.S. Fletcher, Oppenheim), and two were romantic novelists (Deeping, E.M. Savi). Wodehouse and Hales still feature, but are placed lower down. Moreover, of the twenty additional authors on Howe's list, thirteen wrote romantic fiction, thereby bringing the sum of romantic novelists to twenty-three. Romantic fiction, then, had a greater appeal at this library than at any other. Significantly, the number of 'women's' fiction titles is spread across a range of authors. Once again, then, working-class women tended to choose widely. Working-class men again reveal the conservative nature of their reading habits. Not only are the top three authors writers of 'men's' fiction, but the list contains only a few additional authors of the type of fiction men preferred.

There are other continuities in working-class patterns of taste. Along with Wodehouse, Crompton is again the only other author of humorous fiction listed, so the appeal of comedy in its written form is once more shown to be very limited. However, Crompton's sustained popularity does suggest that her 'William' books, which satirised middle-class values and codes of behaviour, went down extremely well with working-class readers. There is an additional author of western fiction (Zane Grey). Notably, though, the popularity of the western genre fluctuated throughout the decade. Indeed, while Batty recommended that '[s]ome western stories must be carried,' he also warned prospective shop-owners, 'but don't ask me how many. Demand for this type of book is incredibly variable'.[9] It is tempting to suggest that male readers only turned to the western genre when other, more favoured, genres were out of stock. There is one surprise addition. The adventure writer H. Rider Haggard, known for his favourable depictions of Empire, is very respectably placed. Haggard does not appear on any other list, and the lack of other 'Empire' adventure writers on all of these lists suggests that this type of writing rarely appealed to working-class readers. Haggard's inclusion undoubtedly had much to do with the release of *She*, the American-produced film based on his novel, in the year the survey took place.

Contemporary surveys thus reveal that there were often gender and geographical differences in the working classes' reading habits. They also show that, for some authors, success remained constant, while for others, popularity drifted in and out like the tide. One trend that remained constant throughout the decade, however, was the desire among working-class readers to consume a specific *type* of fiction. Whatever section of the working classes was being examined, and whatever year in the decade their habits were being surveyed, the overwhelming preference among these readers was for the 'lighter' type of fiction. Twopenny library owners, with an eye on commercial success, obviously understood this. Indeed, Batty wisely advised potential shop-owners to stock their libraries 'with a good preponderance in favour of the lighter type of book'.[10] But twopenny libraries were not the only establishments to respond to the tastes of the working-class reader. Public libraries and the larger commercial lending libraries also began to stock the kind of reading material working-class readers preferred. This is not to say that the working classes completely ignored 'classic' literature. In 1933, a leading article in *The Publishers' Circular* triumphantly declared that the 'thousands of new readers [were] not neglecting a classic background'.[11] According to the paper, the authors doing particularly well were R.D. Blackmore, whose *Lorna Doone* topped the list, and Charles Dickens, who, in fact, dominated it, with *David Copperfield*, *The Old Curiosity Shop*, *Oliver Twist*, *The Pickwick Papers* and *A Tale of Two Cities* all cited as appealing to a broad readership. But none of these authors appear on Batty's, Callender's or Howe's lists, so if they were attracting working-class readers, their novels were not being borrowed from the local twopenny libraries.

Of course, many publishing trade personnel had an uneasy relationship with this new class of readers, and were keen to distance themselves from the type of fiction they preferred. It is not surprising, then, to find them trying to insist that a kinship existed between the new reading public and 'classic' literature. But trade personnel did not, indeed could not, ignore the fact that most working-class readers wanted to read the type of fiction produced by Wallace *et al.* The surveys undertaken by Callender and Howe are, indeed, evidence of the trade's curiosity about the working classes' reading habits. Unfortunately, though, and this undoubtedly stems from the publishing trade's haughtiness regarding popular fiction, forays into understanding the tastes of the mass consumer were nowhere near as extensive or as informative as those conducted by film trade personnel. We must look elsewhere if we are to gain a better understanding of the working classes' relationship with popular fiction.

Mass-Observation Archive and other studies

Mass-Observation's research into society's reading habits is especially fruitful in this respect. As part of their investigation, Mass-Observers studied the activities of consumers in a number of lending libraries. Their research allows us to identify the types of literature working-class readers preferred, and, by turning to their recorded utterances, understand their reasons for choosing it. M-O research thus provides us with the most valuable index of working-class taste in the 1930s. In addition to this material, there are a number of smaller, more academic, studies that offer an equally revealing insight into the working classes' reading habits in our period. Pearl Jephcott produced two books in the 1940s, *Girls Growing Up* and *Rising Twenty*, which investigated the reading habits of working-class girls and women in the 1930s and early 1940s.[12] A.J. Jenkinson's 1940 book *What Do Boys and Girls Read?* also examined the reading habits of school-children in our period.[13] The work of both authors will be deployed here.

Significantly, none of these surveys contradict the conclusions outlined above. But there are a number of minor differences. Mass-Observers also identified a conservatism in the working classes' reading choices, but they did not say whether they detected any gender differences in this matter. In her 1940 report on 'Selection and Taste in Book Reading', Kathleen Box simply noted:

> There is little experimenting, little adventure among unfamiliar literature. It seems almost a state of rut. Moreover people tend to follow the taste of the majority, at public libraries often picking books from those which have just been returned by other borrowers. Thus the same books are constantly kept in circulation, while others especially the classics remain on the shelf. People stick to their own type, and have prejudices in some cases against other types.[14]

The various librarians who were interviewed by M-O researchers also found readers' tastes to be conservative, but they, too, did not distinguish between the sexes. A librarian in Timothy Davies' twopenny library noted, 'A lot of people stick to say a couple of authors. They are conservative, very conservative I think in their ideas of books'.[15] Public librarians observed similar borrowing patterns. 'If you give people short stories,' one public librarian told Box, 'they look at you as though you had given them margarine instead of butter'.[16] As the last comment reveals, many library users left the choice of their reading material to the librarians themselves, so the latter were placed in a prime position to express an opinion on readers' tastes. Time and again, M-O researchers investigating the habits of library users found that it was the novels of the same few authors which were regularly borrowed from both public and twopenny libraries.[17]

Of course, these are the results of an investigation that was not confined to the reading habits of the working classes. But other areas of M-O research that make the reading habits of the working classes more explicit contain material that corresponds with the findings of these less class-specific reports. Responses from working-class library users illustrate that they preferred to borrow books which had a high lending-rate. One female working-class reader told a Mass-Observer, 'I just look at the front page where the date stamps are marked and if there's a lot of dates on it, then a lot of people must have read it, and so it must be a good book'.[18] A male respondent similarly noted, 'The appearance is an added incentive, if "dog-eared", proving considerable handling by various people using lending libraries'.[19] The desire to read books that had been approved by their peers was expressed vocally by a number of working-class readers. A shop assistant told a Mass-Observer that she read Angela Thirkell's *Wild Strawberries* because, 'A friend recommended it'.[20] A preference for particular authors was common; a number of working-class readers admitted they chose only to read books by the same limited range of authors. A nursemaid thus said that she read 'anything by Jeffery Farnol'.[21] A domestic servant 'never [read] anything but her few authors, or rather, author-esses'.[22] The working-class respondents to Mass-Observation's 1938 directive similarly read only the novels of their favourite authors.[23]

The working-class readers investigated by Mass-Observation thus exhibited an intense fidelity towards their preferred type of fiction, their favourite authors, and indeed, the novels that were most popular within their own social group. It is not surprising that Mass-Observers believed the working-class reading habit to be rather conservative. Jephcott's investigations into the reading habits of working-class girls and women detected a similar constancy of conservatism. Only certain novels, Jephcott noted, had 'a considerable circulation' amongst the readers she observed.[24]

To an extent, then, this conservatism in reading choice cut across gender lines. But we must remember that working-class men, rather than women, took fewer risks. In any case, it is wrong to view the working classes as an homogenous group, sharing identical perspectives and attitudes. Indeed, like the surveys conducted by members of the publishing trade, M-O research also revealed differences in the working classes' reading habits. Researchers found that the most avid female readers were aged forty and under, with the greatest proportion aged under twenty-five.[25] The largest numbers of male readers, on the other hand, were aged between twenty-six and fifty-five. As well as identifying variations in reading habits structured by age, M-O researchers also found marked differences in the type of fiction chosen by men and women. One M-O report noted that female readers preferred 'light romantic novels of the family and life kind, with happily-ever-after wedding bells theme', while male readers tended to favour 'Western novels of the sexy and saucy kind. Detective, thrillers, and sticky murders, spy stories'.[26] Like Batty, then, Mass-Observers classified certain genres of fiction as gender-specific.

The majority of comments by M-O's working-class respondents certainly followed these gender-specific distinctions. Most female readers expressed preferences for:

> The love and romance and escape from everyday problems.[27]

> A good old-fashioned love story.[28]

> A nice light romance – not too long as if I get tired of it.[29]

Working-class men, meanwhile, favoured:

> Any big adventure stories … Love books don't interest me or anything like that.[30]

> Mostly what I call blood and thunder.[31]

> I like action books – 'thrillers'.[32]

The reading preferences of some working-class respondents do go against these trends. One working-class female reader told an M-O researcher, 'I like a mixture, something deep about the last war, so that I can more or less understand this one better – or else – a light romance – some light stuff to take my mind off the worries these days'.[33] Nevertheless, the majority of working-class men preferred detective fiction and adventure stories, while most working-class women favoured romances. Interestingly, A.J. Jenkinson's investigation into the reading habits of school-children indicated that this predilection for particular genres of fiction started in childhood. His research also uncovered a distinct preference for adventure stories and detective fiction amongst boys and romances amongst girls.[34] Of course, these children were probably following the reading habits of their parents. Indeed, Jephcott found that many of the working-class girls and women she investigated followed their mother's reading habits, concluding, 'taste does appear to run in families'.[35]

There are other similarities between M-O's findings and those of the publishing trade. Mass-Observation material also reveals that the overriding demand amongst working-class readers was for fiction 'of the light sort'.[36] The working-class interviewees contributing to Kathleen Box's door-to-door survey in Fulham repeatedly said that they read only those novels written by authors of 'light' fiction.[37] In Mass-Observation's 1938 directive, 'light' fiction was identified as the most popular type of reading material.[38] Investigators observing library borrowing habits found that it was 'light' fiction that dominated reading choice.[39] Interestingly, the books which many historians have associated with attracting a large working-class readership, such as those published by Penguin Books and the Left Book Club, were found to be rather unpopular with the working-class readers observed and interviewed by M-O investigators. In fact, not one of Box's working-class interviewees said that they read Penguin or Left Book Club books. Mass-Observers also found that they were not borrowed in any significant number from either public or twopenny libraries. In the 1938 directive, only two of the many working-class interviewees read books published by Penguin Books.[40] These books were not mentioned by Batty, nor were they on Callender and Howe's lists, so we are witnessing a widespread trend. These types of book may have had an increased mass readership, then, but their readers were unlikely to have been found, in any number at least, within working-class communities.

What reasons did working-class readers give for their preferred choice of fiction? Bearing in mind the varying motives given for going to see a particular film, it is perhaps predictable that the working classes also gave various reasons for choosing particular works of fiction. One female respondent told an M-O researcher that she read the romantic novels of Baroness Orczy and Daphne du Maurier because she liked books 'dealing with some costume period when smugglers had the rule of the seas,' adding, 'I like books to take me into another world far from the realities of this'.[41] In sharp contrast, another female respondent declared that she chose to read 'books about plain Mr and Mrs, no lords and princes and dukes – people more in my way of living that I can understand. I like writers that don't exaggerate'.[42] Other working-class readers gave equally contrasting motives to explain their preference for the genre:

> Because they are about possible people and always seem alive.[43]
>
> Light recreation blotting out all immediate worries.[44]
>
> Just to pass the time away like.[45]
>
> Generally light reading.[46]
>
> I like something exciting. Something about the old-time Navy, or adventures abroad, adventures anywhere. Anything exciting.[47]
>
> Something light to take my mind off the war – a straight romantic tale.[48]

Realism, relaxation, excitement, escapism and a need to understand the world – these were the various, and highly contrasting, reasons given by working-class readers for their keen interest in popular fiction. Compare these motives with those offered by Queenie Leavis. Leavis argued that popular fiction merely provided 'reading fodder for odd moments'; it was fiction that was 'only meant to entertain'; it 'made no real mental challenge on the reader'.[49] Not so. To be sure, many working-class readers chose to read popular fiction because it provided a means to escape from the realities of day-to-day life, but the escapist motive was just *one* of the many cultural tasks that popular fiction performed. This factor, no doubt, explains why the working classes were so loyal to their favourite authors. They knew precisely what to expect from, say, Edgar Wallace's adventures or Ursula Bloom's romances; they knew that the work of these authors would answer their cultural needs. The comfort was in the close fit. Of course, authors of popular fiction well understood this. In fact, to gain a better understanding of the nature of the working-class reading habit, we need to analyse the *meaning* of the texts themselves. We need to understand what it was authors *expected* working-class readers to get from their work. Chapter 9 will, therefore, include analyses of a limited number of the most popular novels. For now, I will shift focus slightly, moving away from the working classes' novel-reading habit and looking at the types of magazine they preferred.

Magazine popularity

A large number of new magazines were introduced during the 1930s, reflecting the growing demand among readers for a type of reading material that did not distract from the many requirements of the day. Mass-Observers had, indeed, identified an increased trend towards what they classified as 'scattered' reading. This related to people reading 'while travelling, at meal-times, in bed and in any spare five minutes that [could] be snatched from the urgency of the routine'.[50] Because of their form, magazines could easily fulfil that requirement. Many working-class readers still chose to read novels; they, too, had undergone a major transformation to their form that made them more convenient to read. But many readers preferred to use any spare moments the day afforded browsing through the latest edition of their favourite magazine. In fact, many working-class interviewees in Mass-Observation's Fulham survey continued to believe that novels required time to enjoy, and read magazines because they supposed they had little time to read much else.[51] One female interviewee thus told Kathleen Box that she bought magazines because, 'I don't have much time to read at all'.[52] Besides, many working-class readers saw little difference between a magazine and a book. When one female interviewee was asked by Box whether she read any books, she replied, 'just those 2d ones,' meaning, of course, weekly magazines.[53]

What, then, were the most popular magazines in our period? M-O researchers found that the best-selling magazines were those aimed at women, and of these, it was the 'romance' magazines which gained the highest sales. Those mentioned by M-O as being particularly successful with working-class readers were *Golden Star*, *Lucky Star*, *Miracle*, *Oracle*, *Red Star Weekly* and *Silver*

Star.[54] These were magazines which, as Richard Hoggart has rightly noted, faithfully catered to the needs of the working-class consumer.[55] They were inexpensive (usually costing 2d), contained a number of short and serialised stories, and included a range of regular sections that sought to offer working-class women guidance and advice, often embracing the concerns of the young, female home-keeper. In fact, as Hoggart also noted, publishers took great care to ensure that the material in their magazines 'mirror[ed] the attitudes of the readers'.[56] While we cannot assume that these magazines accurately reflected the attitudes and assumptions of the readers they were aiming to attract, publishers would have endeavoured to ensure that they contained the kind of material that would be popular with working-class readers.

Therefore, all these magazines contained a number of stories (ranging from one-page 'shorts' to long serials that ran over many months) of the type known to be popular with the working classes. These stories featured adventurous and daring characters, forbidden or unrequited love, domestic violence and crime, and were given thrilling and enticing titles. Of course, because they contained fictional stories, these magazines tapped into the market for popular fiction. Perhaps predictably, then, publishers were keen to profit from that association. Both *Lucky Star* and *Red Star Weekly* recruited popular romantic novelist Ruby M. Ayres to write for them. Significantly, though, Ayres was not employed in the capacity of author, but as a 'friend' and 'agony aunt'. The readers of *Lucky Star* were invited to write to 'Ruby M. Ayres Friendship Corner'.[57] *Red Star Weekly*'s readers were encouraged to 'Confide Your Troubles to Ruby M. Ayres'.[58] Clearly, the editors of these magazines expected their readers to be aware of Ayres's status as an author of popular fiction. They were thus using that recognition as a way of bolstering the reputation of their magazines.

However, because these magazines contained more than just fiction, they could perform a different cultural function to novels. Indeed, they were more closely and explicitly tied in to everyday concerns. Along with providing fictional material, they offered their readers guidance and advice ('Stop that Ladder'[59]; 'Keeping Hubby Smart'[60]), contained gossip columns ('Confessions of a Hollywood Fortune-Teller'[61]), gave away free gifts ('lucky cameo ring'[62]), held competitions ('Happiest-Bride-to-Be'[63]) and, most importantly, gave readers the chance to write in and converse with their peers on a variety of issues ('Where Readers Meet Readers'[64]). In fact, readers were greatly encouraged to contribute to their own letters' pages. The editor of *Red Star Weekly*, for example, asked the magazine's readers, 'How would you like to earn a penny for every word you write? ... I am going to devote a special page to readers, and I want you to send me paragraphs for it ... You can write about anything you like'.[65]

Magazines thus offered working-class readers much more than something that was simply easy to read. They offered something that had a reassuringly recognisable element. They allowed readers to feel part of a magazine's reading community. They provided readers with a sense of belonging.[66] Of course, popular fiction could operate in a *similar* manner. Authors, too, endeavoured to provide readers with similar feelings of companionship and belonging. But they could only deal with their readers *indirectly* (unless they were contributing to a magazine column, as Ayres did). It was the role of the librarian (and the library) to provide readers of popular fiction with that sense of belonging. Magazine editors, in contrast, were much closer to their reading public. In a sense, they played the role of the librarian; they provided the personal service. In fact, editors openly fostered that sense of community and belonging by addressing their readers in a very personal and friendly manner. The editor of *Lucky Star* (who referred to herself as 'Your Editress') promoted one of the magazine's features as 'some "true" tales from ordinary people like you or me'.[67] A short story in the same magazine ended with the adjunct, 'but, Reader, haven't *you* ever been stupid like that?'.[68] Editors were also keen to show readers that their opinions were highly valued. *Red Star Weekly*'s editor thus asked readers to comment on the stories it published.[69] Authors of popular fiction could only imagine what their readers thought of their work.

In such ways, then, the publishers of popular magazines tried to attract, and maintain the interests of, working-class readers. They certainly succeeded. Both A.J. Jenkinson and Pearl Jephcott commented on the popularity of these magazines with the working-class adolescent girls they studied. Jephcott found that 'the magazines [were] universally known among young people', and had 'very extensive' circulations.[70] She also found that the magazines attracted a large working-class readership, and that many working-class girls progressed from their 'childhood' magazines to the 'blood-and-thunder' papers read by their mother. 'The girls go straight on from the comics of their childhood's reading,' Jephcott observed, 'to *Silver Star* and the other more suggestive magazines of that constellation'.[71] Once again, then, working-class readers displayed an intense loyalty to their preferred type of reading material. In fact, perhaps the most important indication of the popularity of these magazines with the working classes comes from within the magazines themselves. Many of *Red Star Weekly*'s 'regular section' contributors were from within working-class communities.[72] Quite clearly, the publishers of these 'romance' magazines, and those people working for them, understood, and successfully responded to, the *cultural* needs of their intended audience.

Hitherto, I have concentrated on the differences in approach and orientation of film and literature material, but it would be suggestive to end on an area of similarity rather than difference. Film magazines, aimed specifically for the cinema-going community, provide a fundamental area of overlap between the two cultural forms. Indeed, they provide a vital link between the cultural activities of reading (both novels and magazines) and going to the cinema. Although romance magazines dominated the market during the 1930s, film magazines continued to grow in popularity throughout our period. W.N. Coglan's 1936 survey reveals that film magazines, ranging from the inexpensive and working-class orientated *Picture Show*, to the slightly more expensive, and certainly more up-market, *Film Weekly* and *Picturegoer*, attracted a broad readership from a wide social spectrum.[73] This is not surprising, for film magazines fostered the same sense of community and identification as romance magazines. They, too, identified a discourse that was appropriate to the type of readers they aimed to attract. *Picture Show*, for example, adopted a very friendly and 'chatty' style. One response to a reader's letter ran thus, 'Thanks for your interesting letter, "*Molly*".[74] The emphasis on the letter-writer's name is significant; it visibly identifies the author of the piece while at the same time deeply personalises the correspondence between reader and editor.

Interestingly, though not surprisingly, film magazines also adopted a strikingly similar structural style to the most popular romance magazines. *Picture Show*, like *Lucky Star* and *Red Star Weekly*, included serialised and short stories (often about Hollywood[75]), held competitions and gave away free gifts (often cinema tickets[76]), and contained letters pages that offered readers the chance to converse with their peers. Significantly, though, because film magazines concentrated explicitly on the interests of the film fan, they were always eager to immerse their readers in film culture. Recently released films were frequently reproduced in short-story form. In 1932, for example, *Picture Show* ran a serialised version of the American-produced film *Emma*.[77] Film magazines also serialised film-star biographies. Popular actor Robert Taylor was the subject of a *Picture Show* feature that ran throughout July 1937.[78] As well as these extensive biographies, *Picture Show* also included regular short articles that provided a snap-shot of a film star's life, such as Carol Lombard's 'Our camera interview' in 1938.[79]

Picture Show did more than simply provide an insight into a film star's life. Readers were persuaded to identify with their favourite stars. Bebe Daniels was thus said to have preserved her svelte physique by adhering to the 'Diet for the Worker'.[80] Jessie Matthews kept 'her lovely figure' by 'gardening, walking, cycling'.[81] These were areas of a film star's life that the working classes could emulate with little difficulty. There was thus a democratising element to many of these biographies. In fact, while film magazines regularly focused on the opulent lifestyle of the stars ('Stars at Home'[82]), they also, as Mark Glancy has noted, sought to uncover the artifice of a star's image.[83] *Picture Show* thus invited its readers to mimic their favourite actors or actresses ('Copy Your Star'[84]). Readers were also encouraged to believe that they shared the tastes of the stars. A *Picture Show* feature on the popular star Ramon Novarro thus depicted him declaring, 'This is my favourite film paper'.[85] Of course, this was an excellent advertising strategy, but readers were undoubtedly expected to gain comfort from knowing that they shared Novarro's tastes.

Film magazine editors, then, repeatedly sought to ensure that their readers felt part of the film and film-going 'communities'. As Glancy has noted, they championed cinema-goers' 'active participation' in film culture.[86] *Picture Show*'s editor was not only keen to promote the magazine as 'the intimate Picture paper for Picturegoers,' he was also eager to stress that cinema-goers held a valued place in the film world.[87] One editorial, for example, claimed that the 'Public is responsible for the Big Changes in Pictures'.[88] Similarly, and reflecting the editor's keenness to identify with the magazine's target readership, *Picture Show* launched a new feature in 1935 that focused on 'Popular Cinemas and their Patrons'.[89] The manager of one of the cinemas evaluated, the Rex Cinema in Stratford, London, revealed that his clientele were 'very music-loving, they enjoy comedy and laughter'.[90] Such a broad statement regarding consumers' tastes would have undoubtedly met the approval of the majority of *Picture Show*'s readers; very few, if any, would have felt excluded.

These popular magazines, then, were targeted towards working-class literary tastes. They were answering and responding to working-class cultural competences. They were far from being slaves to highbrow literary tastes. It is no surprise Leavis *et al.* were so troubled by these trends in popular literature.

Notes

1 Batty, *How to Run a Twopenny Library*, pp. 91–96.
2 Ibid., p. 30.
3 Ibid., pp. 30–31.
4 McAleer, *Popular Reading*, p. 88; T.E. Callender, 'The Twopenny Library', *Library Association Record*, March 1933; Garfield Howe, 'What the Public Likes', *Bookseller*, 19 June 1935.
5 The total number of novels in these categories comes to 612.
6 McAleer, *Popular Reading*, p. 10.
7 Rachael Low, *The History of British Film 1929–1939: Film Making in 1930s Britain*, London, 1997, pp. 178–179. For an informative discussion of Wallace's relationship with the cinema see James Chapman, 'Celluloid Shockers', in Jeffrey Richards, ed., *The Unknown 1930s: An Alternative History of the British Cinema, 1929–1939*, London, 1998, pp. 75–97, pp. 82–87.
8 Batty, *How to Run a Twopenny Library*, p. 57.
9 Ibid., p. 31.
10 Ibid.
11 *PC*, 21 January 1933.
12 Pearl Jephcott, *Girls Growing Up*, London, 1942; *Rising Twenty*.
13 A. J. Jenkinson, *What Do Boys and Girls Read? An Investigation into Reading Habits With Some Suggestions about the Teaching of Literature in Secondary and Senior Schools*, London, 1940.
14 M-OA: FR 48 'Selection and Taste in Book Reading', March 1940.
15 M-OA: TC Reading Habits 3/A 'Fulham Reading Survey', January 1940.
16 M-OA: FR 48 'Selection and Taste in Book Reading', March 1940.
17 M-OA: TC Reading Habits 3/A 'Fulham Reading Survey', January 1940.
18 M-OA: TC Reading Habits 4/A 'Library QQ, London', April–May 1942. The respondent was F.70.D.
19 M-OA: TC Reading Habits 2/D 'Directive Replies', January–February 1938, unidentified.
20 Ibid. Reply from Elizabeth Shoenberg.
21 Ibid. See reply from B. de la Z. Hall regarding 'nursemaid'.
22 Ibid. See reply from Hilda Hodges regarding: 'My friend Lily, domestic servant'.
23 M-OA: TC Reading Habits 2/E 'Directive Replies', January–February 1938.
24 Jephcott, *Rising Twenty*, p. 113.
25 M-OA: TC Reading Habits 2/B 'Reading Counts/Observations/Reports', November–December 1938.
26 M-OA: TC Reading Habits 4/D '("Tupenny") 2d Libraries', June 1942.
27 M-OA: TC Reading Habits 2/D 'Directive Replies', January–February 1938, domestic servant.
28 Ibid., hairdresser.
29 Ibid. F.40.D.
30 M-OA: TC Reading Habits 3/A 'Fulham Reading Survey', January 1940, M.30.D.
31 Ibid., M.60.D.

32 M-OA: TC Reading Habits 2/B 'Reading Counts/Observations/Reports', November–December 1938, Post Office sorter.

33 M-OA: TC Reading Habits 4/D '("Tupenny") 2d Libraries', June 1942, F.35.D.

34 Jenkinson, *What Do Boys and Girls Read?*, pp. 21 and 180.

35 Jephcott, *Rising Twenty*, p. 112.

36 M-OA: TC Reading Habits 4/D '("Tupenny") 2d Libraries', June 1942.

37 M-OA: TC Reading Habits 3/A 'Fulham Reading Survey', January 1940.

38 M-OA: TC Reading Habits 2/E 'Directive Replies', January–February 1938.

39 M-OA: TC Reading Habits 3/A 'Fulham Reading Survey', January 1940.

40 M-OA: TC Reading Habits 2/D 'Directive Replies', January–February 1938.

41 M-OA: TC Reading Habits 8/C 'Book Indirects', July 1943, F.25/D.

42 Ibid., F.45/D.

43 M-OA: TC Reading Habits 2/D 'Directive Replies', January–February 1938. See reply from Joan Weston Edwards, housekeeper, 50.

44 Ibid., unidentified.

45 M-OA: TC Reading Habits 3/A 'Fulham Reading Survey', January 1940, M.50.D.

46 Ibid., M.35.D.

47 Ibid., M.60.D.

48 M-OA: TC Reading Habits 4/D '("Tupenny") 2d Libraries', June 1942, F.35.D.

49 Leavis, *Fiction and the Reading Public*, pp. 28 and 51.

50 M-OA: TC Reading Habits 1/A 'Reading Survey No 1 (October Directive)', October 1937.

51 Of course, many working-class readers had no time to read anything. Indeed, one female interviewee rather acerbically told Box that she did not read because she had 'no time my good woman. I have to work for my living'. M-OA: TC Reading Habits 3/A 'Fulham Reading Survey', January 1940, F.55.D.

52 Ibid., F.55.D.

53 Ibid., F.45.D.

54 Ibid. According to this survey, 'women's magazines' accounted for eighty-six per cent of magazine sales, and of those fifty-five per cent were 'mainly romantic'.

55 Hoggart, *Uses of Literacy*, p. 121.

56 Ibid., p. 122.

57 *Lucky Star* (hereafter *LS*), 7 September 1935.

58 *RSW*, 4 January 1930.

59 Ibid., 1 March 1930.

60 Ibid.

61 *LS*, 7 September 1935.

62 Ibid.

63 *RSW*, 26 July 1930.

64 Ibid., 1 February 1930.

65 Ibid.

66 Cynthia L. White, *Women's Magazines, 1693–1968*, London, 1970, pp. 96–99.

67 *LS*, 7 September 1935.

68 Ibid., 2 November 1935.

69 *RSW*, 11 January 1930.

70 Jephcott, *Girls Growing Up*, p. 113. See also Jenkinson, *What Do Boys and Girls Read?*, pp. 214–215.

71 Jephcott, *Girls Growing Up*, p. 101.

72 See, for example, the contributors to the magazine's 'Happiest Bride-to-be' section.

73 According to Coglan, *Picture Show*'s readership was based primarily in the lower-income group, while *Film Weekly* and *Picturegoer*'s readership was in the higher-income groups. Of course, cinema-goers from lower-income groups read the latter magazines too, but they were not their target readership. W.N. Coglan, *The Readership of Newspapers and Periodicals*, London, 1936, pp. 272–273.

74 *Picture Show* (hereafter *PS*), 4 January 1930. In bold in original.

75 Ibid., 25 January 1930.

76 Ibid., 22 February 1930.

77 Ibid., 18 June 1932.

78 See ibid., 3 July 1937; ibid., 10 July 1937; ibid., 17 July 1937; ibid., 24 July 1937 and ibid., 31 July 1937.

79 *PS*, 15 January 1938.

80 Ibid., 9 September 1933.

81 Ibid., 26 October 1935.

82 Ibid., 1 December 1934.

83 Glancy, 'Temporary American Citizens?', pp. 461–484.

84 *PS*, 4 January 1930.

85 Ibid., 5 April 1930.

86 Glancy, 'Temporary American Citizens?', p. 478.

87 *PS*, 12 May 1934.

88 Ibid., 29 January 1938.

89 Ibid., 29 June 1935.

90 Ibid., 27 July 1935.

6

'A very profitable enterprise': South Wales Miners' Institutes

So far, I have concentrated on national and metropolitan tastes. I now want to turn to smaller and more local case studies, and the next three chapters will assess the tastes of working-class consumers in specific regions, starting with the tastes of consumers in South Wales.

The South Wales Miners' Institutes played a central role in the life of the region's mining communities. Established in the nineteenth century, the Institutes became a focal point for these communities, answering many of their social, cultural and educational needs.[1] As former miner Walter Haydn Davies recalls, miners and their families experienced most of their indoor popular entertainment in these Institutes.[2] This is not surprising as most Institutes contained libraries, reading rooms, games rooms and, by the period under review, cinemas. The larger Institutes offered an even wider array of activities, from evening classes and lectures, to concerts, theatre, and dances. All Institutes held regular trade union and political meetings. The South Wales Miners' Institutes thus offered the region's mining communities' political, educational and recreational facilities. Significantly, then, while the mining communities' cinema-going and reading habits are my concern, it needs to be remembered that these were just two of a number of leisure activities that they enjoyed. The Institutes' cinemas and libraries were simply components, albeit highly important components, of the 'social fabric' of leisure offered.[3]

The roots of the South Wales Miners' Institutes can be found in the Mechanics' Institutes, temperance halls and literary societies that were established across the Welsh coalfields in the mid-nineteenth century. These were archetypal middle-class organisations that offered culturally superior entertainment in an attempt to make the workforce 'sober, pious and productive'.[4] The South Wales Miners' Institutes were different. Far from being under middle-class patronage, Miners' Institutes were working-class organisations that were chiefly financed, controlled, and managed by the communities in which they were situated.[5] Moreover, many of the activities offered would have been identified as culturally inferior by most middle-class observers. In this sense, then, the South Wales Miners' Institutes were free from middle-class hegemony. As Christopher Baggs has observed, because '[o]ne industry and one class dominated; a sense of uniqueness and solidarity was born in communities, which looked to themselves to provide social, cultural, even educational facilities'.[6] Miners' Institutes were the expression of that commonality. However, much of the literature appertaining to the running of these Institutes leaves little doubt that the values of the middle classes were filtering through. Miners' leaders were keen to use the Institutes as social spaces in which miners and their families could experience cultural edification. The desire to educate as well as entertain figured prominently in the minds of those sitting on the Institutes' library and cinema committees. It is thus telling, though certainly no coincidence, that Davies recalls that Miners' Institutes were 'openly referred to as Prifysgol Y Glowyr (Miners' University)'.[7]

Given the intended educational role of the Miners' Institutes, committee members in charge of the daily running of the miners' libraries and cinemas saw it as their duty to raise the standard of the mining communities' leisure habits. When recalling his time on the library committee of Tredegar Workmen's Institute, miners' leader Archie Lush acknowledged that he was one of an 'elite' who chose edifying books for the rest of the community.[8] During his time on the committee many works of a political nature were selected: Dietzgen, Marx, and Lenin. As Lush admits, 'this was quite deliberate. This was a conscious education of the proletariat ... The ambition was that the working class were to be in power, well the library was a means of power'.[9] Interestingly, though not unexpectedly, this overtly didactic approach was not an entirely popular enterprise in the eyes of many library customers. Lush tellingly recalls that the committee used to receive complaints 'that out of thirty pounds too little was spent on novels'.[10] Fellow committee member Oliver Powell verifies this, but tellingly admits that many of these political works were never borrowed. '[T]he damn things were left on the shelves,' Powell protests, 'no one ever bothered ... Lenin, oh everything Lenin ever wrote, that was there, no one was interested in Lenin despite our efforts to try and encourage the Communist point of view, nobody was interested anyhow'.[11] While some Institute ledgers do record high levels of borrowing of political texts, particularly during certain crisis periods, this was unusual.[12] As Powell recalls, at Tredegar Library the 'issue of books was by far and away fiction more than any others'.[13] Other Institutes' ledgers confirm this trend.[14]

Miners' Institute cinemas also encountered mixed success in this field. A number of progressive political film companies were successful in placing their films in Institute cinemas. The Federation of Workers' Film Societies' own film company, Atlas Films, supplied Soviet pictures to a number of Institute halls.[15] In 1936, Nixons Workmen's Hall held a lecture on Russia and exhibited a film describing life in the country.[16] 'Spanish films' were booked at both Mardy Workmen's Hall and Tredegar Workmen's Institute.[17] In addition, political parties and organisations with a political bent were sometimes allowed to use Institute cinemas. The Left Book Club was granted use of Tredegar Institute's cinema in 1938, as was the Communist Party in 1939.[18] However, not all Institutes were keen to accommodate this kind of organisation. The Left Book Club applied twice to use Nixons' Workmen's Hall and was twice refused.[19] The Workers' Film Movement made little progress in exhibiting their products, primarily because, as Stephen Ridgwell has rightly noted, they failed to attract sufficiently large audiences, and thus enough revenue, to ensure that the Institutes remained financially secure.[20] David Berry has argued likewise, suggesting that the 'alternative circuit of progressive political films began to peter out in the late 1930s' because of a rise in demand for more commercial film fare.[21] As with Institute libraries, an overtly didactic approach was not entirely successful. Committee members may have had their own opinion of what types of film and literature they wanted to include, but their choices were not always very popular and were greeted with a degree of resistance.

Miners' Institutes not only had a cultural responsibility, then; they had a political one too. They were sites in which miners were expected to become politically conscious. Middle-class values of self-improvement may have been present, but they were seen as a means of changing the lives of the miners and their families while giving them political power. Not surprisingly, committee members expressed concern over the influence of the types of film and literature that *were* being consumed. Echoing the attitudes of many of his contemporaries, Lush remarked, apropos Tredegar Library's customers' favoured type of reading material, fiction, 'we decided you know that novels were misleading the working class'.[22] In fact, Lush and his fellow committee members assumed that reading popular fiction would lead to the degeneration of the mining communities, thus espousing a strikingly similar argument to Leavis *et al.*[23]

Miners' leaders' position regarding the cinema was commensurate. In fact, many of the debates raging in society about the cinema during this period were being played out in Institute committee meetings too. Of most concern, was the belief that the favoured diet of Hollywood films would remove miners from the political arena.[24] However, the educational value of the cinema was also heavily promoted. At Tredegar Workmen's Institute, for example, a member of the cinema committee called upon those present at one meeting to 'uphold the traditions of the Institute' by 'bringing before the public films of an educational and interest nature'.[25] As Peter Miskell has observed, only the 'occasional screening of the "right sort" of film' was welcomed by cinema committees.[26] As with Institute libraries, then, cinemas were supposed to be advantageous to the mining communities' cultural well-being. Indeed, as early as 1913 it had been argued that films should be exhibited not 'for profit, but for the common good of the community'.[27] All the same, officials on both library and cinema committees understood that they had to answer to the needs and desires of those who frequented Institute halls. If Institutes were to thrive they had to bow to the tastes of their customers; popular demand thus predictably ruled the day.

This is no surprise, especially when we consider Institute cinemas. Committee members knew that the Institutes *needed* the revenue made from cinema showings to bolster their funds, especially in the poverty-stricken years of the depression when the revenue from the miners themselves had dwindled. Indeed, according to Lush, who was also one-time chairman of Tredegar Institute's cinema committee, the money raised by the cinema effectively 'replaced the miners' contributions'.[28] Eddie Thomas, a committee member for Fforestfach, recalled that a cinema was set up in his local Institute in 1939 purely 'in order to keep going'.[29] George Baker, committee member at Park and Dare Workmen's Hall Institute, described the cinema as 'a very profitable enterprise'.[30] Of course, during these hard times not all cinemas made a profit. The cinema committee of Abergorki Workmen's Institute and Hall, for example, recorded that their cinema was losing money and requested that the Institute obtain a cinema manager who had a 'large circuit behind him' to assist its financial standing.[31] Unfortunately there is no record of what types of film were being exhibited prior to this declaration of financial hardship. Could it be that the most popular genres of film had formerly been shunned by the committee? The desire for a manager with a 'large circuit' suggests this could have been the case.

On the whole, though, Institute cinemas, like the majority of cinemas across the country, were highly profitable commercial ventures. The reasons for this are many. As elsewhere, cinema-going was a relatively inexpensive leisure activity. At Nixons Institute in 1932, for example, adult prices started from as low as 4d.[32] These were prices that the often financially-strapped mining communities could still afford. Moreover, Institute committees could be highly responsive to their customers' economic needs. Joan Rogers, a child visitor to the cinema at Celynen Collieries and Workingman's Institute and Memorial Hall, fondly remembers the compassionate endeavours of those individuals who managed it:

> On New Year's Day through the 1930s until 1939 when the war started, a film was shown in the afternoon, usually a Tarzan or a comedy; afterwards a tea was given in the dance hall downstairs. This was attended by 200 or more children and was greatly appreciated as it was all free and times were hard.[33]

As well as offering low-cost entertainment, miners' cinemas could also offer luxury. Consider the décor of the cinema at the latter Institute. Built in 1924, and dedicated to the memory of those who had died in the First World War, the 'Memo', the name given to the hall by locals, could accommodate around seven hundred people. Its cinema was an art-deco masterpiece; comparable to many of the country's 'picture palaces'. Its plush interior featured 'an eclectic mix of art nouveau, art deco and classical styles', and was decorated with murals 'depicting industrial scenes with miners toiling underground'.[34] It was, as Stephen Ridgwell has rightly observed of all miners' cinemas, 'very much in tune with local needs and sensibilities'.[35]

Like cinemas across the country, then, miners' cinemas offered their customers entertainment which combined comfort, pleasure and low cost. It was, of course, entertainment that provided an escape route from the deprivations experienced by many mining families. As one 'Memo' cinema poster encouragingly exclaimed: 'DON'T BE DEPRESSED IN A DEPRESSED AREA. GO TO THE PICTURES AND ENJOY LIFE AS OTHERS DO'.[36] More than that, though, it was entertainment in which miners and their families could come together and experience a moment of not only cultural, but social, gratification. Indeed, quite often the films being shown were not the primary attraction. As one cinema-goer recalls:

> My memories of the Memo were mainly on a Friday night, which was teenagers and kids night. No one ever knew what the film was. Girls and boys in the back row snogging, paper darts being thrown everywhere, everyone climbing over the seats, usherettes' torches in your eyes, and just pandemonium. The film was often stopped and an announcement made threatening to throw everybody out unless order was maintained. If Harold Jones the manager appeared everyone was terrified into silence.[37]

These recollections offer a salutary reminder that cinema-going was not always about what was playing on the cinema screen. However, along with Rogers' remarks, they also reveal that miners' cinemas operated as a symbolic centre of the community. Judging by their success, this was a phenomenon not lost on those who both ran and patronised them. Of course, we must not discount the similar role played by the many other leisure activities offered at Miners' Institutes. Indeed, as Ridgwell has asserted, cinemas were seen as one of the many community institutions that epitomised the miners' 'community spirit'.[38] Nonetheless, for the majority of their customers, going to the cinema was *the* most important leisure activity the Institutes offered. In fact, as Bert Hogenkamp has observed, the introduction of cinemas had a profound effect on the Institutes. They not only helped to bring in much needed revenue; they also opened up what were once 'bastions of typically male activities' to the whole of the community.[39]

Of course, for those who ran the Miners' Institutes, the cinema was primarily a way of making enough money to support the Institutes' libraries. As Archie Lush has admitted: 'So the cinema dominated, but all the time the money from that, from my gang's point of view, our chaps was for the library'.[40] In fact, for the likes of Lush *et al.*, miners' libraries played the most important function in the Institutes, not financially of course, but certainly culturally, educationally, and politically. However, while miners' libraries undoubtedly remained incredibly popular throughout the decade, it was not for the reasons people like Lush would have chosen. Lush favoured literature with a political commitment; he wanted his library's customers to be enlightened and instructed by the books they read. But it was primarily fiction that his library's customers demanded, and it was fiction that he and his fellow committee members had to purchase for them.

It is now time to turn to what was actually being consumed. To what can we attribute the *cultural* success of the miners' cinemas and libraries? What types of film featured in Institute cinemas? What types of book found most favour with the libraries' customers?

Film popularity

The South Wales Coalfield Collection, held at the University of Wales, Swansea, contains a number of cinema ledgers from the South Wales Miners' Institutes. To my knowledge, only one cinema ledger from the 1930s remains extant. That ledger belongs to the Cwmllynfell Miners' Welfare Hall cinema and runs from 29 March 1937 to 28 December 1939.[41] There are a number of breaks in the ledger, so we need to cut our coat according to the cloth of the somewhat sporadic material available, but it is nevertheless a highly valuable resource. In fact, given the richness of the material, this is perforce an abbreviated account of my detailed interpretation of the data.[42]

The ledger lists first and second features, along with a number of other programmes, such as shorts and newsreels. I shall assume, though, that the first features were the main draw for the consumer. The cinema's programmes usually changed every Monday and Thursday, but some films were exhibited for a whole week. For example, MGM's earthquake melodrama *San Francisco* (1936) was shown from 31 May until 6 June 1937. No films were shown on Sundays, but on occasions the hall was given over to other users.

Cwmllynfell's miners' cinema opened in 1935 and was advertised in the local press as 'The Valley's Super Cinema'.[43] The cinema played a major role in providing films that answered to the tastes of the majority of people within that region. What types of film were being shown? There are eighty-seven first features listed in the ledger. At twenty-nine features, drama is by far the most highly represented film genre, accounting for one third of the total number of first features shown. These range from the socially conscious Julius Hagen production *Broken Blossoms* (1936), depicting London slum life, to the American-produced *San Francisco* (1936), the melodramatic spectacular that recreates the 1906 earthquake, and centres its narrative on the 'triangle' relationship between Clark Gable, Spencer Tracy and Jeanette MacDonald.

Despite their generic similarities, *Broken Blossoms* and *San Francisco* offer highly contrasting visual and narrative styles. *Broken Blossoms* was a relatively low-budget film produced at Hagen's Twickenham Film Studios. The film marked the directorial debut of Hans (later John) Brahm and starred Emlyn Williams; Williams also wrote the screenplay. Its narrative is especially bleak. Adapted from Thomas Burke's novel, *Limehouse Nights*, *Broken Blossoms* tells the story of Chen (Williams), an idealistic young Chinaman whose beloved Lucy is killed by her violent father. Chen kills the father in retribution. The film's visual style complements the dour theme. The wretchedness of life in London's Limehouse area is poignantly captured. According to *Kineweekly*, the Limehouse scenes were 'sketched with a vividness that catches all the squalor'.[44] *Broken Blossoms* may thus be visually stylish, but it is a dramatic film with a particularly gloomy mode of delivery.

Compare this to the high-gloss, MGM production, *San Francisco*. Directed by one of the American film industry's major figures, W.S. Van Dyke, *San Francisco* is visually rich and has an extremely fast pace. Its lively narrative centres on the relationship between the boss of a beer garden (Gable), a singer employed by him (MacDonald), and a priest (Tracy). Gable, MacDonald and Tracy were all major Hollywood stars. Tracy and Gable's battle to win MacDonald's affections dominates the film's narrative until the earthquake sequence begins. From then on, a range of cinematic techniques are skilfully deployed to beguile the audience. Long, sweeping shots of the devastated city, coupled with a series of rapidly-edited close-ups of individuals struggling to deal with the earthquake's effects, command attention. In fact, the first warning of the impending earthquake is signalled by a low rumble heard by the patrons of a crowded music hall, cleverly drawing a parallel between the two leisure forms while guaranteeing the cinema audience's rapt attention. There was no doubting that this was a Hollywood spectacular. Not surprisingly, the film was showered with critical acclaim. *Kineweekly's* review panel were unrestrained in their admiration. 'Seldom, if ever, has there been a greater show than this,' gushed one reviewer'.[45] *Variety* and *Monthly Film Bulletin* offered similar views.[46]

San Francisco, then, possessed all the qualities that were expected to attract British working-class audiences: action-packed, laden with special effects and star-studded. Its inclusion on the ledger is not surprising. *Broken Blossoms* is another matter. For a start, it was a British film. The home-made product was not expected to appeal to British working-class audiences. Indeed, according to *World Film News*, exhibitors in working-class areas were 'unanimous in regarding the majority of British films as unsuitable for their audiences'.[47] In addition, the film's narrative built slowly; working-class audiences were supposed to demand films 'with tempo and action'.[48]

Considering the type of fare that was supposed to attract working-class cinema-goers, then, it is extremely surprising to see this film was shown at a miners' cinema. However, this taste-community liked dramatic films with a social conscience; films of this type were regularly exhibited at the hall. In addition to this, of course, *Broken Blossoms* was a remake of the popular 1919 American silent film of the same name (which had been directed by the renowned D.W. Griffith), so the reputation of the film's earlier version would probably have influenced the committee's decision to book the film.[49] The film's principal star, Emlyn Williams, was also Welsh; a factor that must similarly have aided the committee's decision-making process. Moreover, film critics generally praised the film's aesthetic and story-telling values.[50]

A number of factors thus combined to make *Broken Blossoms* an attractive booking for Cwmllynfell's cinema committee. Its romantic drive, exoticism and rough action were, of course, expected to provide pleasure. But the cinema's patrons could hardly be expected to gain pleasure from its uncompromisingly brutal exposition of the grim realities of London slum life. Considering that the film's famous silent predecessor was equally bleak, it is highly unlikely that the cinema committee were not aware that this element dominated. The foremost influencing factor must, then, have been the recognition of what this film said about contemporary society. Chen is a deeply idealistic individual who is passionately committed in his attempts to fight society's injustices. *Broken Blossoms* thus made caustic comments about the state of contemporary society.

A large proportion of the dramatic films shown at this cinema are also driven by a socially conscious premise. *Two Wise Maids* (1936), *Fury* (1936), *They Gave Him a Gun* (1937), *The Last Gangster* (1937), *South Riding* (1938), *Blockade* (1938) and *The Citadel* (1938), while markedly different in approach, all possess a strong socially conscious ethos. Like *Broken Blossoms*, these films feature individuals who attempt to deal with society's inequalities. Like *Broken Blossoms*, they made scathing comments about the existing social order. It is, of course, hardly surprising that miners' leaders booked films of a political persuasion, but the repeated booking of films of this type suggests that the cinema's patrons were not averse to them either. Why? Because these films addressed society's problems, and, most significantly, many focused explicitly on the deprivations faced by working-class communities and sought resolutions to them. If we bear in mind the effects of the depression on mining communities prior to this period, it is clear why mining families turned to such fare in the late 1930s.

Of course, not all of the dramatic films shown at Cwmllynfell's cinema were driven by such lofty principles. But one thematic strand is common to all: they suggest that individual effort can overcome adverse circumstances. Some films, such as *Broken Blossoms*, *Fury*, *The Last Gangster* and *The Devil-Doll* (1936), concentrate on the individual's ability to avenge past wrongs. In others, such as *Sworn Enemy* (1936), *Counterfeit* (1936), *I Promise to Pay* (1937), *The Crowd Roars* (1938) and, of course, *San Francisco*, the central characters' efforts to succeed in the face of much adversity is a constant theme. These films offer resolutions to specific problems, and in the manner in which they do so, they seek to comfort the cinema audience. Some films offer a resolution that is, to say the least, extreme. *Broken Blossoms* is a case in point. But these films not only highlighted society's injustices, they also placed the working classes and marginal groups at the centre of the narrative. The working-class consumers at this Miner's Institute cinema were bound to like them.

Of the twenty-nine dramatic films listed, twenty-two were American productions, and only seven were British films. Of course, as the exhibition of *San Francisco* reveals, Cwmllynfell's patrons liked dramatic films to have gloss, and the majority of these films were indeed high-gloss productions. But there was more to it than this. As mentioned, American-produced films were more likely to be highly critical of the inequalities in the existing social system and pose alternatives to them. These films could offer this mining community a more radical interpretation of the social order. They were answering to the cinematic tastes of this community, and the sheer volume of them in this category only serves to underline the point.

After drama, comedy is the next most highly represented genre on the ledger. It accounts for twenty of the total number of first features shown. There are fourteen American films and six British productions. A number of American comedy staples appear on the ledger. Laurel and Hardy were clearly popular with Cwmllynfell's patrons; three of their films were exhibited as first features – *Way Out West* (1937), *Swiss Miss* (1938) and *Block-Heads* (1938). These films are low-status vehicles in which the pair are placed in unfamiliar surroundings and face a number of seemingly insurmountable challenges. Each film incorporates the music-hall staples of physical humour and slapstick. The pair are lampooned throughout, but nonetheless eventually succeed in their respective quests. By doing so, these films both amuse and comfort the audience.

The Marx Brothers, whose highly successful film *A Day At The Races* (1937) was exhibited in May 1938, presented an altogether more nihilistic view of society. Their films, which will be discussed in more detail in Chapter 9, contain amusing sequences in which the comedians mock authority and high society. Their films thus offered working-class cinema-goers a high-spirited release, and sought to give them confidence in their class position. A number of British comedy films exhibited at the cinema operated in an analogous manner. The two Old Mother Riley films shown at the hall, *Old Mother Riley* (1937) and *Old Mother Riley In Paris* (1938), featured music-hall star Arthur Lucan as a larger-than-life Irish washer-woman who ridicules the conventions of the middle classes, but is also completely relaxed with her own social standing.[51] Made cheaply for the small, independent production company Butchers, these low-status films were anarchic, disparaging towards middle-class society, and featured strong working-class characters. It is no surprise this taste-community liked them. Of higher status, but equally anarchic and disparaging, the Gainsborough production *Ask a Policeman* (1939), exhibited in November 1939, featured Will Hay, Moore Marriot and Graham Moffat as representatives of that most respectable of British institutions – the police force. Far from representing 'law and order', though, the protagonists are incompetent buffoons who involve themselves with much of the village's criminal activities. The film celebrates this lawlessness and adopts a decidedly anti-authoritarian stance. It thus constantly rejects the social mores and values of middle-class society.[52] These elements are softened by the film's humour, but they are not removed; they would certainly have played well with Cwmllyn-fell's working-class patrons. Like the Marx Brothers' and Old Mother Riley features, then, *Ask a Policeman* was using the masking properties of comedy to make swingeing comments about contemporary society. No wonder it was booked for this cinema.

If we turn our attention to thematic patterns in the comedy films exhibited at the hall, one strand is common to many: they often serve to warn against the dangers of having or obtaining money. *A Day At The Races*, *The Three Wise Guys* (1936), *Bluebeard's Eighth Wife* (1938) and *The Young In Heart* (1938) made it clear that material wealth did not equate to happiness. *Mister Cinderella* (1936), *Mr Deeds Goes To Town* (1936) and *Way Out West*, meanwhile, alerted the audience to the risks of acquiring wealth. All of these films could operate, to borrow a term used by Jeffrey Richards, as 'cautionary tales'.[53] They demonstrated that monetary gain is no guarantee of happiness. In fact, possessing money is often exposed as the *cause* of extreme unhappiness. In addition, while these films allow social boundaries to be breached throughout, there is always restitution at their dénouement. In this sense, these films can be argued to offer a consensual resolution to society's woes. This is perhaps predictable when we consider both the effects of the depression on society in the 1930s, and the level of fear this generated among society's elites on both sides of the Atlantic. It seems curious, though, that these films were being booked by a cinema committee who would have undoubtedly favoured a more radical resolution to society's problems.

We must remember, however, that these films were performing a number of social and cultural roles. A range of factors combined to make them attractive bookings. Firstly, all of these films were American productions. American comedies were favoured over the British product. This was undoubtedly because American films were glossier affairs that were not afraid to make biting criticisms about contemporary society. Secondly, the films featured a number of the period's most popular stars and were thus expected to draw in large cinema audiences. Thirdly, and finally, the films' directors had a keen eye for popular taste. All of these films thus assume a highly populist perspective.

As a result, not only do the majority of them place lower-class characters at the heart of their narratives, but in the manner in which they are contrasted against other social classes, they are given the upperhand. Without exception, middle- and upper-class society is depicted as pompous, rigid, and staid; working-class society is vibrant and exciting.

There is, then, an imbalance between the films' narrative and textural qualities. The films' lower-class characters may be uncomfortable outside the realms of their known experiences, but they are very comfortable with their own social status. Of course, this can be identified as hegemony at work; there is no threat to the social order. But these films could serve to give working-class consumers *confidence* in their class position. They implied that if there was something deeper wrong with society, the fault lay not with the working classes, but with those members of society higher up the social scale. Rather than soothing social anxieties, then, these films actively sought to arouse them. It seems likely that they were booked by Cwmllynfell's cinema committee because, along with their provenance and star values, they enhanced the self-belief of the hall's working-class patrons. It is, therefore, tempting to suggest that these films were being employed at a conscious level by the cinema committee to awaken the audience's class consciousness. Is this, then, evidence of a displacement between a film's expected meaning and how it was actually being consumed by the audience? Were they reading these films 'against the grain'?[54] If we bear in mind that these films were shown alongside the Old Mother Riley features *et al.*, it would appear that they were expected to do just that.

Of the eighty-seven films listed on the ledger, twelve are musicals, eleven are historical films, and nine are adventures. Between them, then, these films accounted for just over a third of the total of films booked for the hall. This is a respectable proportion, considering that these types of film were usually more expensive to make than dramatic or comedy productions, and, as such, represent a smaller percentage of the total film output.[55] In fact, of most significance is the number of historical films the committee booked. Sue Harper has shown that, during the years 1932–1939, eighty-seven historical films were produced in Britain.[56] This represents just over six per cent of the total British film output. The ledger's eleven historical films account for 12.64 per cent of the total number of films booked; a highly significant figure. What is even more interesting about these figures is that, according to *World Film News*, historical films were supposed to hold little appeal for working-class audiences.[57] Not so. Cwmllynfell's patrons certainly appreciated them.

Three of Alexander Korda's historical films were booked: *Rembrandt*

(1936), *Fire Over England* (1937), and *The Four Feathers* (1939). Significantly, *Rembrandt*, a high-status production which documents various aspects of the famous painter's life, was described by *Kineweekly*'s review panel as a film 'for good and high class halls'.[58] Its inclusion here, then, is perhaps surprising. But, firstly, it was a Korda film. Ever since the phenomenal success of *The Private Life of Henry VIII* (1933) Korda's films were expected to do well at the box-office. Secondly, the committee would have viewed the film as culturally edifying, and thus an ideal booking for improving the cultural capital of the audience. Thirdly, it featured Charles Laughton in the title role; Laughton was a highly popular star attraction in the period. Finally, and perhaps most importantly, the film, like all of Korda's historical films, negotiates a relationship between the aristocracy and the working classes, effectively denying the middle classes their social role. This radical presentation of society was certain to go down well with Cwmllynfell's cinema committee and patrons, especially as Korda's films generally painted working-class society in a very positive light. In fact, the scenes in *Rembrandt* which witness the artist's return to the family home leave one in no doubt about the importance of Rembrandt's lower-class ancestry ('peasants' bread; I'm home') and popular cultural forms (barn-dancing; 'gallon of beer').[59]

The remaining historical films on the ledger are all American productions. *Romeo and Juliet* (1936) was Hollywood Shakespeare with a stellar cast. It was, like *Rembrandt*, a rather ambitious booking, and was undoubtedly expected to be culturally edifying. *The House of Rothschild* (1934), a biography of the Viennese banking family, was shown in January 1939, despite being antediluvian. The committee's minds were probably swayed by the fact that it featured an array of popular stars and included a Technicolor finale. The remaining films, apart from the historical musical *Maytime*, were much less sophisticated affairs. *The Suicide Club* (1936) was a light-hearted black comedy set in Victorian London. *The Texans* (1938) and *Stagecoach* (1939) could equally be classified as 'westerns'. Perhaps surprisingly, considering that they were expected to appeal to male working-class audiences, westerns were not popular as first features here. These are the only two that appear on the ledger (although thirteen were shown as second features). But both of these films featured strong female as well as male characters; an obvious attraction for a cinema committee attempting to draw female cinema-goers to an establishment that had until recently been identified as a predominantly male preserve. *A Woman Rebels* (1936), set in Victorian England, and starring Katharine Hepburn as a rebel against Victorian convention, was probably booked for the same reason.

The Bold Cavalier (1937), which featured the heroic Zorro, held considerable appeal for both sexes.

Of course, *The Bold Cavalier* was as much a swashbuckling adventure film as it was an historical one. In fact, two other historical films, *Fire Over England* and *The Four Feathers*, could also be described as adventure films. By the same token, a couple of the adventure films listed on the ledger could likewise be placed in the historical category: Korda's *The Return of the Scarlet Pimpernel* and Samuel Goldwyn's *The Adventures of Marco Polo* (1937), which traces the life of the thirteenth-century Venetian traveller. However, it seems that, apart from these two films, the adventure films shown here possessed a rather different cinematic appeal from the historical features. Whereas the majority of historical films booked by the committee seem to offer equal pleasure for both sexes, most adventure films possess a more masculine appeal. Take the American-produced spectacle *Trader Horn* (1931). The film, which charts the experiences of African trader Aloysius 'Trader' Horn, was described by *Variety* as a 'Sure money-getter … which has a good-looking white girl romping around scantily clad'.[60] One can imagine why this would be an attraction for Cwmllynfell's miners, but it was hardly likely to appeal to their wives or girlfriends.

This is not to say that adventure films had *no* feminine appeal. They did. *Captains Courageous* (1937), a nautical adventure focusing on the rigours of seafaring life, nevertheless has a tender side. In exploring the relationship, at first indifferent, then compassionate, between rough-edged fisherman Manuel, played by Spencer Tracy (a highly popular star attraction for both male and female cinema-goers) and pampered rich child Harvey, the film constructs a kinship of emotional punch that was sure to appeal to both sexes. *The Prisoner of Zenda* (1937), meanwhile, is an action-packed American-produced swashbuckler, complete with a gripping duel sequence, which carefully develops the romantic union between the King's impersonator and a princess. Both of these films were booked for a whole week – in July and October 1938 respectively – so they were expected to draw in a large, and undoubtedly mixed-sex, crowd. All the same, these films, along with the likes of *Tarzan Escapes* (1936), *Elephant Boy* (1937) and *The Drum* (1938), give prominence to the masculine ideal in their narratives. Some celebrate the male form; all champion masculine endeavour, values and codes of practice. On the whole, then, the target audience for these films appears to be the miners themselves. And, in propelling them into a strange and alien world in which *their* social status was paramount, these films offered both an escape and reassurance. For a miner suffering the emasculating effects of the depression – unemployment, reduced income, loss of status – the appeal of these films is completely understandable.

All of these films were adaptations of famous, and highly popular, novels. Rudyard Kipling's tales were the source material for both *Captains Courageous* and *Elephant Boy*; *The Drum* was based on A.E.W. Mason's novel; *The Prisoner of Zenda* was an adaptation of the novel by Anthony Hope; Edgar Rice Burroughs' stories provided the inspiration for *Tarzan Escapes*; and *Trader Horn* was based on the novel by Ethelreda Lewis. Significantly, all of these authors had novels regularly borrowed from Miners' Institute libraries.[61] They were popular, no doubt, because they functioned in a similar manner to the films. These stories were part of the 'boy's own' tradition of adventure writing which, like the films they inspired, celebrated masculine endeavour and the chivalric code.

In adventure films, then, this taste-community expressed a liking for the spectacular and the exotic. In musicals, for a while at least, they wanted something less florid. Indeed, the most striking feature of the musical films listed on the ledger is the disproportionate split between British and American first features. There were eight British and four American musicals. It is the only genre in which British productions outnumber American ones. It would be instructive, however, to break down these figures year by year, for it would appear that the audience's tastes in musical films changed as the decade progressed. Of the eight musicals booked in 1937, seven are British productions and one is American. Of the two booked in 1938, one is British and one is American. In 1939 two musical films feature – both are American productions. It would appear, therefore, that not only did the audience's interest in musical films wane as the decade drew to a close, they also fell out of love with the British product.

The audience's taste for musical films appears to have grown more sophisticated during these years. Initially, the British films chosen by the committee were extremely low status, crudely-made affairs. Between 5 April and 6 May 1937 they booked the George Formby comedy vehicle *Off the Dole* (1935), romantic musical *The Last Waltz* (1936), the Will Fyffe comedy vehicle *Annie Laurie* (1936), and naval reunion yarn *Shipmates O' Mine* (1936). According to contemporary critics, these films were tailor-made for this type of cinema. 'Should please industrial audiences,' remarked *Kineweekly*'s review panel apropos *Off the Dole*.[62] *The Last Waltz* was considered a '[u]seful "programmer" for the unsophisticated'.[63] *Annie Laurie* was said to be '[g]rand stuff for populous halls and industrial districts'.[64] And *Shipmates O' Mine* was a '[f]air average two-feature booking for the unsophisticated and juveniles'.[65] By being shown at Cwmllynfell's miners' cinema, then, these films were expected to be hitting their target audience. The repeated booking of such fare suggests that they were doing just that.

However, the quality of the musicals exhibited at the hall gradually improved after this run of films. The British musicals featured were, if not exactly high-status, then at least far more glossy cinematic productions. Musical drama *Song of Freedom* (1936), complete with Paul Robeson as a London docker who becomes a famous opera singer, was booked for a whole week in late May 1937. *Calling All Stars* (1937), a variety film that, with its American settings and performers, drew considerable influence from Hollywood, was shown in October of the same year.[66] More culturally ambitious fare came along in November 1937 with *Pagliacci* (1936), a one-act opera that contained a number of colour sequences, and, in January 1938, with *Moonlight Sonata* (1937), a triangle melodrama that incorporated a twenty-minute recital by Paderewski.[67] These films, or at least aspects of them, demanded some measure of cultural competence from the audience; they were far superior to the British musicals shown earlier. Interestingly, though, all of these films were teamed with extremely low-status productions. *Song of Freedom* was accompanied by, firstly *Lawless Nineties* (1936), then *The Singing Cowboy* (1936); *Calling All Stars* was paired with *Oh Susanna!* (1936); *Pagliacci*'s running mate was *Fighting Through* (1934); *Moonlight Sonata* was teamed with *Blarney Stone* (1933). Apart from the latter, which is a Tom Walls comedy-drama, all of these second features are westerns. This raises a number of questions. Were the committee booking the low-status films to ensure audience satisfaction, while hoping that their culturally superior running mates would be edifying? Were they expecting the first features to appeal to the miners' wives, and the second features to the miners themselves? Or did they expect the first features to be so popular that they booked any old tosh to accompany them? It is impossible to be certain which factors came into play. But I believe that it was the first features that were the principal draw for the consumer. It would seem, then, that parts of this audience were demanding more respectable musical fare or that those *booking* the films wanted them to see more respectable fare.

The booking of high-gloss American musicals during this latter period under-scores this. In fact, historical musical *Maytime*, which was booked for a week in May 1938, had only shorts as accompaniment. This musical extravaganza, featuring the ever-popular star pairing of Jeanette MacDonald and Nelson Eddy, is the type of musical spectacular Hollywood did best in the 1930s. It was clearly expected to do well here. The other musicals booked for the hall – *The Great Ziegfeld* (1936), *The Hit Parade* (1937), *The Goldwyn Follies* (1938), and *Sweethearts* (1938) – were similarly glossy affairs. All of these films display textural and narrative balance. Therefore, unlike some of the low-status British musicals which sought to arouse social anxieties – *Off the Dole* for example – these films sought to alleviate them. If this taste-community liked some films to stimulate them in this way, they did not want these musical films to do it.

It is now time to consider the least represented genre on the ledger: the romance film. Perhaps predictably, considering the origins of the Institutes as a male leisure stronghold, only six romantic films were booked by the committee; of these, five are best described as 'romantic comedies'. Three American and three British romance films were exhibited. Significantly, like all of the British-produced adventure and historical films, all three British-produced romances – *Men are Not Gods* (1937), *Storm in a Teacup* (1937), and *The Divorce of Lady X* (1938) – came from Korda's production stable. All of these films are lavish, glossy productions (*The Divorce of Lady X* was made in colour) that, apart from the latter, which foregrounded feminine pleasure, portrayed the working classes in a positive light. *Storm in a Teacup*, for example, focused on the triumph of the 'common man' (or in this case woman). *Men are Not Gods* foregrounded the 'simple' pleasures of working-class life ('the representatives of the gallery, the symbol of the unreserved seats'). This audience, then, and especially the female members of it, were sure to gain satisfaction from watching them. All of the American-produced romances are similarly highly-polished affairs. They rely on humour to carry forward the narrative, and feature some of the period's most popular stars. Like their musical counterparts, the American-produced romance films sought to ease social anxieties rather than stimulate them.

It would appear, then, that for Cwmllynfell's mining community, going to the cinema performed a number of social, cultural, and even political, tasks. The range of films booked for exhibition was far from purely 'escapist' fare. Indeed, many films demanded a high level of cultural competence from the audience. Of course, if these types of film were not popular with the audience, the committee would have had little choice other than to stop booking them. Financial necessity required close attention to consumer demand. It would seem, then, that these working-class consumers were demanding more challenging film fare. And it seems that they were using their highly-valued position in the Institute's financial affairs to do so.

These conclusions go against much of the perceived historiographical wisdom regarding the role of the cinema in the South Wales Miners' Institutes. Much of this stems from the unequal focus on the progressive, political workers' films these Institutes exhibited, and the almost total lack of attention paid towards more commercial film fare. Indeed, while Berry, Hogenkamp, Miskell and Ridgwell have rightly argued that miners' cinemas sought to raise working-class consciousness through the exhibition of films of an overtly political nature, they ignore the role that the commercial product could play.[68] I suggest that cinema committees were carefully choosing the commercial films that could help to work in this way. It seems likely that mining communities were actively using these commercial films to gain both a sense of place in society and confidence in their class position.

This analysis of Cwmllynfell's cinema ledger has, then, modified a number of important issues regarding the role of the Miners' Institute cinemas in particular, and the function of the cinema in the lives of the working classes more generally. It has shown that Hollywood films did not, as Hogenkamp has argued, 'willy-nilly [dominate] the screens of the miners' cinemas'.[69] Indeed, while Cwmllynfell's principal supplier may have been MGM, and while the committee may have also taken films from other American film companies – Columbia, Paramount and United Artists – they also booked a large number of films from a string of British companies – British Lion, Butchers, Mancunian, Sound City and Twickenham. Therefore, while American-produced films did figure in greater numbers, the amount of British productions exhibited at Cwmllynfell's cinema was far from negligible. In fact, thirty British films – over a third of the total number of films listed – is a very significant figure when we consider that many contemporaries, and indeed numerous historians since, have observed that working-class audiences expressed a deep dislike for the British product.

The ledger has also shown that historical films, thought by some cinema exhibitors to hold little appeal for working-class patrons, were well represented here; so were social realist films which, far from containing plenty of action and fast tempo, were slow-moving and replete with dialogue. More highbrow fare – always an expected turn-off for working-class audiences – also featured quite prominently. Conversely, romance films, a genre that was expected to play well with (female) working-class audiences, were not popular at all here. Although this undoubtedly has much to do with the male-centred character of the Miners' Institutes' leisure provision, it does serve to remind us that there are many variations in working-class taste. In fact, these variations in taste are further highlighted when we compare this ledger to Mass-Observation's Bolton Questionnaire. The category of film that featured at the top of the list of preferences among the Palladium's male cinema-goers – and third on the list of preferences among the cinema's female consumers – was crime. Only four crime films are listed on Cwmllynfell's ledger. Moreover, all of these are classified as 'crime-drama[s]'. These cinema-goers, then, appear only to have enjoyed elements of lawlessness and anti-authoritarianism when they were heavily couched in comedy.

Of course, we cannot view the tastes of this mining community as representative of *all* mining communities. What may have played to a packed hall at Cwmllynfell's cinema may have bombed elsewhere. Besides, not all of the Institutes exhibited the same films at the same time. Certainly, an initiative in 1933 by the regional representative of the Miners' Welfare Fund, Captain Mason, to cut costs by organising a united film booking scheme for Halls and Institutes failed to gain much support.[70] Most Institutes were highly independent, and their members cherished (and indeed protected) that independence.[71] However, while each Institute was self-governing, as far as film-booking patterns are concerned, similar arrangements were undertaken elsewhere. The minute books of Tredegar Workmen's Institute, for example, reveal that the committee booked films from a mixture of American and British production companies.[72]

There is indeed another, even more significant, issue to address regarding Tredegar Institute's minute books. It concerns the day-to-day running of Tredegar's cinema, and, more importantly, the nature of the relationship between the Institute's cinema committee and film distributors. Hogenkamp has argued that miners' cinemas were 'at the mercy of the commercial renters'.[73] Not so. Cinema committees had considerable bearing on what films they chose to exhibit. In fact, Tredegar's committee used their extensive authority to ensure they only booked films that would play well at their cinema. In 1937, for example, United Artists – who from 1934 had provided the 'back-bone' of the cinema's programmes – offered them· thirteen films, but the committee were only 'prepared to negotiate for the pictures [they were] interested in'.[74] The committee were also well-versed on film availability. In 1935, the cinema's manager attended a trade show held by Gaumont-British; while in 1936 the committee asked the firm to provide a list of their films to enable them to be reviewed.[75] Far from being 'at the mercy' of these commercial renters, then, Tredegar's cinema committee were not afraid to make exacting demands to ensure they got the films their audiences wanted to see.

The committee were also adept at gaining the best possible prices for the films they wanted to exhibit. In 1938, for example, they agreed to 'pay the percentage asked for *The Drum* provided [United Artists] was prepared to let them have two others at a reduced price'.[76] Financial necessity clearly brought out the best of the committee's business acumen. They also had their fingers on the pulse regarding the local competition. Not only were their admission prices comparable to the rival cinema, the Olympia, but they were also keen to ensure that there was no duplication of programmes.[77] In fact, when, in February 1935, Butchers offered the Olympia a film 'that was booked tentatively for this Hall,' they were quickly dropped.[78] Flexing their muscles again in July 1937, the committee demanded to know why the musical comedy western *Rhythm on the Range* (1936) 'had been played as a second feature at [Markham's Welfare Hall] some weeks ago'.[79] Of course, these examples demonstrate that the committee were, not surprisingly, eager to obtain the best possible audience figures for their film shows. They needed the revenue from the cinema to keep the Institute financially buoyant.

Given this requirement, it is predictable that the committee were highly responsive to their audiences' needs and desires. In fact, they were adept at understanding their customers' tastes and second-guessing what types of film would be popular with them. In October 1935, for example, the committee, displaying an acute awareness of the national success of Shirley Temple's films, and obviously expecting that success to be replicated here, decided to exhibit Temple's first 'star vehicle', *Bright Eyes* (1934), 'twice nightly, with matinée showings for adults on Thursday afternoon and for children on Saturday'.[80] The film must have hit its target because two other Temple films, *The Little Colonel* and *Curly Top* (both 1935), were given similar treatment in 1936.[81] In fact, such was the expected popularity of Temple's films that in 1937 the committee agreed that the manager should be given 'any necessary assistance' to obtain them.[82] This close attention to the mining communities' cinematic tastes is indicative of the importance of the consumer in the field of cultural relations. Without doubt, then, the films shown at this, and indeed Cwmllynfell's cinema, were answering to the tastes of these mining communities. These resources thus offer us an invaluable insight into the cultural lives of these mining communities. They provide us with a clearer understanding of the cinema audiences' desires and aspirations. It is safe to assume that the library registers of the miners' libraries afford us an equally enlightening insight.

Literature popularity

To my knowledge, there are two miners' library registers still extant covering the 1930s. The first, the Cynon and Duffryn Welfare Hall library register, runs from 1927–1952. The second, belonging to the Markham Welfare Association's library, covers 1923–1940. Both registers are reproduced by Jonathan Rose in his article.[83] There are some gaps in the original registers, so we do not gain a full picture of an author or book's popularity. Markham's library register stops recording borrowing activity between January 1926 and February 1932 and November 1936 and March 1937, so the record of popularity is somewhat skewed. Cynon and Duffryn's library register devotes one page to each book in the collection, and once the page was full, the borrowing record ends. Therefore, while Richmal Crompton's *Just William* (1922) is recorded as being borrowed thirty-three times between 1927 and 1936, we do not know how many more times, if any, it was loaned after that date. Despite these inconsistencies, both registers are extremely valuable resources that help draw a map of the reading activities of both mining communities.

The Cynon and Duffryn register is slightly problematic for my purposes, however. In reproducing the register, Rose groups the record of loans over large periods. Alexandre Dumas's *The Three Musketeers* (1846) is thus recorded as being borrowed nineteen times between 1933 and 1948. It is impossible to ascertain *when* each of these loans took place. The majority of them may have occurred between 1940 and 1948 and, therefore, be of no relevance. Then again, the novel could have been loaned eighteen times in the 1930s and once in 1948, and so be of greater significance. There is no way of knowing one way or the other. While some books *are* recorded as being borrowed in our period, they account for less than a third of the three hundred or so titles listed, so the material needs to be treated with some caution.[84] Markham Welfare Hall's library register is less problematic. Borrowing records are divided into five periods, three of which are useful: March 1932–February 1935, March 1935–October 1936 and April 1937–March 1940. Both registers will be employed here, but we can only gain an *impression* of the popularity of certain authors and their work. Who, then, were the most popular authors with the readers using these libraries? Are there significant differences in taste between the two communities? How do the results compare with reading tastes at a national level?

Cynon and Duffryn Welfare Hall library register[85]

Many of the period's most popular authors are listed on the Cynon and Duffryn register. Ruby M. Ayres, Warwick Deeping, Jeffery Farnol, E.M. Savi and, of course, Edgar Wallace, all appear. They do *not* dominate it, though. In fact, of the three hundred and two titles listed, only seventy-three were written by the authors found on the lists drawn up by Ronald F. Batty, T.E. Callender and Garfield Howe. Moreover, when it comes to the books being borrowed, only a few of the period's most popular authors fared extremely well. E.P. Oppenheim, with eight titles on the list, was clearly popular. Edgar Rice Burroughs and Baroness Orczy, with five titles each, were also well represented. Interestingly, though, while Oppenheim and Orczy were regularly borrowed throughout the decade, Burroughs's popularity peaked early. Only two of his five listed novels – *A Princess of Mars* (1919) and *The Return of Tarzan* (1918) – were actually borrowed during the 1930s. The other three – *Beasts of Tarzan* (1918), *Tarzan of the Apes* (1917) and *Tarzan the Terrible* (1921) – were not borrowed after 1929. Chest-beating masculinity must have gone down better with the mining communities' cinema-goers after that date.

In fact, the drift in Burroughs's popularity shows that, far from raising interest in a novel, a filmed version could have a deleterious effect upon it. Having seen the film, these consumers may have felt that the written word had far less impact. Indeed, Anthony Hope's *The Prisoner of Zenda* (1894) was not borrowed once after the filmed version was released in 1937. It was, however, repeatedly borrowed earlier in the decade. Of course, not all authors saw their popularity dip after one of their novels was filmed. Baroness Orczy's *A Spy of Napoleon* (1934) was released as a film in 1937 and was borrowed regularly in that and the following year. But, on the whole, filmed versions of popular novels made little impact in increasing book borrowing in this miners' library. Indeed, we can again use Richmal Crompton's popularity as evidence of these trends. As mentioned, the filmed version of Crompton's *Just William* had little effect on her popularity nationally. It also had little effect here. Two of her novels appear on the register – *Just William* (1922) and *William Again* (1923) – and both were subject to high demand long before the filmed version of the former was released. Moreover, while we cannot be certain whether *Just William* was borrowed after the film's release (the page was filled in 1936 leaving no room for further entries), *William Again* was *not* loaned out. The feature film had no impact at all. Like many readers across the country, then, readers in this mining community already knew what types of fiction they preferred, and needed little encouragement when choosing it.

What, then, did they like? As mentioned, many of the period's most popular authors appear on the register. But only a few experienced significant success. Arnold Bennett's sensational and humorous 'pot-boilers' went down well. The register lists four of his novels, and all except one, which was not returned after its initial loan, were repeatedly borrowed. Jeffery Farnol's romantic adventure *The Money Moon* (1911) was well liked. It was loaned thirty times until it went missing in 1936. Zane Grey's westerns were also popular. *Desert Gold* (1913) was loaned thirty-six times between 1927 and 1936.[86] Jack London was also in high demand, with adventure *Burning Daylight* (1910) and short-story *The Night Born* (1916) doing particularly well. Gertrude Page's romance *The Pathway* (1914) was also highly popular. What becomes clear when analysing the register, though, is how relatively short the time-span was in which an author or novel experienced success. Bennett's star certainly shone brightly, but only for a brief period. After 1932, no-one wanted to borrow his work. Page suffered the same fate after 1933. Zane Grey's *Desert Gold* remained popular, but his two other novels on the register – *Rainbow Trail* (1915) and *The Young Pitcher* (1919) – were not borrowed after 1930. Some authors, such as Jeffery Farnol, enjoyed a longer cycle of popularity, but these were the exception rather than the rule. Readers' tastes were clearly highly volatile.

Moreover, when we compare this register to the lists of popular authors drawn up by Callender and Howe, there are some surprising omissions. P.G. Wodehouse, A.G. Hales, Margaret Peterson and Joan Sutherland, all top ten ranked authors according to Callender's calculations, do not feature. Sydney Horler, Denise Robins and Kathleen Norris, all placed in Howe's top ten, fail to appear. There are other notable absences. Charlotte Brame, Elizabeth Carfrae, Ethel M. Dell, Louise Gerard, Elinor Glyn, Deidre O'Brien, Marjorie M. Price, E. Adelaide Rowlands, Paul Trent and F.E. Mills Young, all known to attract the mass reading public, are not listed. The differences in taste between the users of the Cynon and Duffryn library and working-class consumers at a national level are, therefore, quite striking.

In fact, the most popular authors with readers in this community generally did not appear on any of the popularity lists mentioned earlier. Frederick C. Vernon Harcourt's detective novel *Bolts and Bars* (1905) was by far the most popular book on the register – it was taken out an impressive forty times between 1930 and 1934 – but Harcourt does not get a mention by Batty, Callender or Howe. These individuals are equally silent about H.L. Gates, but his bleak novel *The Auction of Souls: The Story of Aurora Mardiganian* (1920), a translation of Aurora Mardiganian's account of the 1915 Armenian massacre, was highly popular with this reading community. These readers also liked Samuel Lover's tale of Irish life, *Handy Andy* (1842). Lover was similarly not mentioned by Batty *et al*. Indeed, the only authors who we can be certain did exceptionally well with these consumers *and* working-class readers at a national level during this period were Jack London, E.P. Oppenheim and Baroness Orczy. Other authors, such as Richmal Crompton and Edgar Rice Burroughs performed well overall, but they experienced considerable fluctuations in popularity.

It is not surprising, bearing in mind that miners' libraries were intended to be culturally edifying, to find a number of 'classics' on the register. Novels by Jane Austen, Emily Brontë, Daniel Defoe and Charles Dickens feature. What is surprising, though, is that these authors achieved a sustained popularity. Unlike many popular novelists, who, on the whole, achieved success over a brief period, these authors maintained the interests of this reading community across many years. We must be careful not to over-egg the pudding, however, because none of the classics attained a vast readership. Jane Austen's *Pride and Prejudice* (1813), which was the most popular of the classics, was borrowed only sixteen times over a fourteen year period (1934–1948). Charles Dickens had an impressive seventeen titles on the register, but between 1928 and 1949 they were taken out sixty-six times in total. *Oliver Twist* (1841) and *A Tale of Two Cities* (1859) were his most successful novels here; both were taken out a mere seven times each. Compare that to E.P. Oppenheim's success rate. Oppenheim had eight novels on the register, and between 1927 and 1949 they were borrowed a total of one hundred and forty-one times. The most popular among these was the short-story collection *Slane's Long Shots* (1930), which was borrowed twelve times over a one-year period. In fact, it might have been loaned out even more, but it went missing after it was borrowed in 1936. Cynon and Duffryn's library committee would have undoubtedly been far happier if the work of Dickens *et al*. had achieved that sort of popularity.

It is worth saying something at this point about the types of book that were *unpopular*. What books failed to attract many, or indeed, *any* readers? There was little interest in instructional or home-improvement books. Mabel Hodkin's *Rug Making and Designing* (1936), Alfred Keeble's *Handicraft Woodwork* (1935), Charles G. Leland's *Leather Work* (1892), Millicent Vince's *Practical House Decorating* (1932) and Mrs Arthur Webb's *Economical Cookery* (1934) failed to attract a single reader. A few instructional books *did* attract an occasional reader – Louisa Judd-Morris's *The Sampler Book of Decorative Needlework* (1937) in 1938, for example – but, in general, this type of book rarely whetted this mining community's appetites. General interest books hardly fared any better. *Carber's Blue Book of Gardening* (n.d.), Karl M. Bowman's *Towards Peace of Mind: Everyday Problems of Mental Health* (1936) and Donald Mackenzie's *Ancient Man in Britain* (1922) were each taken out on one occasion. Books that dealt with Welsh communities also fared badly. William Johnstone's *The Welsh at Home* (1904) attracted three readers over a five-year period. James Hanley's *Grey Children* (1937) was equally unpopular. This is not surprising, however, for *Grey Children* was a report about unemployed Welsh colliers. Miners were hardly likely to want to read about their suffering; they had lived or were living through extreme deprivation, and did not want or need to be reminded about their torment.

Bearing in mind the politicised nature of many mining communities, it is surprising that books on political and social issues were unpopular with Cynon and Duffryn's library users. Only five are listed. Of these, Matthew Arnold's *Culture and Anarchy* (1869) was the only text that attracted many readers, and that was taken out a mere four times. Of course, H.L. Gates's *The Auction of Souls* was well liked, but there is a significant difference between this and other socio-political texts. *Auction of Souls* was a *novel*. It may have been a bitter diatribe against war, but it was written in a format that this community found more attractive. Bertha von Suttner's pro-disarmament novel *Disarm! Disarm!* (1913), which did well, can be placed in that category too. On the whole, then, readers in this mining community were not interested in educational, instructional or political books. Their interests lay elsewhere. It was *fiction* that they wanted, and, on the whole, a certain *type* of fiction at that. Culturally edifying novels were borrowed occasionally, but for these readers, like many working-class readers across the country, 'light' fiction was by far the preferred type of reading material.

If we turn to patterns of genre popularity, we can identify *some* common trends with readers at a national level. Romance novels did particularly well. There are no fewer than fifteen romantic novelists on the register. Readers liked Rex Beach's *The Barrier* (1908), Marie Corelli's *The Life Everlasting* (1911) and A.S.M. Hutchinson's *If Winter Comes* (1921). They particularly liked the work of Baroness Orczy and E.M. Savi. Both authors had a number of titles in the library and all were regularly borrowed. Significantly, though, romantic fiction does *not* dominate. Therefore, while national reading trends point towards a greater desire for romantic fiction than any other genre, in this miners' library other genres did equally well. Adventure novels were highly popular, for example. R.M. Ballantyne's *The World of Ice* (1859) did very well.

H. Rider Haggard, whose inclusion on other lists appears as something of an anomaly, did quite well. In fact, his romantic adventure *Cleopatra* (1889) was very popular. Readers using this library were clearly not averse to this style of adventure writing, for Robert Service, who was widely known as 'the Canadian Kipling', did particularly well at the beginning of the decade. Interestingly, though, and despite the success of *Cleopatra*, historical adventures got a mixed reception. Anthony Hope's *The Dolly Dialogues* and *The Prisoner of Zenda* (both 1894) did well during the early part of the decade, but only one of the three Alexandre Dumas novels stocked – *The Three Musketeers* (1846) – did particularly well. Readers clearly preferred their adventures to be set in a contemporary, if admittedly alien, world.

Detective fiction and thriller or mystery novels also did well with Cynon and Duffryn's library users. However, there were far fewer of these novels available than there were romantic and adventure fiction titles. Significantly, though, the number borrowed was very high. The keen interest in Frederick C. Vernon Harcourt and E.P. Oppenheim's stories has already been mentioned, but there are other examples. The library stocked two William Le Queux thrillers, and they were taken out twenty-nine times between 1928 and 1932. Arthur Reeve's *The Exploits of Elaine* (1915) was borrowed twenty-eight times over a three-year period. Clearly, then, when it came to these genres, this reading community liked to consume the work of the same few authors. Are we again witnessing a conservatism in the reading habits of working-class men? It would certainly seem so. Of course, men would have read adventure novels and there were many of these listed, but adventure novels could also appeal to women. Detective novels and thrillers were, on the whole, targeted towards, and preferred by, male readers. The limited range of authors thus signifies a conservatism common with male working-class readers nationwide. In fact, this is particularly apparent if we look at the range of western novelists stocked in the library. There are only two: Harold Bindloss and Zane Grey. Both had a number of titles available, and all were borrowed in great numbers. Of course, the popularity of particular authors fluctuated rapidly across the decade, but these trends in *genre* popularity remained constant. There were, then, gender differences in the reading habits of this mining community.

We can thus identify a number of trends in reading habits that are common between users of this miners' library and working-class readers at a national level. Popular fiction was favoured over the classics. Romance novels were the most popular *single* genre. Author popularity varied considerably over the decade. Men were far more conservative than women in their reading habits.

Yet, there are also a number of key *differences* in taste. One is not unexpected. Overall, men had a far greater range of fiction titles available to them. This, of course, befits an institution that was initially used only by *male* consumers. Other differences are more startling, however. Edgar Wallace, the most popular author with the country's working-class readers, fared very badly here. The library stocked only *one* of his books – the short-story collection *The Last Adventure* (1934) – and while it was taken out regularly from 1938 onwards, this is a far cry from the popularity of his work nationwide. This may have had something to do with availability. Perhaps Cynon and Duffryn's library committee found Wallace's novels hard to obtain. But *other* Institute libraries stocked his work. The library committee at Abergorki Workmen's Hall added sixteen of his novels to their range in 1930, for example.[87] Markham Welfare Association's library carried seven Wallace titles. Surely Cynon and Duffryn's library committee could have added more titles too? The answer is probably 'yes', but they chose not to. Why? Well, Wallace did not do that well with readers using Markham's library either. His star was eclipsed regularly by other authors. Remarkably, then, mining communities appeared to care little for his work, and it would be instructive to speculate on why this was the case. I will, therefore, make space at the end of this book to analyse one of Wallace's novels and attempt to understand why miners and their families did not find his work to their taste.

There is one other key difference in taste. Apart from the work of Richmal Crompton, humorous novels did not fare particularly well with the nation's working-class readers. They did very well here. Crompton, of course, was well liked. But other comedy writers were also highly popular. William Darlington's *Alf's Button* (1919) was borrowed twenty-nine times over a four-year period. W.W. Jacobs' *Odd Craft* (1904) was only slightly less popular. Herbert Jenkins had two titles listed, and they amassed a total of forty-four loans during the early part of the decade. Unlike national consumers, then, this mining community favoured, and undoubtedly found comfort in, humorous fiction. But, of course, these are the tastes of readers at *one* Miners' Institute. Are they representative of the tastes of other mining communities? To answer this question we can turn to the register for Markham Welfare Association's library. How do the two registers compare? Can we identify any significant difference in taste?

Markham Welfare Association library register[88]

There is one striking difference in taste between readers using Cynon and Duffryn's library and those using the library at Markham's Welfare Association. The latter expressed a keen interest in works of a socio-political nature. There are a large number of socio-political novels on the register, and they all perform extremely well, especially during the latter part of the decade. Not surprisingly, left-wing writers were particularly popular. Ralph Bates's novel on the Spanish Revolution of 1931 *Lean Men* (1935) was regularly borrowed between April 1937 and March 1940, as was his short-story collection *Sierra* (1933). Halldór Laxness's portrayal of Icelandic fisherman *Salka Valka* (1936), which carried a strong Christian communist message, attracted many readers over the same period, as did Walter Brierley's socialist tract *Means Test Man* (1935), and Robert Tressell's harsh proletarian novel *The Ragged Trousered Philanthropists* (1914). The most popular political novels over those years, however, were Feodor Gladkov's *Cement* (1929), which features a communist hero who overcomes overwhelming odds, and Upton Sinclair's *Oil!* (1927), in which the son of an oil tycoon espouses strong socialist values. Both novels were loaned out an impressive twenty-two times over the three-year period. The most successful political novel overall, though, was William C. Bullitt's portrait of Soviet life in Philadelphia, *It's Not Done* (1926). Between 1935 and 1936, and over the space of a mere nineteen months, the novel was loaned out a massive twenty times; that equates to one loan every four weeks. Compare that to the borrowing record of the most popular socio-political novel at Cynon and Duffryn's library, H.L. Gates's *Auction of Souls*, which was loaned out *thirteen* times over a *three*-year period. With Markham's reading community, then, we can perceive something of the political awareness that we would associate with a miners' library.

This is not to say that Markham's library users did not like lighter fiction. They did. In fact, at the beginning of the decade reading preferences tended towards the types of fiction that attracted working-class readers nationwide. Ottwell Binns's adventures, Warwick Deeping's romances, and E.P. Oppenheim's detective yarns all attracted a wide readership. However, in common with reading patterns at Cynon and Duffryn's library, these popular authors did *not* dominate. Less than a quarter of the authors listed are to be found on the lists created by Batty *et al.* Once again, only a few of these popular authors performed particularly well. E.P. Oppenheim was again the most successful author. Jeffery Farnol also performed extremely well. Interestingly, Edgar Wallace fared better here than at Cynon and Duffryn's library. Seven of his titles were stocked, two of which were repeatedly borrowed. However, as stated, the interest shown in Wallace's work by these mining communities does not compare to that displayed by working-class readers elsewhere. Indeed, the loans of Wallace's novels at Markham occurred over a nineteen-month period between 1935 and 1936. For the rest of the 1930s his books remained firmly on the shelf. As with reading trends at Cynon and Duffryn's library, the most successful novels at Markham were written by authors who did not appear on the lists created by Batty *et al.* Willard K. Smith's detective story *The Bowery Murder* (1929) was the most popular novel overall. Dale Collins's detective novel *The Fifth Victim* (1930) ranked second place. Neither author appears on the popularity lists mentioned above.

There are other similarities in the reading habits of these two mining communities. Reading tastes at Markham were also highly volatile. Only a few authors and novels gained long-term popularity. Detective author Howel Evans's *A Little Welsh Girl* (1918) performed well between 1932 and 1936; Zane Grey's westerns did well between 1935 and 1940. On the whole, though, an author or novel's popularity was extremely short-lived. Indeed, while novels with a political commitment did remarkably well between April 1937 and March 1940, before and after those dates the vast majority of them were left on the shelves. Even Émile Zola's *The Dream* (1893) and *Germinal* (1894), which performed extremely well during those years, were ignored outside that period. The same trend pertains with light fiction. Apart from Howel Evans and Zane Grey, the authors who attracted an extensive readership between March 1935 and October 1936 failed to attract many readers before or after those dates. The library's acquisition of a new batch of novels by lowbrow authors in March 1935 probably accounts for the keen interest shown in their work after that date. The rapid decline in their popularity after October 1936 was undoubtedly caused by circumstances of a different kind. The Spanish Civil War, Japan's invasion of China, and the seemingly inexorable rise of Hitler and Mussolini clearly awakened this mining community's political interest. Fiction with a political commitment thus became the order of the day.

In fact, even 'classic' literature, which maintained a constant interest at Cynon and Duffryn during the 1930s, could not attract even a modest readership at Markham after February 1935. The library may have stocked thirteen Dickens titles, but they were more or less left on the shelves from March 1935 onwards. Novels by Jane Austen, the Brontë sisters, Benjamin Disraeli and George Eliot suffered the same fate. Interestingly, they had all performed well during the 1920s, and quite respectably during the early 1930s. The allure of new books and an awareness of international events clearly dimmed this community's interest in the 'classics'. Reading tastes may, then, have been even more unpredictable at Markham than at Cynon and Duffryn. Indeed, it would appear that Markham's library users were more easily swayed by contemporary affairs, for it is noticeable that the Second World War caused a significant shift in reading tastes. After June 1940, readers were generally drawn towards authors who had not attracted them at all before. G.W. Barrington, Ethel M. Dell, Arthur Conan Doyle and W. Somerset Maugham achieved borrowing numbers in double figures between June and December 1940; only Maugham had attracted any readers in the previous decade.

There are, then, *some* similarities in the reading habits of these mining communities. But there are some significant differences. Markham's reading community expressed a desire for fiction with a political commitment, and their reading tastes were even more changeable, but there are important variations in the *types* of light fiction Markham's library users chose. Humorous fiction fared less well here than at Cynon and Duffryn. The library may have stocked three Richmal Crompton novels, but only one – *William's Happy Days* (1930) – did well. The other two were not taken out once during the 1930s. Moreover, no other author of humorous fiction attracted many readers. Other authors who were popular at Cynon and Duffryn's library likewise raised little interest here. H. Rider Haggard's writing held no appeal. Alexandre Dumas's *The Three Musketeers* was not borrowed once. Despite the success of Ottwell Binns's novels, then, adventure writing was much less popular at Markham. Romantic fiction also fared considerably less well at Markham than at Cynon and Duffryn. Samuel Lover's *Handy Andy* was left sitting on the shelves. Only one of the three Marie Corelli romances stocked was borrowed during the 1930s, and that was taken out a mere two times. Rafael Sabatini's novels were similarly undervalued. In fact, only a few authors of the genre did well. Rex Beach, Warwick Deeping, Gertrude Page and Ida Wylie were popular. Ethel Savi did particularly well. But these were the exceptions. The library register announces loud and clear that romantic fiction was not very popular with Markham's library customers.

Detective fiction, mysteries and thrillers were extremely popular, though. They were particularly well represented, with no fewer than sixteen authors available, and were regularly borrowed. Oppenheim was the most popular author, but many other writers did remarkably well. Herbert Adams, Francis Beeding, Guy Clifford, G.D.H. Cole, Dale Collins, J.J. Connington, J.S. Fletcher, George Goodchild, Howel Evans, A.E.W. Mason, Frank Packard,

John Rhode, Willard K. Smith and Hugh Walpole all attracted a great many readers. Even Edgar Wallace did significantly better than the majority of the library's stock of romantic fiction authors. There was, in fact, a far greater range of fiction aimed primarily at male readers at Markham than at Cynon and Duffryn, and all male-targeted genres did well. It would appear, therefore, that at Markham, unlike at Cynon and Duffryn, and indeed, many libraries nation-wide, it was not male readers who were conservative in their tastes, but female readers. Women tended to consume the work of the same few authors, while men appeared to cast the net more widely (even if their preference was for a similar type of story). There were, then, clear variations in genre popularity between the two mining communities.

This analysis of the Cynon and Duffryn and Markham library registers reveals that there could be significant differences in the reading habits of the mining communities of South Wales. Reading tastes not only varied consid-erably over time and between the sexes, but even over short geographical distances. Of course, as Rose has noted, book availability, library acquisition policies and the librarian's guiding influence could account for these variations in taste.[89] Peer pressure, too, could affect reading choice. Archie James, for example, a keen library user who claimed to have read many political texts, recalled that he was influenced in his choices by a fellow miner who had been 'pouring questions and relating different things of what he had known and read and all that kind of thing'.[90] However, while it is important to remember that other determinants may affect consumer choice, we need to be cognisant of the agency of the consumers themselves. The most popular books at both libraries were borrowed with remarkable frequency; miners and their families would not have kept reading them if they were not answering their tastes. Markham's library users, then, *wanted* to read political novels between 1937 and 1940; Cynon and Duffryn's customers did not.[91]

Of course, in general, both reading communities displayed an overriding fondness for light fiction. It is not surprising, therefore, that the number of light fiction titles far outnumbers any other type of literature in both libraries. In fact, despite the ever-present rhetoric regarding the culturally edifying responsibilities of the Miners' Institutes, library shelves in *all* Institute libraries were crammed with light fiction.[92] Clearly, then, library committees were responding closely to the demands of the consumer. Indeed, such was the importance of the consumer in this relationship, that librarians were expected to be familiar with the work of the most popular authors. Thus, when the library committee at Nixons Workmen's Hall and Institute were appointing a new librarian, it was presumed that candidates would be 'acquainted with writers of fiction', and that they would be able to answer questions on a variety of popular novels, such as Marie Corelli's *God's Good Man* (1904) and Wilkie Collins's *Woman in White* (1859).[93] Regardless of the aims of those individuals running Institute libraries, then, what the miners and their families wanted to read undoubtedly guided stock acquisition. In short, library committees, like the Institutes' cinema committees, had to keep in step with consumer demand.

Notes

1 Will Picton, oral history recording, 18 May 1973 (University of Wales, Swansea, South Wales Miners' Library). All subsequent references with UWS in parentheses refer to oral history recordings from this archive.

2 Walter Haydn Davies, *The Right Place – The Right Time (Memories of Boyhood Days in a Welsh Mining Community)*, Llandybie, 1972, p. 224.

3 Stephen Ridgwell, 'South Wales and the Cinema in the 1930s', *Welsh History Review*, 17:4, 1995, pp. 590–615; p. 599.

4 Rose, *Intellectual Life*, pp. 237–238.

5 See Jonathan Rose, 'Marx, Jane Eyre, Tarzan: Miners' Libraries in South Wales, 1923–52', *Leipziger Jahrbuch zur Buchgeschichte*, 4, 1994, pp. 187–207; p. 187. See also Christopher Baggs, '"The Whole Tragedy of Leisure in Penury": The South Wales Miners' Institute Libraries during the Great Depression', *Libraries and Culture*, 39:2, 2004, pp. 115–136; p. 115.

6 Christopher Baggs, 'How Well Read was My Valley? Reading, Popular Fiction, and the Miners of South Wales, 1875–1939,' *Book History*, 4, 2001, pp. 277–301; p. 278.

7 Haydn Davies, *The Right Place*, p. 224.

8 Archie Lush, 11 May 1973 (UWS). See also Oliver Powell, 29 November 1973 (UWS). Powell was also on the library committee at Tredegar and recalled that many books were chosen to raise the general reading level.

9 Lush, 11 May 1973.

10 Ibid.

11 Powell, 29 November 1973.

12 Rose, 'Marx, Jane Eyre, Tarzan', pp. 193–194.

13 Powell, 29 November 1973.

14 See the library registers for Cynon and Duffryn Welfare Hall and Markham Welfare Association, reproduced in Rose, 'Marx, Jane Eyre, Tarzan', pp. 195–206. See also, Christopher Baggs, 'The Miners' Libraries of South Wales from the 1860s to 1939' (PhD thesis, Aberystwyth University, 1995).

15 Bert Hogenkamp, 'Miners' Cinemas in South Wales in the 1920s and 1930s', *Llafur*, 4:2, 1985, pp. 64–76; p. 67.

16 Nixons Workmen's Hall and Institute Minute Book 1935–1943, 14 July 1936.

17 Ridgwell, 'South Wales', pp. 604–605; Tredegar Workmen's Institute Hall Committee and Cinema Committee Minutes, 1933–1940, 2 September 1937.

18 Tredegar Workmen's Institute, 14 July 1938; 3 November 1939.

19 Nixons Workmen's Hall and Institute Minute Book 1935–1943, 4 April 1939. See also 2 May 1939.

20 Ridgwell, 'South Wales', pp. 604–605.

21 David Berry, *Wales and Cinema; The First Hundred Years*, Cardiff, 1994, p. 142.

22 Lush, 11 May 1973.

23 Ibid.

24 Hogenkamp, 'Miners' Cinemas', pp. 68–69.

25 Tredegar Workmen's Institute, 26 April 1934.

26 Peter Miskell, *A Social History of the Cinema in Wales 1918–1951: Pulpits, Coal Pits and Fleapits*, Cardiff, 2006, p. 151.

27 *Gazette*, letter to editor, 27 June 1913, in Gwilym Richards, newspaper cuttings, MNA/PP/98/17/1.

28 Lush, 11 May 1973.

29 Eddie Thomas, 4 February 1974 (UWS).

30 George Baker, 18 July 1974 (UWS).

31 See Abergorki Workmen's Hall and Institute; General, finance, library and film committee minute books, 1928–37, 5 November 1935.

32 See Nixons Workmen's Hall and Institute Minute Book, 1927–1937, 11 October 1932.

33 The Institute is also known as Newbridge Memorial Hall and Institute. Rogers' remarks were retrieved from www.newbridge-memo.net/jewel/index.html, accessed on 22 February 2006.

34 All information retrieved from www.newbridge-memo.net/jewel/index.html, accessed on 22 February 2006.

35 Ridgwell, 'South Wales', p. 603.

36 Retrieved from www.newbridge-memo.net/jewel/index.html, accessed on 22 February 2006.

37 Ibid.

38 Ridgwell, 'South Wales', p. 602.

39 Hogenkamp, 'Miners' Cinemas', p. 66. See also Baggs, 'Miners' Libraries of South Wales', pp. 230–234.

40 Lush, 11 May 1973.

41 Cwmllynfell Miners' Welfare Hall, cinema secretary's diaries. The ledger is located in the South Wales Coalfield Collection, University of Wales, Swansea.

42 Robert James, '"A Very Profitable Enterprise": South Wales Miners' Institute Cinemas in the 1930s', *Historical Journal of Film, Radio and Television*, 27:1, 2007, pp. 27–61. The ledger is reproduced in this article.

43 Ridgwell, 'South Wales', p. 603.

44 *Kineweekly*, 28 May 1936.

45 Ibid., 23 July 1936.

46 See *Variety*, 1 July 1936 and *Monthly Film Bulletin* (hereafter *MFB*), July 1936.

47 *WFN*, February 1937.

48 Ibid.

49 Indeed, it was championed by *Kineweekly* partly because it held 'valuable box-office heritage in its title'. *Kineweekly*, 28 May 1936.

50 See ibid.; *FW*, 20 June 1936. For a negative view, see *Variety*, 10 June 1936.

51 See Richards, *Age of the Dream Palace*, pp. 298–299; Sutton, *Chorus of Raspberries*, p. 148–152.

52 For a discussion of these aspects in Hay's films see Steven W. Allen, 'Will Hay and the Cinema of Consensus', *Journal of British Cinema and Television*, 3:2, 2006, pp. 244–265.

53 Richards, *Age of the Dream Palace*, p. 304.

54 Morley, 'Theories of Consumption', pp. 300–301.

55 See figures supplied by Stephen Guy, 'Calling All Stars: Musical Films in a Musical Decade', in Richards, ed., *Unknown 1930s*, pp. 99–118, p. 99, and Sutton, *Chorus of Raspberries*, pp. 246–282.

56 Harper, *Picturing the Past*, p. 10.

57 *WFN*, February 1937. The paper noted that 'history is almost universally condemned' among working-class consumers.

58 *Kineweekly*, 12 November 1936.

59 The barn-dancing sequence is intercut with images of Laughton, filmed from below and well-lit, smiling at the scenes he is witnessing. His 'peasants' bread' utterance takes place immediately after a particularly solemn reading from the bible. As he utters those words he gives a knowing nod towards the camera.

60 *Variety*, 11 February 1931.

61 See the library registers for Cynon and Duffryn Welfare Hall and Markham Welfare Association, reproduced in Rose, 'Marx, Jane Eyre, Tarzan', pp. 195–206.

62 *Kineweekly*, 25 April 1935.

63 Ibid., 23 July 1936.

64 Ibid., 16 July 1936. See also *MFB*, 31 July 1936.

65 *Kineweekly*, 21 May 1936.

66 Low, *History of British Film*, p. 107; Guy, 'Calling All Stars', pp. 114–115.

67 Richards, *Age of the Dream Palace*, p. 27.

68 Berry, *Wales and Cinema*, p. 133; Hogenkamp, 'Miners' Cinemas', p. 65; Miskell, *A Social History*, pp. 150–152; Ridgwell, 'South Wales and the Cinema', p. 604.

69 Hogenkamp, 'Miners' Cinemas', p. 68.

70 Tredegar Workmen's Institute supported the initiative, but 'complete unity could not be reached'. See Hogenkamp, 'Miners' Cinemas', p. 68.

71 See comments of George Baker, 18 July 1974 (UWS).

72 Films were booked from Anglo-Cosmopolitan, Ambassador, Butchers, Fox, Gaumont-British, Mancunian, Paramount, United Artists and Warner Brothers. See Tredegar Workmen's Institute, Hall Committee and Cinema Committee Minutes, 1933–1940.

73 Hogenkamp, 'Miners' Cinemas', p. 65.

74 Tredegar Workmen's Institute minutes, 8 February 1934 and 15 April 1937.

75 Ibid., 31 January 1935 and 12 March 1936.

76 Ibid., 14 July 1938.

77 Ibid., 16 May 1935.

78 Ibid., 21 February 1935.

79 Ibid., 8 July 1937.

80 Ibid., 3 October 1935.

81 Ibid., 23 January 1936 and 28 May 1936.

82 Ibid., 28 April 1937.

83 Rose, 'Marx, Jane Eyre, Tarzan', pp. 195–206. Rose reproduces the Cynon and Duffryn Welfare Hall register in its entirety; the Markham Welfare Association register is, however, selectively reproduced.

84 Rose states that the registers are held by the library of the University of Wales, Swansea. I intended to analyse these ledgers in person, but, despite repeated searches by the library staff during the duration of my visit, the registers could not be found.

85 All the data used here can be found in Rose, 'Marx, Jane Eyre and Tarzan', pp. 195–201.

86 The page is filled in 1936 so we cannot be certain how many times the novel was loaned after that year.

87 Baggs, 'Miners' Libraries', p. 281.

88 All the data used here can be found in Rose, 'Marx, Jane Eyre and Tarzan', pp. 201–206.

89 Ibid., p. 192.

90 Archie James, 14 November 1973 (UWS).

91 Readers often borrowed different types of book from various Institute libraries. George Baker thus chose to read both fiction and political works, but went to three different libraries to obtain them. Baker, 18 July 1974.

92 Fiction accounted for 75%–95% of book loans. Baggs, 'Miners' Libraries', p. 431.

93 Nixons Workmen's Hall and Institute minute book, 1927–1937, 21 March 1933.

7

'Gunmen, rustlers and a damsel in distress': working-class tastes in Derby

I have shown that working-class cultural tastes in South Wales were predicated on the particular set of socio-economic circumstances in which consumers were living. If we now turn to another geographical area, the Midlands, we can see that, here too, the nature of the region's socio-economic structure influenced consumers' taste preferences.

The Midlands town of Derby had a diversified industrial structure by the 1930s, but engineering and textile industries dominated.[1] While unemployment levels remained relatively low throughout the period, there were fluctuations which affected the working classes' leisure participation. In 1932, for example, the *Derbyshire Advertiser*, the region's weekly paper, observed that libraries in industrial areas were well utilised because they provided 'a means of recreation and study in this period of industrial and financial depression'.[2] Derby's library committee, who recorded library issues and were well aware of variations in borrowing, shared this view, noting: 'Unemployment undoubtedly had something to do with [the] big jump in [borrowing] figures'.[3] By 1934, however, the library committee had recorded a sharp decrease in borrowing which they attributed partly to rising employment levels.[4] There were, then, clear shifts in reading habits structured by employment patterns. To my knowledge, there are no complete records of cinema attendance, so we cannot identify equivalent shifts in cinema-going habits. However, in 1939 one observer noted that 'more than 35,000 people' visited Derby's cinemas every week, with just under half that number attending on Saturday nights.[5] Participation in cinema and literature culture was, therefore, well established among the town's working-class population.

Derby was, in fact, particularly well served by cinema and library facilities. With an estimated population of 140,000 in our period, the town supported eleven cinemas in 1930, and seventeen by 1939.[6] These ranged from the large 'super-cinemas' such as the Coliseum and the Gaumont Palace, which were located in more affluent areas of the town and accommodated 1,250 and 2,175 patrons respectively, to the smaller, less glamorous halls, such as the Allenton and the Alvaston, that were situated in largely working-class neighbourhoods and housed around 600 patrons.[7] Derby was also well populated by libraries. The town's central library opened in 1871.[8] By the 1930s, Derby supported a large number of public, twopenny and mobile libraries, leading the *Derbyshire Advertiser* to note 'that no one, not even in the most isolated places, and whatever his taste, needs go without books because he cannot obtain them'.[9]

Information on the organisation and provision of reading material in Derby is scanty. There are few records that tell us of the attitudes and values of those responsible for providing reading material to the town's citizens. Information on cinema provision is more abundant. We can, therefore, gain a sense of how valued working-class consumers were for the town's cinema industry. Not surprisingly, the owners and managers of Derby's cinemas were keen to foster a close relationship with their patrons. The owners of the Cosmo cinema, Mr and Mrs France, for example, distributed sticks of rock and an orange to children in the audience after returning from their summer holidays.[10] They also financed the Cosmo Athletic football team, which was formed by regular cinema-goers in the early 1930s, and offered free admission to the team's players on Saturday evenings.[11] If the team won, Mr France displayed the score on the cinema screen. Similar practices can be seen elsewhere. Cinema staff at the Coliseum would enter the auditorium and announce both half- and full-time football scores through a megaphone.[12] Staff at many other cinemas also distributed fruit to children in the audience.[13] Derby's cinema managers, then, understood that going to the cinema was an integral part of working-class life. It was not so much a separate and distinct cultural activity for the town's working classes, but one that coalesced fully with every aspect of their lives. Reflecting that, cinema owners were not shy in establishing links with other prominent community figures. Mr and Mrs France thus had links with the local chemist and butcher. The former sold the 'Cosmo Cough Cure', while the latter was often called into the cinema's auditorium – 'complete with apron and long carving knife' – to calm excitable children attending Saturday matinées.[14]

Following national trends, then, cinema-going and reading were key cultural activities for Derby's working-class consumers. Can we discern any changes or continuities in taste between this town's working-class consumers and those at a national level or in the South Wales mining communities? In order to draw a map of the film tastes of this community, I will turn to the weekly advertisements placed in the town's sole daily paper, the *Derbyshire Evening Telegraph*, for the Allenton cinema, which was used predominantly by working-class consumers. To my knowledge, there are no records regarding specific books borrowed from Derby's public and commercial libraries. Fortunately, though, the *Derbyshire Evening Telegraph*, along with recommending which films to watch, regularly recommended new book releases. To establish reading patterns, therefore, I will look at the recommendations made in this newspaper along with the more general and impressionistic material available from library committee minutes.

Film popularity

The Allenton cinema opened on 17 December 1928. It was located in Osmanton Road, at the centre of a shopping and residential area, and had a seating capacity of 670.[15] In 1937, prices ranged from 6d to 1s 3d.[16] It shared the same circuit as its sister cinema the Alvaston, which had opened in 1925, and the two alternated as third- and fourth-run cinemas. Both cinemas were owned and managed by Mr T. Swift (until 1939 when a new manager, Mr H.V.B. Goodson, took over).[17] Films changed twice-weekly.

The Allenton's managers booked films from a range of American and British production companies. First National, Fox, Metro-Goldwyn-Mayer, Paramount and Warner Brothers were the main suppliers of American films; British and Dominions, British International Pictures, British Lion, Gaumont-British, Twickenham and, by the end of the decade, Herbert Wilcox Productions supplied the majority of British films. In many ways, then, exhibition patterns at the Allenton closely follow the national model (although there were sometimes significant delays between the films' initial release and the time they were shown here). Many Hollywood spectaculars were exhibited throughout the decade. *Sunny Side Up* (1929) was shown in September 1931; *Smilin' Thru* (1932) and *I Am a Fugitive from a Chain Gang* (1932) played in November 1933; *San Francisco* (1936) was exhibited in November 1938; *Sweethearts* (1938) was shown in October 1939. British-made comedies also featured regularly. *The Middle Watch* (1930) was booked in October 1931; *The Last Coupon* (1932) played in April 1933; *Oh, Mr Porter!* (1937) was exhibited in November 1938. This is not surprising, for these films contained elements that attracted working-class audiences nationwide; they were bound to go down well with Derby's working-class cinema-goers too. We cannot draw too simplistic conclusions based on these similarities, however. There were some noticeable differences from national trends.

The ratio of American to British films is a case in point. Admittedly, American-produced films consistently outnumber the home-made product. In 1935, American films outnumber British productions four to one. In 1933, the figures are only slightly more favourable towards the British product. But this highly disproportionate ratio does not obtain every year. In 1931, the ratio of American to British films was two to one. Bearing in mind the number of films that exhibitors needed to book to meet the quota, this is a very respectable figure. The Allenton's managers must, then, have thought that their customers *wanted* to watch British films. In fact, in some years the ratio of American to British films suggests that the latter were in very high demand with these working-class cinema-goers. In 1937, a third of the films shown were British. Of the 104 films booked in 1938, fifty-four were American, and forty-nine were British (one Indian film – *The Street Singer* [1938] – was also shown). British films thus represented almost half of the films exhibited. This is an astonishing figure, especially if we consider that many film trade personnel expected working-class audiences to snub the home-made product. Of course, without accurate attendance figures we are unable to determine the number of patrons these films attracted. But, the sheer number of British-produced films booked suggests that the attendance figures must have been sufficiently high.

In fact, during certain periods British films were shown with such regularity that they *must* have been attracting very large audiences. For example, in January 1938, seven British films were booked (*For Valour, London Melody, Please Teacher, Splinters in the Air* [all 1937], *No Exit, This'll Make You Whistle* [both 1936] and *Yes, Mr Brown* [1933]), while only two American features were exhibited (*The Magnificent Brute* and *Three Smart Girls* [both 1936]). Similarly, in October of the same year, six British films were shown (*Dishonour Bright* [1936], *The Elephant Boy, Jericho, Smash and Grab, Gangway* [all 1937] and *The Sky's the Limit* [1937]), while three American films were booked (*The Last of the Mohicans* [1936], *Big City* and *The Man Who Cried Wolf* [both 1937]). Of course, there are periods during which this pattern is reversed (in July 1938, for example, six American and three British films were shown), but the sheer fact that, on occasions, British films far outnumbered American productions reveals that some working-class consumers were more than happy to watch the home-made product. What types of film were they consuming?

Dramas were the most popular film genre with these cinema-goers, with comedy features running a close second. In most, although not all, years, dramatic films dominated. In 1931, 1933 and 1935, roughly half of the films booked were dramas or contained highly dramatic elements. This pattern obtained until the latter years of the decade, when the number of dramatic films declined slightly. In 1937, dramas only accounted for a third of film bookings. In fact, in this year, comedy films outnumbered dramatic productions. While the proportion of dramatic films rose again in 1938, they were never to attain their earlier dominance. Other film genres were gaining popularity instead. This may have had something to do with the uneasy international situation, for comedy films continued to be screened regularly, and musicals, romances and adventures – all types of film which promised to transport the audience, metaphorically of course, into a world free from worry – were booked with increasing regularity. Perhaps surprisingly, the ratio of war films also increased. It may just be that these film-goers were turning to some films to escape from their daily concerns, while using others to help resolve them.

The Allenton's patrons, then, consumed a rich tapestry of films to answer their cultural needs. This was substantially different from the more 'war-like' garrison town of Portsmouth. Nevertheless, booking patterns reveal that the Allenton's patrons found some films more to their tastes than others. The large number of Wheeler and Woolsey films exhibited suggests that the American comedy duo's blend of verbal and visual humour held particular resonance for these consumers. Most of the duo's films were shown, from *Rio Rita* (1929) in July 1931 to *On Again – Off Again* (1937) in June 1938. It is not hard to understand why. Wheeler and Woolsey's films portrayed the world as a chaotic place where *anything goes* and where every institution is essentially ineffective. In addition, the pair always triumphed through a combination of bluff, shrewdness and good fortune. These films would have been highly reassuring for these working-class consumers. They placed them in a position of confidence by showing them that *anything* was possible. In fact, the ability to come out on top despite facing seemingly overwhelming odds is a theme common to many comedies exhibited here. Laurel and Hardy's low-status vehicles, which similarly featured a pair of hapless individuals who endured difficulties from which they ultimately emerged victorious, were also repeatedly booked. The run of Joe E. Brown comedies exhibited, including *The Tenderfoot* (1932), *Alibi Ike* (1935), *Sons O' Guns* (1936) and *Fit for a King* (1937), were structured around a similar premise.

All the abovementioned films were American productions, but the types of British comedy most frequently booked at the Allenton likewise featured social misfits on a triumphant pursuit of success. Many of Will Hay's films were exhibited, including *Windbag the Sailor* (1936), *Oh, Mr Porter!* (1937) and *Old Bones of the River* (1938). Hay's films constantly rejected the social mores and values of middle-class society, while at the same time seeking to assuage any anxiety working-class audiences may have felt regarding their social position. They were bound to go down well with the Allenton's working-class patrons. A number of Crazy Gang features were also booked, including *Okay for Sound* (1937) and *Alf's Button Afloat* (1938). The Crazy Gang's films offered this audience similar pleasures to the Will Hay comedies. They relentlessly lampooned authority and elite society, while simultaneously championing working-class life. In *Alf's Button Afloat*, for example, the Gang parody the upper classes by speaking in a pronounced and humorous manner; their visual and oral performances satirise the aristocratic stereotype. Meanwhile, when the Gang are granted a wish they ask for beer and women, because these are the things 'really worth having'. All these films thus aimed to amuse and comfort working-class audiences. Their repeated booking at the Allenton suggests they were doing just that, and that patterns of consumption *are* class-specific.

Bearing the popularity of these films in mind, it is somewhat surprising to see that a number of Ben Travers farces were also exhibited here. These films did not champion working-class life; they mocked it. And, unlike the majority of other comedies exhibited at the Allenton, they offered few solutions for the working-class characters that populated them. They could, therefore, be quite discomfiting for working-class audiences. Of course, the Travers films appealed little to working-class consumers in some areas. They failed to attract many customers to Bernstein's 'working-class' cinemas, and do not appear on Cwmllynfell's miners' cinema ledger. It is also interesting to note that the Allenton's manager, Mr Swift, did not book these films until long after they had been released. *Turkey Time* (1933) was not shown until August 1936, three years after its initial release, while *A Night Like This* (1931) was exhibited in April 1938, a full seven years after it was first released. It is not clear why these delays occurred, but I would suggest that there was some doubt in the cinema manager's mind regarding the suitability of these films for his working-class patrons. It would seem, though, that after his initial hesitation Mr Swift took a risk and booked *Turkey Time*, found it attracted reasonably-sized audiences, and then booked as many films as he could get his hands on. Indeed, after *Turkey Time* was exhibited the next Travers farce to be released – *For Valour* (1937) – was promptly booked, and two earlier films (*A Night Like This, Dishonour Bright* [1936]) were shown in very quick succession after that.

What was it about these films that attracted the Allenton's patrons? Well, these films did contain elements that we know pleased this cinema's audiences. All these films displayed a real disdain for society's institutions (the army in *For Valour*, for example). Moreover, they lampooned *all* social groups, not just the working classes. However, we know that *many* working-class cinema-goers across the country liked these comedic elements, but they did not much like the Travers farces. Why did the Allenton's patrons like these films while many working-class cinema-goers did not? I would suggest that in this small cinema in a working-class area of Derby, a large part of the audience felt secure enough in their class position to enjoy being challenged by these films' radical depiction of society. This may have had something to do with Derby's diversified industrial structure. As mentioned, the effects of the Depression varied across different regions. Derby was one of the towns in which employment levels remained relatively stable, with wages comparatively higher than many of the older industrial heartlands. For many of the Allenton's patrons, then, in a more secure socio-economic position than most working-class cinema-goers, the Travers farces' portrayal of a highly individualistic and status-bound society would have offered much pleasure. What was there not to like about a series of films that confirmed that middle-class notions of respectability and morality were something of a façade, especially when one's own earning capabilities ensured that, economically at least, one held an equivalent place in society? Of course, these elements were undoubtedly too challenging for many working-class cinema-goers, who, perhaps worried about their place in the social structure, preferred to be comforted when they went to the cinema. Indeed, in comparison to the quantity of other types of comedy exhibited here, the number of Travers farces booked was relatively small. The films' capacity to discomfort rather than reassure unquestionably accounts for this disparity.

The other types of British film comedy that found favour at the Allenton were Jack Buchanan's musical burlesques.[18] From *A Man of Mayfair* (1931), shown in July 1932, to *The Gang's All Here* (1939), exhibited in December of the year of its release, Buchanan's films were a regular feature. In fact, during the latter part of the decade his films were shown with astonishing frequency. In 1938, for example, three of his films were exhibited: *Yes, Mr Brown* (1933), *Smash and Grab* (1937) and *The Sky's the Limit* (1937). Interestingly, in all of these films Buchanan plays characters in an elevated social position. In *A Man of Mayfair* he is a lord, in *Yes, Mr Brown* a businessman, in *The Sky's the Limit* an aircraft designer, in *Smash and Grab* a detective, and in *The Gang's All Here* an insurance investigator. What did the Allenton's working-class audiences find to relate to in these films? Firstly, we must remember that this was Derby, home to a more affluent, higher-status, working-class cinema-goer. Secondly, Buchanan's characters were always strong, but fair, individuals, and we know that working-class audiences liked these traits in their male film characters. Finally, in all of these films Buchanan's characters prove themselves to be equal to any situation that may befall them. Like Wheeler and Woolsey, Laurel and Hardy, Joe E. Brown, Will Hay or the Crazy Gang, therefore, Buchanan showed that *anything* was possible. Place him in any situation and he would come up trumps. Working-class cinema-goers were sure to like that.

Of all the musical films shown at the Allenton, Buchanan's burlesques were the most popular. It is important to note, though, that other British-produced musicals also fared well here. In fact, for much of the decade, British musicals outnumbered the American product. An array of narrative styles was on offer. There were variety films that took advantage of their stars' music-hall roots: Will Hay in *Radio Parade of 1935* (1935); Stanley Holloway in *In Town Tonight* (1935). There were films that played with notions of identity: *Lucky Girl* (1932), starring Gene Gerrard as a Ruritanian king who is mistaken for a gem thief; *Sleepless Nights* (1932), featuring Stanley Lupino posing as an heiress's husband. There were films that championed community spirit: *Say It with Flowers* (1934), in which a group of Cockneys come to the aid of Mary Clare's sickly flower-girl. There were rags-to-riches tales: *Indiscretions of Eve* (1932), in which an earl falls in loves with a poor girl. There were films featuring regional characters: *Let's Be Famous* (1939), starring Betty Driver as a stage-struck North Country girl and Jimmy O'Dea as her Irish companion. And there were films featuring strong, female characters: Bebe Daniels as a flirtatious singer pursuing Claude Hulbert in *The Song You Gave Me* (1933); Gracie Fields demonstrating fighting spirit in *Sally in Our Alley* (1931), *Looking on the Bright Side* (1932) and *Sing As We Go* (1934).[19]

Despite their varying narrative drives, these films share a number of similarities. Most of them incorporate humour into the narrative. Most feature plucky, resilient and self-assured individuals who manage to overcome any obstacle in a carefree and confident manner. Many feature identifiable working-class characters. All seek to provide resolutions to specific problems. These films, then, offered to soothe social anxieties rather than stimulate them. But, and this is important, many of these films propelled the audience into a world in which *their* social status was celebrated. They championed working-class life, kinship and popular culture. Even for those working-class consumers feeling the worse effects of the depression, these films offered comfort and reassurance. Moreover, films such as *Lucky Girl* and *Sleepless Nights* confirmed that concepts of identity were socially and culturally constructed. These cinemagoers, especially those whose economic status was equal to many members of the middle classes, were bound to like watching films that allowed notions of identity to be pushed to their very limits.

The Allenton's patrons' preference for British musicals is clear, but glossy, big-budget American productions did begin to grow in favour as the decade progressed. Astaire and Rogers's sophisticated musicals were booked with increased frequency, for example. *Top Hat* (1935) was exhibited in October 1936, *Swing Time* (1936) in June 1937, *Shall We Dance?* (1937) in April 1938 and *Carefree* (1938) in July 1939. Nelson Eddy and Jeanette MacDonald's sweeping musical romances also did well as the decade drew to a close. *Maytime* (1937) was shown in December 1938, while *Rose-Marie* (1936), *The Girl of the Golden West* (1938) and *Sweethearts* were all exhibited in 1939. In fact, 1939 represented something of a high point for American-produced musicals. *Hitting a New High* and *Merry-go-round of 1938* (both 1937) were shown in January 1939. *You're a Sweetheart* (1937) was shown in February. *A Damsel in Distress* (1937), starring Fred Astaire, was shown in March 1939, along with *Goodbye Broadway* (1938). *Radio City Revels* (1938) was exhibited in April. *Rose-Marie* (1936) was shown in May. *The Girl of the Golden West* was booked in June. *Carefree* and *Garden of the Moon* (1938) were exhibited in July. *That Certain Age* (1938), starring child star Deanna Durbin, was shown in August. *Sweethearts* and *Honolulu* (1939) were booked in October. *The Goldwyn Follies* (1938) was exhibited in December.

All these films display textural and narrative balance. Like the British musicals exhibited here, they sought to alleviate social anxieties rather than arouse them. Crucially, though, American musicals performed a different cultural role from the British films. The American musicals offered to take the audience away from an identifiable world into a strange and, more often than not, exotic one. If they dealt with the social problems of the day, it was on a subliminal level only. Many British musicals, however, dealt with these problems more directly. It would appear, then, that the Allenton's patrons were using American musicals to help them forget their worries, while using some British musicals to help come to terms with them. Indeed, the increased exhibition of American musicals during the latter part of the decade suggests that, as the international situation worsened, this audience increasingly wanted to watch films that took their minds off it. The extraordinarily large number of American musicals booked during 1939, as Europe slid gradually, but inexorably, towards another war, only serves to underline this.

If the Allenton's patrons were using American musicals to help them forget their worries, they were using many American dramas to help them deal with them. As stated, dramatic films dominated for most of the decade. And it was American gloss that the Allenton's managers must have thought this audience wanted to see, because, in *all* years, a far greater number of American films were booked. British-produced dramas were exhibited in respectable numbers, especially as the decade progressed, but the fondness for American films is clear. There are also clear patterns regarding the type of drama shown. At the beginning of the decade, films with strong moral messages dominated. Consider anti-war melodramas *The Enemy* (1927) and *Out of the Ruins* (1928); consider *White Shadows in the South Seas* (1928), which explores the influence of white traders over South Seas islanders; consider *Sins of the Fathers* (1928), which deals with the evils of prohibition; or consider *Adoration* (1928), a revolutionary epic dealing with the Petrograd uprising. These are all serious, respectable features that demanded an element of cultural competence from the audience. They were undoubtedly booked because they offered to teach these patrons important lessons about the social structure and world affairs. Significantly, though, and despite their moralistic tone, these films were not overtly didactic. They may have said much about social obligation and duty, but, in all cases, it was the role of society's governing bodies that was brought into question; society's lower orders were invariably innocent bystanders. More importantly, these films always offered a satisfactory resolution to any problems that may have arisen. We can interpret their popularity as an indication of the audience's need for comfort during a time of economic and social instability.

All these films were shown in 1930. In 1931, when dramas accounted for almost half of the films booked, a different type of dramatic vehicle dominated. Consider *Halfway to Heaven, Trial Marriage* (both 1929), or *A Lady Surrenders* (1930). These were films that dealt with affairs of the heart, and they would have appealed principally to the Allenton's female patrons. In 1932, when the number of dramas booked dipped slightly, the types of film shown focused on the criminal underworld: *The Lawyer's Secret, Silence, Smart Money* and *The Star Witness* (all 1931). These films were targeted primarily towards the male consumer. When it came to watching dramatic films, then, a greater proportion of this cinema's customers were women. Indeed, in 1933, when, once again, dramas accounted for roughly 50% of films booked, the number of romantic dramas had also increased. Significantly, though, there were some interesting developments in the style of films being shown. Many mixed romantic and criminal elements: *Panama Flo* (1932), in which a cabaret dancer gets romantically involved with a gangster; *Hotel Continental* (1932), in which two villains find redemption in love. These films could appeal equally to both sexes. It would appear, then, that the Allenton's manager was now booking the types of dramatic film that would draw in a mixed-sex audience. This was, of course, an ideal way of achieving maximum seating capacity.

But there is more to it than this. These films performed different cultural tasks from the types of drama booked in 1930. These were not films dealing with grand societal issues. These films did not place their characters on a world stage. No, these films wrestled with the individual's emotions and morality (or, more importantly, their lack of them). These were films in which women were strong and assertive; not yet independent, but willing to breach gender conventions, and in which men (and sometimes the women) were sharp and calculating; operating outside the realms of respectable society. These films, then, opened up a space in which the Allenton's patrons could imagine a world free from convention and obligation (except to one's peers). They did caution against transgressing social and gender boundaries; rebellious individuals are always punished or redeemed. But audiences were expected to take great pleasure in watching the excesses of these characters. In fact, it is important to remember that these films were produced before the rigorous enforcement of the Hays Code, so they could, and indeed did, take risks. As one of *Kineweekly*'s reviewers observed apropos *Panama Flo*: 'This melodrama is not a bedtime story, it is strong meat cut to the bone [...] it provides arresting fare, full of suspense, for the masses [...] sordid, grim, and unrelenting'.[20] These films, then, were undoubtedly popular with the Allenton's patrons because they allowed them to envisage a world without limits. In addition, these films could act as a moral compass; they offered cinema-goers the chance to negotiate a path between acceptable and improper behaviour. Some working-class patrons certainly appreciated that.

While these types of drama continued to be shown in respectable numbers throughout the decade, there was a clear shift in booking patterns from the mid-1930s. The majority of American dramas booked from this time dealt, once again, with more worldly issues. Consider *Storm at Daybreak* (1933), shown in June 1934, which examines the events leading up to the assassination of Archduke Ferdinand; or consider *The Witching Hour* (1934), shown in February 1935, in which a corrupt politician is killed. There is also *The Informer* (1935), shown in June 1936, in which an IRA leader is betrayed by a former embittered associate. And there is *The Plough and the Stars* (1934), shown in September 1937, which examines the causes of the 1916 Dublin uprising. Consider, too, *The Road Back* (1937) and *Three Comrades* (1938), shown in September 1938 and June 1939 respectively, which deal with the disillusionment and despair of former soldiers adjusting to civilian life in post-war Germany. These American dramas performed similar cultural roles to those shown at the beginning of the decade. They reminded the audience of their responsibilities and those of the state's representatives. More importantly, though, many of these films also focused explicitly on the human tragedy caused by a breakdown in social relations. We could attribute this shift in booking patterns to the Allenton's managers' desire to help their patrons come to terms with the ever-worsening international situation. Certainly, the exhibition of this type of drama greatly increased in volume in the latter years of the decade. In fact, if we consider the types of dramatic film booked shortly after the outbreak of war, with such morale-boosting titles as *Stand Up and Fight* and *Let Freedom Ring* (both 1939), it would certainly seem that this was the case. The Allenton's managers, then, sensed that their patrons needed to be reassured and encouraged by the types of drama they were watching, and chose to book the types of film that could operate in that way.

We must remember, though, that the number of dramatic films being booked after 1936 was somewhat lower than in earlier years. The Allenton's patrons must, then, have only wanted to watch a certain number of films that reminded them about the world's problems. Indeed, it is important to stress that none of these dramas dealt explicitly with contemporary issues; all of them dealt with them indirectly. The majority of these working-class cinemagoers, then, wanted to watch films that helped them forget about their worries. Indeed, as stated, by the end of the decade other film genres were getting booked with greater frequency, and these films promised to transport the audience into a world where their worries could be forgotten. Consider the regularity in which British-produced comedies were shown from 1937 onwards, for example; or consider the number of American musicals that appeared during the latter years of the decade. These films offered to encourage or reassure these audiences. Indeed, even the highly radical Travers farces offered *these* working-class cinema-goers the chance to feel good about themselves. The Allenton's managers, then, were undoubtedly intimately attuned to the moods of their patrons, and were quick to respond when the need demanded.

One final point needs to be made regarding the film tastes of Derby's working classes, and it is one which provides a healthy warning against complacency in any research into the tastes of the country's consumers. There were a number of British-produced films shown at the Allenton that, while not numerically significant when considered on their own, are highly significant when judged together. These were films made by small, independent production companies such as Butchers, Mancunian and Rock Studios. The many films made by these and other companies like them were shown in considerable numbers here. Consider *Cotton Queen* and *King of Hearts* (both 1936), which featured Scottish character actor Will Fyffe; or consider *Off the Dole* (1935), starring popular Lancastrian comedian George Formby. These films were extremely low-status, cheaply-made and targeted specifically for working-class audiences. Many had a regional – principally northern – focus and relied heavily on the fact that cinema audiences would be familiar with both their stars and their exclusively working-class environments. As David Sutton has noted, these films were 'defiantly local, extraordinarily unsophisticated' and were aimed at 'a purely regional' market.[21] The fact that many of them were shown here, and with such regularity, especially during the latter years of the decade, illustrates that many of these cinema-goers wanted to watch films that dealt explicitly with aspects of their own lives. They wanted to watch films that championed their experiences.

Of course, some of the most frequently booked films (the American musicals in particular) offered to transport the audience into an unfamiliar world, but the types of film that appeared to do best were those that focused on working-class life or featured clearly identifiable working-class characters. They were booked with most regularity. They must have been in greatest demand. These films did not usually offer to help the audience forget their worries; they did not always offer to resolve them. What they did offer, though, was an arena in which the working classes were *central* to social life. For these cinema-goers, what was there not to like?

Literature popularity

In addition to being affected by changes in unemployment levels, borrowing patterns in Derby's public libraries also witnessed slight seasonal fluctuations. Peak borrowing periods always occurred between October and March (though December saw a dip in borrowing numbers).[22] The lowest borrowing numbers were recorded in June, July and August.[23] Cold, winter weather clearly drew people towards the book and the fireplace, while the warmer summer months enticed people away. To my knowledge, there are no records extant belonging to the twopenny or mobile libraries that populated the town, so we cannot produce any evidence about the borrowing habits of their readers. There is, however, evidence of what books were available in the town's public and commercial libraries. The *Derbyshire Evening Telegraph* included a section each week in which an anonymous reviewer recommended a number of new books available. Of course, these are the recommendations of the *reviewer*, so while he or she was certainly tied into the market, the views espoused are his or her own. What taste patterns can we observe?

Not surprisingly, fiction was the most regularly borrowed type of book in Derby's public libraries.[24] Fiction titles were also the most recommended books in the local paper. Derby's reading tastes thus closely followed, or were expected to follow, national trends. There were many similarities in the various genres of fiction being recommended. Romantic novels dominated; detective fiction ran a close second; westerns and humorous fiction were rarely reviewed. The majority of novels recommended, meanwhile, were written by authors who were popular with readers nationwide. Consider the favourable review in February 1936 for *Feather* (1935), a tale of two sisters who fall in love with the same man, by romantic novelist Ruby M. Ayres.[25] Ayres was, of course, recommended by Batty and also featured on the lists of Callender and Howe. Consider also *No Hero* (1936) by Warwick Deeping, *Thursby* (1933) by Geoffrey Moss, *Frances Fights for Herself* (1933) by Effie A. Rowlands, or *Parents are a Problem* (1933) and *I Lost My Heart* (1934) by Maysie Grieg.[26] All of these novels were by romantic novelists who featured in at least one of the lists drawn up by Batty *et al.*

Similar trends obtain with detective fiction. E.P. Oppenheim, one of this genre's most popular authors, had novels reviewed in the period (*The Gallows of Chance* [1933] and *The Spymaster* [1938]).[27] Many other detective fiction authors who had likewise gained widespread popularity appear in the paper's reviews section. Consider Ben Bolt's *The Lavenham Mystery* (1933); Freeman Wills Crofts's *12.30 from Croydon* (1933); or J. Jefferson Farjeon's *The Windmill Mystery* (1933).[28] These authors had attracted a wide readership nationally; they were expected to go down well in Derby too.

While humorous fiction and westerns were rarely reviewed, there were occasions when these less popular genres were championed. Virginia Faulkner's *The Barbarians* (1935) was afforded a rapturous review in 1936, for example. According to the paper's reviewer, the novel was 'full of fun, innuendo and farce'.[29] In the same year, Tavis Miller's western *Slumgullion Trail* (1935) also received a very favourable review. The novel, which featured a winning triumvirate of '[g]unmen, rustlers and a damsel in distress,' was, according to this reviewer, 'written in an attractive and racy style' and contained 'plenty of thrills'.[30] Interestingly, neither of these authors appeared on any of the popularity lists mentioned earlier, but there was clearly much about their work that was expected to attract Derby's reading public. Despite these positive recommendations, though, reviews for these types of fiction were very uncommon. Romance novels and detective fiction *always* dominated in this paper's reviews section. The attraction of the western or comedy novel with the town's reading public, then, was undoubtedly expected to be as limited as it was with readers nationally.

While there are clear similarities between the reading habits of this town's consumers and those across the country, there are some interesting differences. The paper's reviews section regularly featured novels that had regional settings and/or were written by local authors. Consider *White Ladies* (1935) by West Midlands novelist Francis Brett Young, with its Black Country setting; *Flo* (1933) by Derbyshire miner-author F.C. Boden; or R.J. White's *The Young Wife's Progress* (1934), with its Derbyshire/Nottinghamshire coalfield setting.[31] And there are the sophisticated thrillers of Long Eaton author J.G. Lenehan, which were heavily supported by this reviewer.[32] Like the town's working-class cinema-goers, then, Derby's readers were encouraged to appreciate material with a strong regional focus. Whether these novels were borrowed in any significant number is, of course, impossible to ascertain. We cannot also be certain that the town's working-class readers were expected to appreciate them. But the very fact that they were regularly recommended suggests that at least some part of Derby's reading public was expected to want to read them, and it would be unwise to believe that the working classes were not being considered by the paper's reviewer.

While the work of the country's most popular novelists dominated the paper's reviews section, the work of emerging novelists was not ignored. Robert Hill's revolutionary tale *Adam's Daughter* (1934) was highly rated by the paper's reviewer.[33] Readers were also cautioned about material deemed to be of rather poor quality. The reviewer thus wrote tersely of Violet Keniball's *Marrying Mark* (1938): 'It is seldom that a completely unsophisticated book comes from an American author, but [this novel] seems to be the exception'.[34] Such responses, then, provide an insight into this reviewer's attitudes towards certain types of popular literature. Clearly, fiction with a political bent was liked; low quality writing was not acceptable. Whether the reviewer's recommendations were heeded by the paper's readers is, of course, unknowable. But one thing is clear. This reviewer had a firm grasp of popular taste and was unwilling to chastise the reading public for their reading tastes. Indeed, despite the negative appraisal of Keniball's novel, the reviewer admitted that it managed to 'hold [his] attention throughout'.[35] On the whole, then, this reviewer was keen to champion light fiction, and there was little of the stuffiness that could be found in the writings of many highbrow contemporaries regarding this most popular type of reading material.

As elsewhere, patterns of book recommendation point towards a gender imbalance in the reading habits of Derby's working-class consumers. In every year of the decade, more romantic novels were reviewed than any other type of fiction. Because romantic novels were primarily favoured by female readers, we can assume one of two things: either more women than men were turning to the written word for pleasure; or women were more likely to choose from a wide variety of material. If we consider previous reading patterns, we should favour the latter. Indeed, the authors appearing in Batty's 'Novels' category, and who were expected to attract a primarily female readership, were also reviewed with considerable frequency. Jeffery Farnol, Eden Philpotts and Lady Eleanor Smith thus appear in the paper's reviews section.[36] Detective fiction was also frequently reviewed, but, in most years, for every one work of detective fiction recommended two romantic fiction titles were reviewed. Men were reading avidly too, then, just not as avidly as women.

There were, then, many similarities between the reading habits of Derby's consumers and readers up and down the country. The types of literature that found most favour (or was expected to find most favour) in this relatively small Midlands town were very similar to the types of literature that found most favour nationwide. The same authors appear time and again. The reading habits of the different sexes, too, followed the national model. However, while these similarities existed, regional variations were in evidence too. Readers in this town were undoubtedly expected to champion the work of local authors, and the fact that these types of fiction were repeatedly reviewed suggests that they did just that. These variations, then, remind us that while there may have been similarities in the reading habits of the country's readers, we should not view the latter as an undifferentiated mass. As with the country's cinema-goers, there were variations in taste that were geographically specific.

Notes

1   T. Cauter and J.S. Downham, *The Communication of Ideas; A Study of Contemporary Experiences on Urban Life*, London, 1954, pp. 11–20.

2   *Derbyshire Advertiser* (hereafter *DA*), 19 August 1932.

3   County Borough of Derby Public Libraries, Museum and Art Gallery Sixty-First Annual report for year ending 31 March 1932.

4   County Borough of Derby Public Libraries, Museum and Art Gallery Sixty-Third Annual report for year ending 31 March 1934.

5   See 'Going to the Pictures', *Derby by Night 1939*, Derby Ram, Volume 2–12.

6   *Kineweekly Year Book* appeared annually. It lists all cinemas, their location and price bands. The town's population is also indicated.

7   For a history of the town's cinemas see Sam Winfield, *Dream Palaces of Derby*, Derby, 1995.

8   Cauter and Downham, *The Communication of Ideas*, pp. 189–190.

9   *DA*, 2 October 1931.

10 Winfield, *Dream Palaces*, p. 73.

11 Ashley Franklin, *A Cinema Near You: 100 Years of Going to the Pictures in Derbyshire*, Derby, 1996, p. 18.

12 Ibid.

13 Ibid., p. 44.

14 Ibid.; Winfield, *Dream Palaces*, p. 73.

15 Winfield, *Dream Palaces*, pp. 95–97.

16 *Kineweekly Year Book*, 1937.

17 Goodson took over the running of these cinemas in July 1939, changing the names of both. The Allenton became the Broadway; the Alvaston became the Rex. Goodson had previously managed the Coliseum in London Road, Derby. *DA*, 7 July 1939.

18 For an analysis of Buchanan's films, see Andrew Spicer, 'Jack Buchanan: the "Man About Town" of British musical-comedies in the 1930s', in Ian Conrich and Estella Tincknell, eds, *Film's Musical Moments*, Edinburgh, 2006, pp. 71–83.

19 *Sally in Our Alley* must have gone down well with the Allenton's patrons for it was exhibited twice, in April 1931 and October 1935.

20 *Kineweekly*, 7 April 1932.

21 Sutton, *Chorus of Raspberries*, p. 152. Sutton makes these remarks apropos Mancunian films.

22 County Borough of Derby Council Minute Books, 1930–1940. For example, in November 1933, 82,995 books were borrowed; in December 1933, 68,664 books were taken out; in January 1934, 84,786 books were loaned.

23 Ibid. In June 1934, 65,109 books were borrowed. The figures for July and August (which were always combined) totalled 129,887.

24 The *Derby Advertiser* observed that the town's library-borrowing habits were similar to those around the country, with 'light fiction' being the most sought-after reading material. *DA*, 19 August 1932. The *Derbyshire Evening Telegraph* (hereafter *DET*) also noted that 'the greatest need is for fiction'. *DET*, 15 December 1933.

25 *DET*, 7 February 1936.
26 Ibid., 9 October 1936; 5 May 1933; 23 February 1934; 20 October 1933 and 16 August 1935.
27 Ibid., 2 March 1934 and 17 March 1939.
28 Ibid., 20 October 1933 and 23 February 1934.
29 Ibid., 7 February 1936.
30 Ibid., 14 February 1936.
31 Ibid., 16 August 1935, 5 May 1933 and 15 February 1935.
32 Ibid., 9 October 1936 and 11 March 1938.
33 Ibid., 15 February 1935.
34 Ibid., 13 March 1939.
35 Ibid.
36 See ibid., 2 April 1937, 2 March 1934 and 11 March 1938.

8

'The home of the brave'?: working-class tastes in Portsmouth

My third, and final, case-study is of the town of Portsmouth, located in the South. Once again, the taste preferences of working-class consumers were influenced by the region's socio-economic structure.

Despite being geographically restricted, Portsmouth had a much larger population than Derby, standing at approximately 258,000 by 1939.[1] This had much to do with Portsmouth's importance as a naval town. As Sue Harper has shown, Ordnance Survey maps of the period reveal that about 20% of the available land was occupied by Naval installations and the Royal Navy Dockyard. Moreover, because Portsmouth's principal employer was the Dockyard, it remained a poor town.[2] Despite, or maybe because of this, the town's reading and cinema cultures flourished in our period, and Portsmouth's working classes were exceptionally well served by cinema and library facilities.

Portsmouth had 22 cinemas in 1930, and 29 by 1939.[3] The Regent was the town's principal cinema. It was extremely plush, accommodated 1,992 patrons and was located in a lower-middle-class area of the city. There were few comparable cinemas, but some did compete with the Regent for custom. The Odeon, which opened in 1936, was situated just along the road and was similarly luxurious. However, while the Odeon's manager mounted many lavish publicity campaigns for the films he booked, there is no evidence of this from the Regent's manager. Clearly, the managers of Portsmouth's other large cinemas saw the Regent as *the* major competitor and responded accordingly. Of course, managers of the larger halls were trying to attract cinema-goers from across Portsmouth. In contrast, the many smaller cinemas catered principally for cinema-goers living in the immediate vicinity, and their managers did not, indeed could not, compete with the larger picture palaces for custom. Many of these smaller cinemas, such as the Arcade and the Queens, were located in working-class areas of the city, accommodated fewer than 600 patrons, and were frugally adorned in comparison to the larger halls. These were the *working-class* cinemas, and the films that were shown in them answered to the tastes of their working-class patrons. It is the tastes of the patrons of the Queens cinema that will be considered here.

Despite the size of the town's population, Portsmouth's first public library did not open until 1883. This was much later than Derby, and indeed most other large towns in England. In fact, there was some reluctance within the Council to set up a free library service, and a report in 1944 admitted that 'in the early days of the [free library] movement Portsmouth was not "library conscious"'.[4] However, after the first public library proved to be a popular and well-used amenity, Portsmouth Council embarked upon providing branch libraries in other areas of the city.[5] Moreover, in the mid-1930s, the library committee decided to publish a quarterly magazine that aimed to both keep established readers up to date with new developments and encourage greater interest in the library service among the population as a whole.[6] There is, then, a great deal of evidence relating to public library policies in Portsmouth. Evidence on twopenny libraries is, as with Derby, limited. But there is one interesting piece of information that reveals something about Portsmouth's readers' relationship with this type of library. In a 1936 edition of the *Portsmouth Evening News*, the town's sole daily paper, there is a report on the bankruptcy of twopenny library owner George Bernard Samuelson. Samuelson owned 25 twopenny libraries across the country, and had opened a library in Portsmouth in 1934. The paper reported that, of these 25 premises, only two – in Worthing and Portsmouth – were unsuccessful.[7] Quite possibly, then, twopenny libraries faced a mixed reaction from Portsmouth's readers. Can we discern any other differences between the tastes of these working-class consumers and those previously addressed?

Film popularity

The Queens cinema opened in 1914. It was located in Queen Street, Portsea, a working-class area of the town, and was situated alongside and opposite the naval barracks, with the Dockyard just along the road. It accommodated around 450 patrons.[8] The Queens had an unsettling history, for in April 1931 its owner and manager Mr H.E. Bingham took his own life after an (unnamed) second feature failed to arrive in time for the undoubtedly busy Easter holiday weekend.[9] The event had been precipitated by a recent change in the Council's housing policy.[10] Slum clearance in the Portsea area, and the relocation of a large number of working-class families to a new housing estate in Hilsea, in the northern area of the town, ensured that Bingham lost a large number of his regular patrons. According to reports, he had repeatedly threatened to close the cinema due to falling box-office takings.[11] Despite these troubled conditions, the cinema was taken over later in the year by Mrs L.H. Scott and renamed the New Queens Cinema.[12] After her (natural) death in 1935, the cinema changed hands again.[13] It was now owned and managed by J. Petters; it retained the latter name.[14]

Admission prices fluctuated across the period. Under Bingham's management prices ranged from 5d to 1s; Scott increased the lower price band in 1934 to 6d; in 1935, Petters reduced the lower band to 5d but increased the upper band to 1s 3d.[15] Until the introduction of Sunday opening in 1933, films changed twice weekly.[16] After 1933, films changed three times a week.[17] The Queens operated as a third- and fourth-run cinema.[18]

Unlike the Allenton in Derby, the Queens did not advertise regularly in the local press. In fact, under Mr Bingham's management, the cinema did not advertise at all. Mrs Scott began advertising in December 1931, and regular advertisements were placed in the *Portsmouth Evening News* until the cinema was acquired by Mr Petters. After that, advertisements were, rather curiously, sporadic. Because of these inconsistencies, it is not possible to get a full picture of what films were exhibited across the whole decade. We have no way of knowing, for example, what features Mr Bingham decided to book between 1930 and 1931. It is also interesting to note that, while the local paper's film critic reviewed all the films being shown at Portsmouth's other cinemas, the films being exhibited at the Queens were *never* considered. This says much about how low this cinema was on the critic's cultural register. Despite these irregularities, though, there is ample material from 1932 until around 1937 to identify exhibition patterns.

Distribution practices at the Queens were similar to the locally-owned cinemas discussed elsewhere in this book. The Queens' managers thus booked films from a number of American and British production companies. But there are a few minor differences. RKO was the major supplier of American films. The majority of British films were supplied by British International Pictures (BIP); very few films were booked from the Gaumont-British production stable. The strong showing of BIP productions suggests that the Queens' managers privileged films from the Associated British Picture Corporation (ABPC), which owned two medium-sized cinemas in the town (the Commodore and Gaiety).[19] The Gaumont-British subsidiary Associated Provincial

Picture Houses (APPH) owned Portsmouth's two largest cinemas (The Regent and Plaza), which may explain why fewer of their films were chosen. Perhaps the Queens' managers were concerned that many potential customers would have already travelled to the town's plushest cinema to see their favourite films. In fact, the Queens exhibited far fewer 'big' films than either Cwmllynfell's miners' cinema or Derby's Allenton. The combination of higher booking costs and lower audience numbers probably deterred these managers from booking films that were undoubtedly more expensive. Whatever the reasons, many of the films exhibited at the Queens were cheaply-made, low-status productions.

What booking patterns can be identified? In all of the years that evidence is available, American films outnumbered British productions. In fact, only in 1932, 1933 and 1934 did the latter get booked in respectable numbers (roughly half of the films booked in 1932 and 1934 were British; in 1933, British films accounted for around a third of film bookings). Between 1935 and 1937 (after which evidence begins to get patchy), British films made up a quarter of films booked – just enough, then, to meet the quota. In contrast to Derby's Allenton, which exhibited an increasing number of British films as the decade progressed, the number of British films shown at the Queens declined. There are occasions when there is an impressive run of British film exhibition. In November 1932, for example, four British productions were shown consecutively – *Girl in the Night, Glamour, The Bells* (all 1931) and *Gipsy Blood* (1930). Nevertheless, the ratio of films shown that month still favoured the American product (5:4), and all but three of the first features' running mates were American films. The Queens' managers must, then, have believed that their customers preferred to watch the American product.

In common with the Allenton and Cwmllynfell's miners' cinema, dramas were the most popular film genre, with comedy films running a close second. In 1932, approximately 50 per cent of films booked were dramatic productions, while comedy films accounted for around a third of those shown. The evidence suggests that, as with the Allenton, the number of dramatic films booked declined as the decade progressed, with other film genres gaining popularity. However, the erratic nature of the evidence towards the end of the decade ensures that any firm conclusions cannot be drawn. What is clear, though, is that there are marked differences between the *types* of dramatic and comedy films shown at the Allenton and the Queens. In almost all years, the Allenton's patrons favoured dramas that dealt with more worldly or worthy issues. The trend is reversed at the Queens. By far the most frequently booked type of dramatic film here was the crime drama. Consider the American-produced gangster drama *Losing Game* (1930); the James Cagney and Jean Harlow star vehicle *Enemies of the Public* [U.S. title: *The Public Enemy*] (1931); the British-produced *Loyalties* (1933); detective yarn *Murder in Trinidad* (1934); and the Spencer Tracy star vehicle *The Murder Men* (1935).

These films feature tough men and feisty women: Walter Huston in *The Ruling Voice* (1931) and *Beast of the City* (1932); Spencer Tracy in *The Murder Men* and *The Painted Woman* (1932); Jean Harlow in *Enemies of the Public* and *Beast of the City*; Peggy Shannon in *The Painted Woman* and *False Faces* (1935). As is clear from these few examples, many of these films featured the same popular stars. Moreover, these stars played very similar roles. Indeed, one of the most significant points about these films is that they share very similar thematic patterns. This cinema's audiences would certainly have known what to expect from them. As mentioned earlier, crime dramas opened up a space in which the audience could imagine a world with very few, if any, restrictions. But, as I have also stressed, those individuals who transgressed social boundaries were always punished or redeemed. Consider the tag-line for *Losing Game*: 'The final reward is DEATH'. These films, then, could perform a dual function. They let cinema-goers enjoy a sense of abandon *and* they acted as a moral compass. The Queens' patrons were undoubtedly using them to gain a sense of proportion.

There are some similarities between the tastes of these cinema-goers and those at Derby's Allenton regarding the types of comedy preferred. The respectable number of Wheeler and Woolsey films shown suggests that the American comedy duo's blend of cynicism and wit went down well here too. Laurel and Hardy also appear to have been well liked. While their films were never shown as first features, many were booked as second features. Interestingly, the films' titles were never given; the duo's names were enough to draw in custom. Joe E. Brown's films were also regularly exhibited, suggesting that he, too, was popular with the Queens' patrons. When we look at the types of British comedy shown here, however, we can observe clear differences in taste. Consider the run of Leslie Fuller vehicles exhibited in 1932: *Why Sailors Leave Home* (1930) and *Old Soldiers Never Die* (1931) were shown in January; *Poor Old Bill* (1931) in March; and *Bill's Legacy* (1931) in September. This is an extraordinary number of films to be shown in one year. Fuller's type of humour must have struck a chord.

Interestingly, there are no Will Hay films listed; there are no Crazy Gang films either; Jack Buchanan's burlesques and the Travers farces are also notice-able by their absence. Of course, the incomplete nature of the evidence may skew the results slightly, but the Queens' patrons seem to be attracted to a different type of British film comedy. Many of the British-produced comedies favoured by the Allenton's patrons were highly anarchic and featured working-class characters who were not only deeply disrespectful to their social superiors, but were also vigorously anti-authoritarian. Fuller's films were never that anarchic, and his 'Bill' character was never that impudent. Certainly, the films were structured around a similar premise, but they were gently mocking; not outrageously so.[20] The Queens' patrons preferred their comedy films to show a little more *respect* for these institutions. This surely had much to do with the town's naval connections, where a strict social structure, with a clear order, and where an unambiguous respect for authority, is fully expected. To be sure, Ernie Lotinga's *Josser Joins the Navy* (1932), in which 'Josser' displays a total lack of respect for any authority figure he encounters, was also shown here, but this film was booked principally for its title, for while no other Lotinga film was shown during the decade, many films with a seafaring theme (or title) were.

The regular booking of seafaring films in a naval-town cinema is perhaps predictable, but the consistency with which such films were exhibited at the Queens is staggering. Consider, along with the aforementioned *Why Sailors Leave Home*, Fay Wray adventure vehicle *Beneath the Sea* (1933), which was shown in June 1933; or consider this run of films in 1934: musical comedy *Melody Cruise* (1933), risqué romance *Pleasure Cruise* (1933), British comedy *Three Men in a Boat* (1933), crime drama *Channel Crossing* (1933), and *The Battle* (1934), which featured an all-star cast and was advertised by the Queens' manager as a 'Thrilling Naval Drama'.[21] There is also *Miss Pacific Fleet* (1935), a Joan Blondell comedy vehicle, drama *Gentlemen of the Navy* (1935), musicals *Shipmates For Ever* and *Ship Café* (both 1935), all-star drama *China Seas* (1935), British comedy *Love at Sea* (1936), and musical drama *Hell Ship Morgan* (1936), exhibited in 1936. These films have varying narrative drives, but one thing is clear: this cinema's managers must have thought that their patrons wanted to watch films that reminded them of their close connections with the sea. It is, of course, not surprising that the managers of cinemas in the landlocked town of Derby were less inclined to book such fare. We also need to remember that Portsmouth's working-class cinema-goers preferred films that did not challenge the social order; films depicting a life at sea, with its rigorous social structures, were hardly likely to do that. Derby's working classes were, of course, more confident in their class position, and were less inclined to worry about such challenges to the social order.

One further point needs to be made regarding the booking patterns at the Queens. They suggest that the majority of the cinema's patrons were male. Crime dramas – typically male-targeted fare – were the most frequently booked film genre, while seafaring films – again, usually targeted towards the male cinema-goer – were also regularly exhibited. The types of comedy booked here would also have been more likely to attract male cinema-goers. Of course, women could enjoy these films too, but they were never really the target audience. Indeed, the limited number of musical and romance films shown at the Queens confirms that this cinema's managers were not really aiming to attract female cinema-goers.[22] No, the Queens' location ensured that the majority of its patrons were more than likely to be male, and the types of film being booked reflected the male-dominated nature of the audience. It is interesting to note, though, that romance films did poorly in *all* of the cinemas discussed in this book. Perhaps, as Portsmouth CEA delegate F. Blake believed, when brought to the fore, the 'love' element invariably had a negative effect on a film's success.[23]

Literature popularity

As with Derby, there are few records extant that provide details of the reading tastes of Portsmouth's working-class consumers. There are the reports of the town's public library committees that, while not specifically dealing with the tastes of working-class readers, undoubtedly include them. Indeed, in the first edition of *The Portsmouth Reader*, the library service's quarterly in-house magazine, officials reminded library users that they always 'endeavour[ed] to provide a well-balanced stock of books on all subjects and for *all* classes of readers' (emphasis added).[24] Portsmouth's working classes were, therefore, expected to use the town's public libraries to obtain their favourite books. In fact, library officials were keen to point out that books by the most popular novelists were 'frequently being added to the libraries'.[25] Not surprisingly, many of the authors who were identified by Batty *et al.* as favourites among working-class readers feature on the town's public library accessions lists.[26]

Further confirmation that Portsmouth's working-class readers were turning to the town's public libraries to obtain their reading material can be found in a report produced by the city librarian in 1932.[27] The report gave the number of readers at each of the town's six libraries by wards. The library with the most members per ward was located in the lower-middle-class district of North End.[28] But the town's Central Library, which was highly popular with readers from across the town, was much used by borrowers from the purely working-class district of Portsea.[29] With this in mind, we must also consider the dramatic increase in lending figures from all of Portsmouth's libraries across the decade. In 1930, readers borrowed just under 700,000 books; by 1936, that figure had jumped to well over a million.[30] During the same period, the number of registered readers leaped from under 40,000 to approximately 60,000.[31] Portsmouth's readers – and this includes the working classes – were thus enthusiastically using the library services offered in the town. This may, in fact, explain why the twopenny library opened by George Bernard Samuelson in 1934 failed to meet with any success. Working-class readers could obtain their favourite books for free elsewhere. By looking at the policies of the various library committees, then, we can gauge the reading tastes of Portsmouth's working classes. Are there any changes in taste between readers in Portsmouth and those in the localities previously discussed?

Unlike in Derby, the local newspaper did not review recently published books. However, the paper did feature a weekly section that listed some of the new additions to the town's public libraries. The list was supplied by the library committee, so it is a guide to the types of book library officials deemed worthy of attention. Significantly, *no* fiction books were listed. General interest and instructional works were the only types of book included. In 1930, for example, the range of books included A.J. Dawson's *Everybody's Dog Book*, *The Art of Well-Being* by C. Jeffery, *Realities of Bird-Life* by E. Selous, and the rather dour-sounding *Sanitary Law and Practice: A Handbook on Public Health* by W. Robertson and J. Porter.[32] Some quite adventurous texts were mentioned. Consider O. Rühle's renowned biography *Karl Marx: His Life and Works*.[33] But it is clear that members of this committee were determined to try and get readers to turn to more edifying fare than the usual fiction staples. Interestingly, the committee believed, quite wrongly it would seem, that these lists would 'prove of great assistance to readers'.[34] Not so. Fiction continued to be borrowed in significantly higher numbers than any other type of book.[35] In fact, by 1937, the library committee had started to respond to this demand, for, in the 'Recent additions' section of their quarterly magazine, a great many works of fiction were listed. The library committee now had its fingers firmly on the pulse of public taste and was willing to shout about it. It is, then, to these lists that I shall turn for an assessment of the tastes of the town's working-class readers.

Portsmouth's working-class readers were expected to enjoy the types of fiction that were popular with readers across the country. The public library accession lists thus feature many novels by authors who can be found on Batty, Callender and Howe's lists of favourites. However, in common with acquisition patterns at the South Wales Miners' Institute libraries, the work of these authors does not dominate. Only approximately one quarter of the novels acquired by Portsmouth's public libraries between 1937 and 1939 were written by novelists who appear on the lists of Batty *et al.* Therefore, while novels by the likes of Sheila Kaye-Smith, Warwick Deeping and Jeffery Farnol feature heavily, the majority of fiction acquired during this period was written by authors whose popularity was far less widespread. Of course, without accurate borrowing figures, there is no way of knowing how popular any of these authors were, but we can use the library committee's acquisition patterns to identify which authors, and, indeed, which genres, were expected to attract a broader readership.

Of the authors who attracted a nationwide readership, Eric Linklater was the most popular here. Four of his novels were added to the town's libraries over the three-year period: *Juan in China* (1937), in which Linklater poured scorn on an ineffective Chinese leadership; *The Sailor's Holiday* (1937), a satirical novel which charts the exploits of a merchant seaman on shore leave; *The Impregnable Woman* (1938), Linklater's version of Aristophanes' Greek comedy *Lysistrata*; and the more sober *Judas* (1939), a retelling of the dramatic biblical tale. Apart from *The Sailor's Holiday*, these were highly ambitious novels that required considerable cultural competence from their readers. We cannot be sure that they were brought into Portsmouth's public libraries to attract the working classes, but we cannot dismiss that possibility either. In fact, all four novels were added to the stock in the town's Central Library, which was frequently used by working-class readers from the Portsea district.

Eden Phillpotts and Hugh Walpole were also nationally popular authors who were expected to do well with readers in Portsmouth. Both authors had three titles added to the Central Library (among others) during this period. The only other author who had three novels added to the Central Library (and, indeed, *every* other library in the town) in this period was H.G. Wells. The innovatory novel *Brynhild, or the Show of Things* (1937) was acquired in 1938, while the equally adventurous *Apropos of Dolores* (1938) and *The Holy Terror* (1939) were added in 1939. Interestingly, Wells does not feature on the lists of Batty, Callender or Howe, so his popularity was certainly not deemed to be assured. But he was undoubtedly expected to be popular in Portsmouth. Why?

Like much of Wells's work, these novels focus on the failings of power-crazy and image-conscious individuals. *Brynhild* features a highly intelligent character, Rowland Palace, whose calculated manipulation of his public image results in his spectacular downfall. *The Holy Terror* deals with the evolution of a dictator. Bearing in mind the international situation, these novels were surely brought into the town's libraries to warn readers about the corrupting nature of power and the risks of following the wrong path. These novels could thus play on the reader's fears; they reminded them about their own frailties. However, because they also feature individuals with highly contrasting characteristics to those just mentioned – consider Wilbeck in *Apropos of Dolores*, or Palace's wife, Brynhild – they could also provide a solution to them. Wilbeck and Brynhild were honest, selfless characters, and they always sought to follow the right path. Readers could learn much from them. Like the crime films much favoured by the Queen's patrons, then, Wells's novels could provide a sense of proportion. Of course, whether Portsmouth's readers took any of these notions on board is unknowable. But the library committee clearly expected them to appreciate such challenging fare, and the acquisition of these three novels over a fourteen-month period certainly suggests they were hitting the mark.

In fact, it is important to note that Portsmouth's working-class readers were not turning to crime or detective fiction to gain a sense of proportion. For these genres, firm favourites in the other locations mentioned in this book, were rarely added to the town's libraries. Of course, there were exceptions. Laurence Housman's crime novel *What Next? Provocative Tales of Faith and Morals* (1937) was added in 1938, for example. But this probably had more to do with the success of Housman's earlier novel, *King John of Jingalo: The Story of a Monarch in Difficulties* (1937) than it did with this one. The addition of *King John of Jingalo* is, in fact, highly significant. The novel was first published in 1902, but because it was believed that its narrative bore much relation to Edward VIII's abdication predicament, it was re-issued in 1937.[36] Portsmouth's library committee, undoubtedly intimately attuned to the national mood, and expecting the story to strike a chord with *their* readers' sensibilities, acquired the novel in the same year. In reality, there were few similarities between the story of King John and Edward VIII. But the novel must have fared well because Housman's crime novel was added to the library in the following year.

While crime and detective fiction fared badly in Portsmouth, romantic fiction was the preferred genre overall. Many of the nationally popular authors who had two novels added in this period wrote predominantly romantic fiction. Consider Warwick Deeping's *The Woman at the Door* (1937) and *The Malice of Men* (1938); Jeffery Farnol's *The Crooked Furrow* (1937) and *The Lonely Road* (1938); Sheila Kaye-Smith's *Rose Deeprose* (1936) and *The Valiant*

Woman (1939); and Compton MacKenzie's novels from *The Four Winds of Love* series, *The East Wind of Love* and *The South Wind of Love* (both 1937). Many romantic novelists who do not feature on the lists of Batty *et al.* also had two novels added in this period: Margaret Irwin's *The Stranger Prince: The Story of Rupert of the Rhine* (1937) and *The Bride: The Story of Louise and Montrose* (1939); Leo Walmsley's *Sally Lunn* (1937) and *Love in the Sun* (1939); and Sigrid Undset's *Gunnar's Daughter* (1936) and *The Faithful Wife* (1936).

While romantic fiction was the most favoured genre with Portsmouth's readers, there was a clear preference for a specific *type* of romance novel: the *historical* romance. Both of Irwin's novels were set in the English Civil War period, for example. *The Stranger Prince* explores the role of Rupert the Devil, the fearsome Cavalier fighter. *The Bride* was a biographical novel about Louise Hollandine. Farnol's *The Crooked Furrow*, which I will analyse in the next chapter, focuses on the experiences of two Regency heroes; *The Lonely Road* deals with the adventures of a courageous young Jacobite. Undset's *Gunnar's Daughter*, whose central character is a feisty, uncompromising Norwegian maiden, is set in Norway and Iceland at the beginning of the eleventh century. In fact, Portsmouth's readers had a particularly strong interest in historical fiction generally. Consider John Masefield's *Eggs and Baker* (1936), which was set in London in the 1870s and featured an Engels-like figure railing against slum conditions. Consider, too, Kenneth Roberts's *Northwest Passage* (1937), the story of the celebrated Indian fighter Robert Rogers, and *Rabble in Arms* (1933), his second epic about the American Revolution. Historical novels, then, and in particular historical romances, were the most popular types of reading material among the town's readers.

There is a marked difference here between the tastes of Portsmouth's working-class readers and those across the country. Historical fiction did respectably well with the reading public nationally, but it *never* dominated, either on the lists of Batty *et al.*, on the registers of the South Wales Miners' Institute libraries, or in the recommendations of Derby's book reviewer. Neither did Mass-Observation's team of researchers identify historical fiction as especially popular with the working-class readers they investigated. But, it was repeatedly acquired for Portsmouth's libraries between 1937 and 1939, so it was performing, or was *expected* to perform, exceptionally well here. How are we to interpret this preference for historical fiction? Part of the answer lies in the fact that this genre could be enjoyed equally by both sexes. In fact, the lack of traditionally male-targeted fiction genres in Portsmouth's libraries suggests that the town's male working-class readers were more than happy to turn to other fiction genres to answer their cultural needs. But, in this period of social, political and economic uncertainty, Portsmouth's readers also felt the need to turn to the past, not simply to escape the present, but to gain a sense of proportion and solace. Wells's novels may have served as a warning about contemporary events, but many historical novels also drew parallels with contemporary society. They could thus provide solutions to the many problems the town's working-class readers may have faced. In addition, because these novels invariably presented the past in an overtly nostalgic manner and featured noble, courageous men and strong, spirited women, working-class readers could gain both comfort and confidence from reading them.

Why, though, were Portsmouth's readers more likely to turn to this type of fiction than any of the readers discussed elsewhere in this book? Well, just as the town's working-class cinema-goers disliked films that presented challenges to the social order, its readers preferred novels that mentally transported them to a time when things were a little more stable. Indeed, Portsmouth's voters were less likely to champion left-wing politics than those in either Derby or South Wales. Sue Harper has argued that Portsmouth was the 'home of the brave'.[37] But perhaps the town's working classes were feeling a little less brave in this period, and wanted to be comforted by novels that reminded them of a time when they were. It would, of course, have been interesting to see if film provision at the Queen's during the last three years of the decade repeated this shift towards historical fare, but with very scanty evidence available it is, alas, impossible to determine.

So, while working-class consumers in Portsmouth shared many similarities with those in Derby, South Wales and at a national level, they also displayed a number of differences. And it is these differences that offer a salutary reminder of the need to recognise that consumers' tastes varied, not simply between generation and gender, but geographical location also. In addition, these analyses of local taste-communities have also revealed that tastes varied *within* these locations too; thereby warning against complacency in any research we may conduct into working-class taste. We must *never* take the leisure habits of the working classes for granted.

Notes

1 *Kineweekly Year Book*, 1939.
2 Harper, 'A Lower Middle-Class Taste-Community', pp. 565–566.
3 *Kineweekly Year Book*. See also John Sedgwick, 'Cinemagoing in Portsmouth during the 1930s', *Cinema Journal*, 46:1, 2006, pp. 52–84.
4 See comments in 'Portsmouth is Now Library Conscious: A Review of 60 Years' Work in the City', *Portsmouth Evening News* (hereafter *PEN*), 30 May 1944. See also Adele Roper, 'The Development of Public Libraries in Portsmouth 1853–1934', *Portsmouth Paper* (n.d.), p. 5.
5 Roper, 'Development of Public Libraries', pp. 9–12.
6 Ibid.
7 *PEN*, 6 April 1936.
8 J. Barker, R. Brown and W. Greer, *The Cinemas of Portsmouth*, Horndean, 1981, pp. 31–32. Barker *et al.* put the Queens' seating capacity as 550, but in the town's Watch Committee minute book seating capacity is never listed as more than 452. See Minutes of the Corporation Watch Committee Book, 5 December 1933, p. 1016.
9 See *Kineweekly*, 9 April 1931, 16 April 1931 and 14 May 1931. See also *PEN*, 8 April 1931.
10 For an analysis of the Council's housing policies in this period see Walker, 'Municipal Enterprise'.
11 *PEN*, 8 April 1931; *Kineweekly*, April 16 1931.
12 *Kineweekly Year Book*, 1933.
13 *Kineweekly*, 13 June 1935.
14 *Kineweekly Year Book*, 1936.
15 Ibid., 1930, 1933, 1934 and 1936.
16 *Kineweekly*, 18 May 1933.
17 The films shown on Sundays differed to those booked on the other weekdays.
18 Sedgwick, 'Cinemagoing in Portsmouth', p. 56.
19 For a discussion of the town's cinema booking practices see ibid., pp. 55–59.
20 For a discussion of Fuller's work, see Sutton, *Chorus of Raspberries*, pp. 104–109.
21 *PEN*, 6 December 1934.
22 Only in 1936 did the number of musical films exhibited at the Queens achieve anywhere near the amount booked at Cwmllynfell's miners' cinema and Derby's Allenton.
23 Blake noted: 'Whenever the word "love" was introduced, that was also seemed to have a fatal bearing on the success of a film'. See *Kineweekly*, 2 June 1938.
24 *The Portsmouth Reader: A Quarterly Magazine Devoted to the Interests of Book Lovers and Museum Visitors*, January 1937, vol. 1, no. 1. Local History Department, Norris Central Library, Portsmouth.
25 Ibid.
26 Ibid. See also 1937, vol. 1, nos. 2–4; 1938, vol. 2, nos. 1–4; and 1939, vol. 3, nos. 1–4.
27 City of Portsmouth Index to Minutes of Meetings of the Council and Committee, 1932.

28 North End library had 6,098 members, 3,236 of whom were from that ward.

29 Central Library had 9,158 members in total, and, of these, 1,361 were from Portsea.

30 See City of Portsmouth Forty-Sixth Annual Report on the Public Libraries and Museums, 1929–1930 and City of Portsmouth Fifty-Third Annual Report on the Public Libraries and Museums, 1936–1937.

31 Ibid.

32 *PEN*, 18 March 1930 and 12 September 1930.

33 Ibid., 5 February 1930.

34 City of Portsmouth Forty-Sixth Annual Report on the Public Libraries and Museums, 1929–1930.

35 In 1937, for example, fiction accounted for three-quarters of all books borrowed. City of Portsmouth Libraries and Museums. An Account of the Year's Work, 1937–1938.

36 Retrieved from www.time.com/time/magazine/article/0,9171,758061,00.html, accessed on 15 April 2007.

37 Harper, 'A Lower Middle-Class Taste-Community', p. 571.

9

Popular film and literature: textual analyses

Any discussion of working-class taste should take into account the nature of the products being consumed. I have borne this in mind throughout, particularly in the chapters assessing working-class film and literature popularity. However, in order to more fully understand the nature of working-class taste, this chapter will conduct some close textual analyses of a number of films and novels known to have been popular with working-class consumers during the 1930s. Of course, the range of popular texts is vast, and space limitations ensure the number analysed here will be small. What I have chosen to do, though, is analyse what *I* consider to be a representative sample of films and novels. They have been chosen because they were among the most popular in the period, and reveal the varied nature of working-class taste, drawing attention to the wide-ranging choices working-class consumers made when deciding which films to watch and what types of novel to read.

Sample film texts

Hard-hitting drama *I Am a Fugitive from a Chain Gang* (1933) was one of the most successful films of the 1930s. It was one of *Film Weekly*'s 'principal picture successes' of 1933, secured a *Picturegoer* 'Award of Merit' and is placed 35th in Sedgwick's POPSTAT index.[1] The film was exhibited at cinemas principally populated by working-class cinema-goers, so it was particularly popular with that social group. It is not hard to see why. *I Am a Fugitive* centres its narrative on the plight of innocent convict James Allen (Paul Muni) who falls foul of corrupt state officials. Significantly, Allen's ordinariness ensures that his plight has the maximum impact. He is an ex-serviceman who is eager to escape the monotonous daily routine of factory work. When he makes vocal his dreams in an impassioned speech to his parents, he is afforded much narrative and textural space (he dominates the frame, is well-lit, and filmed from a low angle). Any working-class cinema-goer could identify with him. Allen's idealistic vision could be argued to have been his folly, and the film could have served as a warning to those seeking to transgress social boundaries. However, Mervyn LeRoy's direction ensures that the audience's sympathies lie with Allen. He is not to blame for his vision. The brutal authoritarian figures who strip him of his strength and dignity in the chain-gang, and the dishonest and corrupt officials who remove him from a life in which he had prospered, are the social pollutants; he is not. This message is compellingly made in the film's harrowing dénouement when Allen's sweetheart Helen affectionately asks how he manages to survive a life on the run. Allen – the embodiment of a broken man, recoiling from the camera in a low-lit long-shot – rasps, 'I *steal*'. This disturbing utterance, chillingly filmed, serves as an indictment against those individuals who drove him to that desperate state.

I Am a Fugitive is perhaps unusual in its ferocity. No other 1930s film could match LeRoy's masterful exposition of the penal system's sheer brutality. But other directors were equally adept at attracting a large working-class following by cloaking swingeing social criticism with high-gloss entertainment. Norman Taurog's sentimental drama *Boys Town* (1938), which despite its sugary coating had at its core an unsettling narrative railing against the failings of the reformatory system, was *Kineweekly*'s second biggest box-office winner of February 1939.[2] It attracted many working-class cinema-goers. Once again, it is not hard to see why. The film's opening sequence allows death-row prisoner Dan Farrow significant narrative and textural space to launch a venomous verbal attack on the reformatory system.[3] During his tirade Farrow is well-lit and dominates the frame, and the closing line of his outburst – 'When I went in, copping a loaf of bread was a job; when I came out, I could rob a bank' – highlights the inadequacies of a system that receives petty criminals and turns them into hardened offenders. Visual and verbal stimulants thus combine to ensure that the message is forcefully made. More revealing are the effects of Farrow's outburst on Father Flanagan (Spencer Tracy). A series of intercuts reveal a soft-focus Flanagan, bathed in a crown of light, visibly trembling as Farrow's words are spoken. Later, while travelling on a train, Flanagan repeats fragments of Farrow's rant to the train's rhythm:

> Twelve years old, twelve years old,
> One friend, one friend,
> Starving kid, starving kid,
> Never had a chance, never had a chance,
> Reformatory, reformatory.

Life's chances are thus shown to be determined by external forces. The system is to blame, not the individual. From then onwards *Boys Town* descends into sentimental mush, but the effects of these opening sequences certainly linger.

Of course, these films were produced in America and contained plenty of action and an array of popular stars. Working-class cinema-goers were expected to gain pleasure from these aspects. They were also expected to obtain satisfaction from the films' socially conscious principles. Certainly, *I Am a Fugitive* offers a resolution that is extraordinarily bleak, but both films feature deeply passionate individuals who fight society's injustices with dogged perseverance. In addition, both films placed the working classes and marginal groups at the centre of the narrative. It is not difficult to see why they attracted cinema-goers from lower social groups.

These themes are also evident in Frank Lloyd's swashbuckling adventure *Mutiny on the Bounty* (1935). The film, which denounces the bullying meted out by Charles Laughton's sadistic Captain Bligh, was one of the biggest successes of the decade. It topped Bernstein's 'Outstanding' films list in 1937, was runner-up among *Kineweekly's* box-office winners of 1936, secured two *Picturegoer* awards, and is placed second in Sedgwick's POPSTAT ranking for 1936.[4] Significantly, the film played to packed houses at Portsmouth's Regent cinema.[5] It was thus answering to the tastes of middle- and working-class cinema-goers. It seems likely that the film appealed to the middle classes because it was set on a ship where discipline and a strict social hierarchy were imperative to order. But, it could also serve as a warning to them: abuse your power and face the consequences. Indeed, Fletcher Christian's (Clark Gable) unheeded warning to Bligh, 'My advice Sir, if you'll take it, is not to be too harsh with them. We're sailing 10,000 miles locked up together on this ship for the next two years, it's … it's like a powder-magazine', must have played heavily on the minds of those individuals in the audience fearing social revolution. That Gable is placed higher in the frame than Laughton only serves to reinforce his message. Of course, the film's satisfactory resolution – the promise of a 'new understanding' between officers and men – ultimately served to dispel these anxieties, but its even-handedness offered to comfort working-class audiences who would have identified with the ship's tormented lower orders. *Mutiny on the Bounty* is thus an historical adventure that comments on social inequalities. As Franchot Tone's idealistic Roger Byam (commanding the frame during an impassioned two-minute long speech) proclaims in his address to the courtroom during the film's finale, it is a 'story of greed and tyranny'.[6] In fact, in Laughton's ruthless Captain Bligh, *Mutiny on the Bounty* contains an authoritarian figure as villainous and corrupt as any of the officials in the abovementioned films. He is the social pollutant that spreads discontent among the ship's company with calamitous results. It is not surprising working-class cinema-goers liked it.

Working-class cinema-goers thus favoured films that gave them confidence in their class position and bolstered their sense of self. They wanted to come out of the cinema *feeling good about themselves*. These preferences continue regardless of the type of film being consumed. The Marx Brothers anarchic comedies, for example, played extremely well at many cinemas used by working-class cinema-goers. Their films contain highly amusing sequences in which the comedians are not afraid to mock authority and high society. Consider the sequence in *A Day at the Races* (1937) in which hypochondriac socialite Mrs. Upjohn (Margaret Dumont) haughtily remarks to Dr Hackenbush (Groucho Marx), a horse-doctor masquerading as a medical doctor: 'Why, I've never been so insulted in my life'. Hackenbush's biting riposte: 'Well, it's early yet'. Consider too the hilarious racecourse finale during which Hackenbush casually observes: 'I haven't seen so much mud-slinging since the last election'. Similarly, in *A Night at the Opera* (1935), Groucho Marx, playing phoney business manager Otis B. Driftwood, addresses an opera house audience thus: 'Ladies and gentlemen … (long pause while he scans the audience) … I guess that takes in most of you'. These films did not seek to build an alliance between these social groups; they actively sought to expose their differences.

Indeed, while these Marx Brothers' films portray society's elites as stuffy, obdurate and unhappy with their lot, individuals lower down the social scale are depicted as vivacious, accommodating and, most importantly, *happy*. 'Maybe haven't got money, maybe haven't got shoes, [but] rhythm [will] push away the blues,' runs one musical interlude in *A Day at the Races*. The sequence in *A Night at the Opera* in which the lower orders dance on a ship is filmed by a high-angle camera which pans across the crowd capturing the lively, joyous nature of the occasion; this is intercut with close-ups of smiling individuals. In contrast, the elite crowd attending the opera are languid and sombre. There are, then, differences in the higher and lower classes' appreciation of, and engagement with, culture. The elites' experience of high culture is shown to be passive in nature, whereas the lower orders actively engage with popular culture. It is made clear, too, that the latter was the more enjoyable. These films thus address a specific audience, and their makers were highly aware of their intended audiences' cultural capital. Indeed, in *A Night at the Opera* Driftwood echoes Tarzan's jungle cry to the opera house audience, and remarks, to their obvious bewilderment, 'It's alright, it's just the Tarzan in me'. Working-class cinema audiences would have been well aware of the reference. These films not only offered working-class cinema-goers a high-spirited release, then, they also sought to give them self-belief.

Neither of these films gained an 'Award of Merit' or similar distinction. They were far too lowbrow for that. However, they were highly successful, and both films appeared on popularity lists based on box-office revenue.[7] Significantly, though, neither of them ranked as high as the previous three films analysed in this chapter. Now, the box-office, as Arthur Dent observed in *Kineweekly*, was the 'barometer of public taste'.[8] If these films did not perform as well as *I Am a Fugitive et al.*, they were clearly not appealing to as broad a range of cinema-goers. It is tempting to suggest that they were not attracting both middle- *and* working-class cinema-goers, but the working classes alone, and a particular *type* of working-class cinema-goer at that. The key, of course, is the manner in which they depict social relations. While middle-class cinema-goers could find some comfort in the resolutions offered in the previous three films, they were hardly likely to enjoy watching a film which questioned and ridiculed *their* codes of behaviour and presented no satisfactory resolution for their social group. Of course, some working-class cinema-goers also found this type of humour too strong for their tastes. Indeed, Marx Brothers films gained a mixed reaction at some cinemas.[9] But many did like them, and it was with these, undoubtedly more radical, cinema-goers that they gained recognition.

Romantic musical *Sweethearts* (1938), unlike the Marx Brothers films, had a very broad appeal. Filmed in Technicolor and loosely based on Victor Herbert's 1913 operetta of the same name, *Sweethearts* principally functioned as a star vehicle for the ever-popular Nelson Eddy/Jeanette MacDonald partnership. It was, in fact, *the* most successful of the couple's musicals, and featured as a *Kineweekly* 'box-office success' in 1939.[10] It is not hard to see why. *Sweethearts* was a particularly highly polished affair in which Eddy and MacDonald play married Broadway stars Ernest Lane and Gwen Marlowe. The film allows much narrative space for the pair to do what they did best – and what the cinema audience *expected* from them – *perform*. Significantly, Lane and Marlowe (similar to music-hall stars) share a close rapport with their audiences, and in one sequence, get them to accompany them while singing the show's theme song. Cinema audiences were undoubtedly expected to appreciate this interaction between the stars and their audience, for a series of intercuts reveal the theatre audience's rapturous responses.

Cinema audiences were also expected to appreciate the film's rather nostalgic tone, for the 'threat' of the 'modern' is heavily played. Lane and Marlowe, put upon by their producer and families, dream of escaping to Hollywood for a more 'simple' life ('I've always wanted to dig in the earth'; 'to put on overalls and get out and chop down your own fruit tree, ah, that's living'). Of course, the studio system in place in Hollywood at the time would have meant that the stars were placed on an equivalent treadmill to the one from which they were trying to flee, but the pair are led to believe (by devious Hollywood agent Norman Trumpet) that the famous film studios were the path to Elysium. Significantly, though, through a series of cleverly contrasting scenes, cinema audiences are informed otherwise. The scene during which Trumpet sings Hollywood's praises to Lane and Marlowe, for example, is preceded by one in which brash Hollywood studio boss Mr Silver – dominating the frame, his name in flashing lights behind him – reveals the truth while on the telephone to Trumpet ('Sure I'm still at the studio, do you thinks it's a holiday out here? Always there's something'; 'She's in the hospital through overwork'; 'she got sore because she was doing two pictures at once'). These scenes were meant to be humorous. Cinema audiences could laugh along knowing they were 'in the know' while the stars were not. But they could also serve as a warning against changes to the status quo.

In fact, verbal and visual techniques repeatedly combine to warn about breaking from the past. Costume design is deployed to function in this way. The anticipated move to Hollywood is signalled by Marlowe trying on a range of clothes which are 'modern' and flamboyant in style; at times, overtly sexual, and at others, quite masculine. These are far removed from the refined, flowing, and, quite frankly, sexless costumes she had previously worn. Marlowe's femininity is changing. She is becoming an independent, commanding woman, and thus a potential threat. The warning is bolstered by her assistant's reluctance to relocate because 'It's much better for one and all if I stay where I belong'. So, neither she, nor indeed, Marlowe or Lane, actually *belong* in Hollywood. This is pushed forcefully home in the film's dénouement when the pair decide to remain with their antiquated Broadway producer ('I'm an old man, and I don't get many pleasures'). More to the point, they are *happy* to do so. Cinema audiences could, then, leave content in the knowledge that the stars had not suffered at the hands of Hollywood; nor had their dreams about the fabled land been spoiled. But audiences could also go away safe in the knowledge that their lives too, hard though they may be, might not be better for change. *Sweethearts* offered to comfort them. And it must have done, for it was one of the decade's biggest hits.

This close analysis of a few film favourites has revealed that, while working-class cinema-goers could be rather partial to films that made venomous attacks on society or challenged them in some way, they also wanted to be comforted by their film fare. They wanted to consume films that offered a satisfactory resolution to the problems presented; films that left them in no doubt as to their importance in the social structure; films that assuaged any anxieties they may have felt regarding the social structure itself; films whose narrative and visual style explicitly promoted their place in society. Working-class cinema-goers thus chose to watch films that bolstered their sense of self; films that made them feel good about themselves. It was rarely simply a matter of watching whatever film happened to be playing.

Sample novels

Popular literature, too, performed a number of complex cultural tasks. Like popular films, novels by the most popular authors of the period responded to the various cultural needs of working-class consumers. Ursula Bloom's *The Passionate Heart* (1930), for example, gave great latitude to its female characters, and can be read as responding to the changing social aspirations of working-class women precipitated by the First World War.[11] In fact, in the manner in which the novel is constructed, it completely redefines women's role in society. While the novel's heroine Mary does marry, the union is portrayed as an unhappy one. Her clergyman husband George is a philanderer, and only through her liaison with sailor Peter can Mary express herself fully. Marriage is thus presented, not as a fitting feminine ambition, but as something which is stifling and oppressive, or to put in Bloom's words – 'a cage'. The way in which Bloom contrasts the two men and their relationship with Mary encapsulates this most precisely. Mary's first proper meeting with George is in her mother's 'prim and proper dining-room, with its suggestion of austere chastity, and its spruce lumbering furniture, and its gilt ornaments'. By contrast, her first meeting with Peter is described thus: 'there was the opal mist filming the harbour with amethyst, where lights, slung yellowly from destroyers at anchor, were like stars'. Mary's life with her husband, then, is portrayed as bleak and pedestrian; with Peter it is passionate and sensual.

In addition, while Mary's relationship with Peter is identified as something which is forbidden, the language used when the couple meet clearly expresses where the reader's sympathies were supposed to be located. One encounter, in which Mary is meeting Peter in a wood, ran thus:

> a little wood fenced round by thick grey hedge; a green wood, where firs and tamarisks waved, but mostly brown and seared by the ravages of winter ... Grass was thrusting its spiked blades up through the soggy clay. Just ahead, the wood in its sweet spring wetness.

Clearly, the wood and its surroundings are being used as a metaphor for Mary's stifling life with George, the taboo nature of her liaison with Peter, and, upon her rendezvous with the latter, as a metaphor for female sexual pleasure. This final element is made explicit as the narrative continues:

> He drew her closer into the deepness of the wood, where the hedge, red with bramble and lightly sprigged by swelling buds, parted for them. He drew her within, where dappled larches lifted masts like proud ships, and undergrowth and scrub grew tattered and close. Here they were close to the heart-throbs of the trees. Closer and closer, his binding, imprisoning arms, the touch of his lips, and the swift sensation of sinking into some fathomless sea; his mouth cupping hers, drinking her very soul from her. A mouth ripe with the promise of a hundred kisses.

The Passionate Heart, then, can be read as a celebration of a new feminine identity, one in which transgression from prescribed gender roles is positively championed. In this sense, Bloom was responding to the altered mood and experiences of working-class women in the period, and the novel can be interpreted as a nod towards their changing social aspirations. In fact, because the novel is set in the period leading up to, and including, the First World War, and because Bloom highly personalises the narrative ('When you come to think of it, it was so funny'; 'There comes a time when you can cling no longer') she was ensuring maximum readership recognition. It is, then, not surprising that Bloom was mentioned by Batty and Mass-Observation researchers as an author who the working classes found much to their tastes.

Edgar Wallace was also extremely popular with working-class readers and was regularly named by contemporaries as a sure-fire attraction for that social group. The narrative drive of his detective novel *The Flying Squad* (1929) partly reveals why.[12] The novel gives considerable narrative space to the activities of those individuals placed on the margins of society – the criminal fraternity. In fact, Ann Perryman, the novel's heroine, is allowed great latitude, and in her association with drug smuggler Mark McGill she, like Bloom's heroine, transgresses traditional feminine behaviour. The novel thus takes an implicitly anti-authoritarian stance and could be read as a celebration of lawlessness. However, by the end of the novel Ann has seen the error of her ways and marries Chief Inspector Bradley (who had been her chief adversary throughout). Mark McGill and his many associates, meanwhile, are punished; McGill by hanging. What are we to make of these highly contrasting elements?

Ken Worpole has argued that, in this period at least, the detective novel 'was a form of fictional reassurance for a middle-class readership that the continuity of the class system was safe'.[13] Certainly, *The Flying Squad*'s dénouement – Ann's domestication, McGill's death – can be interpreted as an attempt by Wallace to assuage any latent fears of the middle-class reader. However, because Wallace gave greater narrative space to the activities of the criminal classes and made it clear that Ann's decision to reform was her own (she is not ruled by Bradley, but is a highly independent woman who is mistress of her own destiny), he was actually trying to encourage readers to take pleasure in his characters' excesses. In addition, the role of the middle classes, which is exemplified in the form of Tiser – 'a twittering, nervous man' who ran a 'Home of Rest' for the 'general reformation of the criminal classes' – is depicted as something of a façade. In fact, Tiser is a 'reformed' criminal, and his philanthropic objectives are portrayed as a cover for his continuing relationship with McGill. Wallace's popularity was based, then, on his ability to allow these socially marginal groups to gain vitality from their dubious social position. *The Flying Squad* thus had a double function for working-class readers; it could comfort and challenge.

This aspect of detective fiction is highlighted by *The Bookseller*'s A.C. Hannay. 'Class feeling,' Hannay observed, 'oddly enough, comes out strongly in the average detective novel. Though the police may be foolish enough occasionally to arrest a gamekeeper, the murderer is always a gentleman'.[14] It could seem odd, then, that many readers in the South Wales mining communities failed to find Wallace much to their taste. But Wallace assigns a highly elevated role to society's outcasts. Miners' leaders would have frowned upon including in their libraries novels which celebrated such dubious qualities. After all, they were expected to be educational centres. The majority of library users must have felt the same way. Interestingly, then, we can identify differences here between the tastes of readers and cinema-goers in these communities, for miners and their families liked films that championed these qualities. But, then, Miners' Institute cinemas did not carry such an esteemed position as centres of enlightenment.

Jeffery Farnol's novels performed consistently well over the decade. His historical adventure *The Crooked Furrow* (1937), which warns against the abuses of power and champions the labouring classes, reveals why he remained so popular with the country's working-class readers.[15] The novel, set in Sussex and London during the 1820s, deals with the experience of two cousins, Oliver and Roland, who are sent on a 'character building' exercise by their wealthy uncle in order to decide which of them inherits his fortune. Throughout the course of their journey the cousins are taught a series of lessons that remind them of their social obligations. As their uncle points out, the acquisition of wealth will bring great power *and* 'heavy responsibility'. *The Crooked Furrow* thus carries a strong socially conscious message. At times Farnol is very heavy-handed in delineating this message. For example, after Oliver had been robbed by a starving child, he tells a policeman, 'not one creature should be permitted to die of hunger, – there's the crime – that any child should want … Someday … when the world is sufficiently civilized, no one will be permitted to starve'. Farnol was undoubtedly drawing parallels with events in contemporary society. It was rather clumsily done, but the working classes clearly appreciated it.

Part of the appeal of *The Crooked Furrow* lay in its celebration of working-class life. The labour of the lower classes is heavily romanticised. Before sending the cousins on their quest, for example, their uncle tells them: 'Hard work never degraded anyone and never will'. On their journey from Sussex to London, meanwhile, the cousins meet a tinker who recalls, 'simple things and ordinary people … hard work, the heroism of ceaseless effort … the romance of labour'. *The Crooked Furrow* is thus highly nostalgic in tone. It is also deeply conservative. Farnol is clearly harking back to the period before rapid industrial and urban growth changed completely the nature of British society; a period in which the various social groups were firmly bound by obligations of duty and deference. In fact, the city is seen as a polluting force. London is described thus:

> Such horrors … poor little children, terrified women, and none to shield or pity them! … Oh London, poor, dreadful, cruel, sorrowful, London!

In contrast, the countryside is described in glowing terms:

> The broad, green sweep of hill and dale where clean, sweet winds played; the hush of trees in leafy solitudes lit by the murmorous glory of sun-kissed stream or sparkle of chattering mill; the fragrant dusk of bosky, winding lanes; broad golden meadow and daisied mead, farmstead, cottage and sleepy village with its good, homely sounds; – the peaceful countryside, the sight, sound, smell of it, and the calm, slow, kindly voices of its folk.

Many working-class readers were clearly responding to this overtly nostalgic message. They were undoubtedly uneasy with the current state of affairs in British society.

Farnol's *The Crooked Furrow*, then, yearns for a return to a time that had been forever lost. Simon Dare's *Adventure Beautiful* (1937) similarly displays a certain uneasiness with contemporary society.[16] It can be read as a stern warning against transgressing gender and social boundaries. Dare allows none of her female characters the same measure of latitude which Bloom or Wallace permit their heroines, but she was also highly popular with working-class readers, being identified by Batty and M-O researchers as an attraction for them. Certainly, Dare's female characters explore the outer limits of feminine behaviour, but they are not permitted to transgress them; and while they enjoy a 'beautiful adventure', their escapades remain just that, adventures only. Indeed, the novel's dénouement witnesses each character's return to traditional gender roles.

Political and social criticisms are also crucial parts of *Adventure Beautiful*'s narrative. During a series of intimate conversations, Dare allows her characters to express disdain at totalitarian regimes (Communists are 'herds of animals, mad and lost and terrified'), the worsening international situation ('what a mess of a world we live in') and modernity ('Such advance of science, such inventions ... And most of them of a destructive kind'). The benefits of democratic government, by contrast, are clearly defined: 'They do their best. It must be a terrible position to be in to rule a country. There must be so many hundreds of reactions and stupid little details and difficulties that we know nothing about. At least let us give them their due'. In this way, Dare pointedly illustrates that any social ills could be resolved only when working with the system, not against it.

Adventure Beautiful is deeply influenced by the ideological concerns of the period. It could thus strike subconscious chords with the country's working-class readers. One would assume that such an apparently overtly didactic text would be disliked by the working classes, but Dare was one of their most favoured authors. How, then, can we square this apparent anomaly? Well, *Adventure Beautiful* does far more than instruct the reader. It entertains and allows them significant agency. Indeed, by giving her characters free rein to explore the limits of the prescribed social norms, Dare implicitly allows her readers considerable creativity also. Consider Hilary's affair with Dominick Hurry. It is depicted as an exotic and freeing experience ('the strange magic of the fragrant room'; 'something different from everyday life'). Nevertheless, because Dare also *gently* checks her characters' behaviour if they begin to push too far (Hilary is chastised thus by her sister, Sally: 'Free love *isn't* right, it can't be'), she is also warning of the dangers of crossing these boundaries.

In these diverse ways, authors and film-makers responded to the tastes of Britain's working-class consumers. They sought to challenge and comfort; to influence and encourage. The success of these films and novels with the working classes suggests that they were achieving their aim.

Notes

1 *FW*, 29 December 1933; *Picturegoer*, 28 April 1934; Sedgwick, *Popular Filmgoing*, p. 265.

2 *Kineweekly*, 11 January 1940. The film also gained a *Picturegoer* 'Award of Merit' for Spencer Tracy's role as the sanctimonious Father Flanagan. *Picturegoer*, 18 May 1940.

3 *Boys Town* is also critical of the death penalty. Consider Father Flanagan's softly spoken comments: 'Life and death should be left to the creator of life'.

4 Bernstein Questionnaire, 1937; *Kineweekly*, 14 January 1937; *Picturegoer*, 12 March 1938; Sedgwick, *Popular Filmgoing*, p. 272.

5 The film attracted 26,136 patrons. Harper, 'A Lower Middle-Class Taste-Community', p. 584.

6 Tone is filmed in extreme close-up for much of this sequence and is always at the centre of the frame. There are four brief intercuts in which the reactions of those he is addressing are shown.

7 *A Day at the Races* was a *Kineweekly* 'box-office success'. *Kineweekly*, 13 January 1938. Both films feature in Sedgwick's POPSTAT index. Sedgwick, *Popular Filmgoing*, pp. 273 and 275.

8 *Kineweekly*, 14 January 1937.

9 See *PS*, 26 November 1932.

10 *Kineweekly*, 11 January 1940.

11 Ursula Bloom, *The Passionate Heart*, London, 1930.

12 Edgar Wallace, *The Flying Squad*, London, 1929.

13 Ken Worpole, *Dockers and Detectives. Popular Reading: Popular Writing*, London, 1983, pp. 33–34.

14 *Bookseller*, 3 October 1934.

15 Jeffery Farnol, *The Crooked Furrow*, Bath, 1937.

16 Simon Dare, *Adventure Beautiful*, London, 1937. Simon Dare was a pseudonym for Marjorie Huxtable.

Conclusion:
'giving the public what it wants'

'Taste is about consumption and, in consuming, we reveal ourselves'.[1]

This book has been concerned with popular cultural tastes in the 1930s. This was a particularly contentious period in which there were a range of controversies about the relationship between class and culture, and the study of working-class taste in this period is of particular interest to the historian. Significantly, working-class leisure has tended to be viewed as either oppositional or compliant, but this survey has shown that, while both elements certainly existed, neither dominated. Leisure products were closely tailored to the demands of the consumer, and these demands varied according to a number of determinants, which could be centred on class, gender, generational or geographical difference. What this book has highlighted most of all, of course, is the need to recognise that working-class consumption patterns vary over time, and that, whatever period we are assessing, we need to remain alert to the specific set of social circumstances that influence leisure habits. It is now time to build on the conclusions made thus far and sketch out precisely how working-class consumption patterns varied over the period.

The markets for film and literature clearly flourished in Britain during the 1930s. Encouraged by the changes in both media and the environs in which to experience them, working-class people became avid consumers of film and popular fiction. Evidently, for many highbrow contemporaries this was something to regret. For them, not only did it appear to signal a debasement of elite culture, it was also believed to lead to all manner of social ills. Despite an increased interest in, and scrutiny of, the working classes' leisure activities, highbrow contemporaries invariably read the situation wrongly. Parts of the Establishment believed that one of the principle roles of popular leisure was to raise class consciousness. It was this aspect, the potential political challenge from below, that they feared most. However, while there were attempts to use leisure activities for these purposes – cinemas and libraries in the South Wales Miners' Institutes were clearly expected to be sites of political awakening – working-class consumers were usually highly resistant to this type of indoctrination. Of course, at times political texts were appreciated. But radical politics only occasionally featured as a significant element in the majority of working-class leisure pursuits. In fact, it was the supposed depoliticised nature of popular leisure that so concerned the likes of Q.D. Leavis. For these cultural critics, the working classes' participation in popular leisure was merely a form of escapism; something to wile away the hours; a 'drug' to help working-class consumers forget their troubles. Undoubtedly, for some consumers, this may have been the case. For the majority of working-class consumers, though, going to the cinema or reading a book performed a range of differing cultural functions; the ability to escape was simply one of them.

Moreover, if we do view escapism as one of the reasons behind the working classes' leisure participation, we need to contextualise it. It is only by doing so that we can begin to unravel the complex threads that run through the working classes' cinema-going and reading habits, and only then do we start to realise that taking part in these activities was predicated on far more than simply the need to escape. For example, we could argue that miners and their families visited Cwmllynfell's Institute cinema simply to escape the deprivation they undoubtedly faced in the period, but the preference for films with a strong social conscience was triggered by the particular set of circumstances in which they were living at the time. The elevated social standing of some working-class consumers in Derby was also the reason behind their appreciation of the Travers' farces and films that played with the constructed nature of identity. The unstable nature of the employment market in Portsmouth likewise played a role in the town's working-class consumers' preference for historical romance novels which offered to imaginatively transport readers into a more stable and secure past. Portsmouth's working-class cinema-goers' reluctance to watch comedy films that depicted society as chaotic and combative was generated by the same concerns, for these types of film offered no resolution for them; they afforded no comfort or reassurance.

It was, in fact, the need to be comforted, to be reassured, to gain confidence, to gain a sense of belonging or proportion, which drew most working-class consumers to the cinema or the library. Taking part in these cultural activities thus acted as a coping mechanism; they provided an emotional release. However, these texts functioned in varying ways for different consumers. In Portsmouth, for example, male working-class consumers turned to crime films, but not crime fiction, to gain a sense of proportion. To gain comfort and reassurance they turned to films that reminded them of their affinity with the sea, but in fiction they, and, indeed, working-class women, turned to stories set in the past to fulfil that task. In Cwmllynfell's miners' cinema, where films with a social conscience went down best of all, crime films rarely whetted the audiences' appetites. But, when turning to the written word, Markham's library users clearly favoured crime fiction; novels closely tied with contemporary events were only liked between 1937 and 1940. For Cynon and Duffryn's reading community, meanwhile, all genres of fiction were appealing, but romantic novels most answered this taste-community's cultural needs. Because romantic fiction was preferred by female readers, Cynon and Duffryn's library patrons, unlike Markham's, must have consisted primarily of women and girls. The same gender balance surely existed in Derby, because romantic fiction was expected to go down well with this town's working-class readers. However, Derby's male *and* female working-class consumers were expected to like literature with a strong regional dimension. Indeed, they liked films that contained this element. Interestingly, there is no evidence of such trends in the other taste-communities surveyed here. Obviously, Derby's working classes, living in a region that generally prospered during the 1930s, were content to be reminded of the area in which they lived. Other taste-communities, living in areas that did not, were less keen to do so.

There are, of course, similarities in taste. Indeed, to draw attention to these differences risks ignoring elements of unity and consistency that existed too. In all of these taste-communities romantic fiction generally did well, while romantic films fared badly. Comedy did much better in visual than in written form. The period's most popular films and authors were (with a few exceptions) well liked in all of these locations. However, these areas of similarity were undoubtedly driven by other factors; and these factors were influencing working-class consumers at a national level. For example, romantic films arguably fared worse than romantic fiction because of the deeper cultural roots of the reading habit among women. In fact, while women were clearly experiencing greater social freedoms, they were still more likely to visit a cinema with a male chaperone (who would probably have found little joy in watching a romance film). The preference for film comedy undoubtedly reflects a continuity between music-hall entertainment and the cinema. The widespread popularity of specific films and authors, meanwhile, was unquestionably driven by the similar promotional and distribution practices of the major producers. But, when we come down to matters of taste, the evidence shouts loud and clear that both cultural forms *and* the various types of genre contained within them performed different cultural functions for the working-class taste-communities surveyed here. So, while some working-class cinema-goers may have delighted in watching the antics of Jeanette MacDonald as a Spanish dancer in *The Firefly*, others were more content when watching her rather sober performance in *Sweethearts*. This brings us neatly back to George Szanto's remarks mentioned in the Introduction, that the comfort was in the close 'fit' between what was on offer and what consumers desired.[2]

Film and publishing trade personnel recognised the need to respond to these desires. They, too, understood that consumers' tastes varied from region to region, by age, between the sexes, and between the various fractions of the working classes. The recommendations of *Kineweekly*'s review panel were structured along these very lines. However, what *these* critics failed to do was allow for displacements in the process. Working-class consumers enjoyed a wider range of films than was expected of them. Indeed, while working-class cinema-goers in South Wales watched a great many films that were expected to appeal to them, they also saw films that were not. These displacements reveal that while *Kineweekly*'s critics were closely attuned to working-class taste, it was the local cinema managers who were likely to know their patrons best. Indeed, many of these individuals were not shy in reminding these arbiters of taste that *they* knew their customers' tastes better than anyone. Certainly, the local case-studies developed in this book illustrate that they did, and that both cinema-managers and librarians were constantly responding to their customers' demands.

The producers and suppliers of cultural goods, then, may well have questioned the nature of working-class taste too, and they may well have had their own ideas about the role of leisure in working-class communities, but, despite a few grumblings, they repeatedly sought to respond to the various social and cultural needs of their customers. This book's closing analysis of a few films and novels produced during the period has allowed us to recognise that the genres remained rich and varied in style, despite the tangible effects of the various determinants on those working in the film and publishing industries. In fact, the structure of these industries, often informal and flexible, and with a considerable amount of emphasis on entrepreneurialism, aided and intensified the growth of the different styles and genres of film and literature. In fact, so extraordinarily rich were these film and literary cultures that this analysis has (perforce) omitted a whole range of texts. The representative sample of films and novels that have been analysed, though, shows us that the form, the style, the structure and the content of these cultural goods had a significant bearing on the working-class consumer's appreciation of them.

So, working-class consumers were enjoying a rich tapestry of films and literature in the 1930s, and this survey of a number of taste-communities has shown that patterns of taste were never uniform, that acts of consumption are highly complex, that working-class consumers chose leisure activities to fulfil a range of cultural roles, and that these roles are never easy to define. As Stephen Bayley, whose comments served as the starting point for this Conclusion, argues, taste involves choice and meaning and reveals much about the consumer.[3] And these working-class consumers were revealing that they had considerable cultural competence and took from these cultural products elements that were relevant to their lives and used them for varying ideological purposes. Films and literature were never simply used as media where messages presented in the narrative were passively received by an apathetic audience.

Such conclusions may appear to represent a celebration of working-class consciousness; they may appear hagiographic. However, these concluding points have been emphasised because they remind us that working-class consumers *should* be accorded equal complexity in the act of consumption as other classes have been in the past. Only by doing so can we begin to draw a more representative map of British society's relationship with leisure in a period during which its engagement with it was highly significant. It would, of course, have been profitable, if time and space allowed, to include a more wide-ranging geographical analysis of working-class taste-communities. How, for example, did working-class consumers in Scotland, Ireland, or, indeed, the north, east and west of England experience these leisure activities? Was working-class taste equally variable in these regions? The evidence presented here suggests that this would have been the case. But we have to draw a line somewhere, and the geographical areas chosen for examination were based on the highly contrasting experiences of working-class consumers in these regions.

This book, then, has set out to broaden our understanding of working-class taste in 1930s Britain. There is little *direct* access to working-class consumers' feelings due to their lack of access to the printed media, so different interpretative skills are required of the cultural historian. My method, charting the relationship between the producer and the consumer, and establishing the booking practices of managers of cinemas in working-class areas and the acquisition policies of librarians, has allowed me to draw some representative maps of working-class taste. This has, in turn, allowed me to *speculate* on the meanings and significance of film and literature for working-class consumers

in the period. Clear patterns of taste are evident, and they illustrate that the specific social, political and economic circumstances of the working classes had a significant impact on their participation in both film and reading cultures. This has important implications for our understanding of the role of leisure in the 1930s. The interesting task now would be to see how such research methods would broaden our understanding of working-class taste in other historical periods. But that, of course, is an undertaking for another time.

Notes

1 Stephen Bayley, *Taste: The Secret Meaning of Things*, London, 1991, p. xviii.
2 Szanto, *Narrative Taste*, p. 155.
3 Bayley, *Taste*, p. xviii.

Appendix I:
Broader patterns of
film popularity

1930

Table I. Best British films of 1930, *Film Weekly*

Rank	Title (inc. year of release)
1	*Rookery Nook* (1930)
2	*Atlantic* (1929)
3	*White Cargo* (1929)
4	*Under the Greenwood Tree* (1929)
5	*Juno the Paycock* (1930)
6	*High Treason* (1928)
7	*The Hate Ship* (1929)
8	*Balaclava* (1928)
9	*Elstree Calling* (1930)
10	*Splinters* (1929)
11	*Alf's Button* (1930)
12	*At the Villa Rose* (1930)
13	*The Return of the Rat* (1929)
14	*Song of Soho* (1930)
15	*Piccadilly* (1929)
16	*The American Prisoner* (1929)
17	*Cottage on Dartmoor* (1929)
18	*The Manxman* (1929)
19	*The Informer* (1929)
20	*Taxi for Two* (1929)

Source: *Film Weekly*, 16 May 1931, p. 6.

Table 2. Best voices of the talkies, *Film Weekly*

Male	Female
Ronald Colman	Ruth Chatterton
Clive Brook	Norma Shearer
George Arliss	Gloria Swanson
John Boles	Betty Compson
William Powell	Janet Gaynor

Source: *Film Weekly*, 7 June 1930, p. 10.

Table 3. Films with the widest appeal in 1930, *Film Weekly*

Title (inc. year of release)
Atlantic (1929)*
The Big House (1930)
Bulldog Drummond (1929)
The Desert Song (1929)
The Four Feathers (1929)
Gold Diggers of Broadway (1929)
High Society Blues (1930)
The Love Parade (1929)
Raffles (1930)
Rio Rita (1929)
Romance of the Rio Grande (1929)
Rookery Nook (1930)*
Sunny Side Up (1929)

Source: *Film Weekly*, 27 December 1930, p. 9.
* denotes a British production

1931

Table 4. Most popular types of British film in 1931, *Film Weekly*

Rank	Genre	Film (represented by)
1	Comedy	*The Middle Watch* (1930)
2	Drama	*The Woman Between* (1931)
3	Bedroom Farce	*Almost a Honeymoon* (1930)
4	Melodrama	*The Man From Chicago* (1930)
5	Musical Comedy	*The Yellow Mask* (1930)
6	Farce	*Compromising Daphne* (1930)
7	Underworld Drama	*Night Birds* (1930)
8	Tragedy	*Cape Forlorn* (1931)
9	Child Picture	*The Black Hand Gang* (1930)
10	Victorian Comedy	*How He Lied to Her Husband* (1931)

Source: *Film Weekly*, 22 August 1931, p. 6.

Table 5. Best British films of 1931, *Film Weekly*

Rank	Title (inc. year of release)
1	*The Middle Watch* (1930)
2	*The Outsider* (1931)
3	*Young Woodley* (1930)
4	*Murder!* (1930)
5	*A Warm Corner* (1930)
6	*My Wife's Family* (1931)
7	*Loose Ends* (1930)
8	*Plunder* (1931)
9	*Tons of Money* (1930)
10	*The Chance of a Night-time* (1931)
11	*The Sleeping Cardinal* (1931)
12	*The 'W' Plan* (1931)
13	*On Approval* (1930)
14	*City of Song* (1931)
15	*The Skin Game* (1931)
16	*The Man from Chicago* (1930)
17	*Dreyfus* (1931)
18	*Tell England* (1931)
19	*Escape* (1930)
20	*The Sport of Kings* (1931)

Source: *Film Weekly*, 29 April 1932, p. 12.

Table 6. Best performance in a British film in 1931, *Film Weekly*

Rank	Performer	Title (inc. year of release)
1	Harold Huth	*The Outsider* (1931)
2	Edmund Gwenn	*The Skin Game* (1931)
3	Gordon Harker	*Third Time Lucky* (1931)
4	Adrianne Allen	*Loose Ends* (1930)
5	Herbert Marshall	*Murder!* (1930)
6	Cedric Hardwicke	*Dreyfus* (1931)
7	Madeleine Carroll	*Young Woodley* (1930)
8	Ralph Lynn	*The Chance of a Night-time* (1931)
9	Gene Gerrard	*My Wife's Family* (1931)
10	Frank Lawton	*Young Woodley* (1930)

Source: *Film Weekly*, 29 April 1932, p. 12.

Table 7. Most popular film stars in 1931, Bernstein questionnaire report

Rank	Male	Female
1	Ronald Colman	Norma Shearer
2	Clive Brook	Constance Bennett
3	George Arliss	Marie Dressler
4	Robert Montgomery	Ruth Chatterton
5	Maurice Chevalier	Janet Gaynor
6	John Boles	Greta Garbo
7	Ralph Lynn	Jeanette MacDonald
8	Tom Walls	Joan Crawford
9	William Powell	Ann Harding
10	Wallace Beery	Marlene Dietrich

Source: *Picturegoer*, 4 June 1932, p. 1.

1932

Table 8. Best British films of 1932, *Film Weekly*

Rank	Title (inc. year of release)
1	*Sunshine Susie* (1931)
2	*Service for Ladies* (1932)
3	*Michael and Mary* (1931)
4	*Jack's the Boy* (1932)
5	*The Faithful Heart* (1932)
6	*Hindle Wakes* (1931)
7	*Mr Bill the Conqueror* (1932)
8	*The Lodger* (1932)
9	*Thark* (1932)
10	*The Frightened Lady* (1932)
11	*The Ghost Train* (1931)
12	*After Office Hours* (1932)
13	*Carnival* (1931)
14	*Goodnight Vienna* (1932)
15	*The Calendar* (1931)
16	*Keepers of Youth* (1931)
17	*Looking on the Bright Side* (1932)
18	*Love on Wheels* (1932)
19	*Men Like These* (1931)
20	*A Night Like This* (1932)

Source: *Film Weekly*, 26 May 1933, p. 7.

Table 9. Best performance in a British film in 1932, *Film Weekly*

Rank	Performer	Title (inc. year of release)
1	Emlyn Williams	*The Frightened Lady* (1932)
2	Leslie Howard	*Service for the Ladies* (1932)
3	Herbert Marshall	*Michael and Mary* (1931)
4	Jack Hulbert	*Jack's the Boy* (1932)
5	Renate Muller	*Sunshine Susie* (1931)
6	Edna Best	*Michael and Mary* (1931)
7	Ivor Novello	*The Lodger* (1932)
8	Tom Walls	*Thark* (1932)
9	Edmund Gwenn	*Hindle Wakes* (1931)
10	Garry Marsh	*Keepers of Youth* (1931)

Source: *Film Weekly*, 26 May 1933, p. 7.

Table 10. Award of Merit 1932, *Picturegoer* – male stars

Rank	Star	Title (inc. year of release)
1	Ronald Colman	*Arrowsmith* (1931)
2	Ricardo Cortez	*The Melody of Life* (1932)
3	Fredric March	*Dr Jekyll and Mr Hyde* (1932)
4	Emlyn Williams	*The Frightened Lady* (1932)*
5	George Arliss	*The Silent Voice* (1932)
6	Herbert Marshall	*The Faithful Heart* (1932)*
7	Jack Hulbert	*Jack's the Boy* (1932)*
8	Wallace Beery	*Hell Divers* (1932)
9	Lowell Sherman	*What Price Hollywood?* (1932)
10	Walter Huston	*The Wet Parade* (1932)

Source: *Picturegoer*, 24 February 1934, pp. 10–11.

* denotes a British production

Table 11. Award of Merit 1932, *Picturegoer* – female stars

Rank	Star	Title (inc. year of release)
1	Marie Dressler	*Emma* (1932)
2	Barbara Stanwyck	*Forbidden* (1932)
3	Greta Garbo	*As You Desire Me* (1932)
4	Norma Shearer	*Private Lives* (1931)
5	Marlene Dietrich	*Shanghai Express* (1932)
6	Joan Crawford	*Letty Lynton* (1932)
7	Edna Best	*The Faithful Heart* (1932)*
8	Helen Hayes	*Lullaby* (1931)
9	Winifred Shotter	*Love Contract* (1932)*
10	Hertha Thiele	*Mädchen in Uniform* (1931)**

Source: *Picturegoer*, 24 February 1934, p. 10–11.

* denotes a British production **denotes a German production

1933

Table 12. Best British films of 1933, *Film Weekly*

Rank	Title (inc. year of release)
1	*I Was a Spy* (1933)
2	*The Good Companions* (1933)
3	*Rome Express* (1932)
4	*Soldiers of the King* (1933)
5	*Wedding Rehearsal* (1932)
6	*Bitter Sweet* (1933)
7	*Maid of the Mountains* (1932)
8	*Loyalties* (1933)
9	*This Week of Grace* (1933)
10	*Falling for You* (1933)

Source: *Film Weekly*, 4 May 1934, p. 9.

Table 13. Best performance in a British film in 1933, *Film Weekly*

Rank	Performer	Title (inc. year of release)
1	Madeleine Carroll	*I Was a Spy* (1933)
2	Conrad Veidt	*I Was a Spy* (1933)
3	Edmund Gwenn	*The Good Companions* (1933)
4	Cicely Courtneidge	*Soldiers of the King* (1933)
5	Basil Rathbone	*Loyalties* (1933)
6	Jessie Matthews	*The Good Companions* (1933)
7	Gracie Fields	*This Week of Grace* (1933)
8	Anna Neagle	*Bitter Sweet* (1933)
9	Matheson Lang	*Channel Crossing* (1933)
10	Cedric Hardwicke	*Rome Express* (1932)

Source: *Film Weekly*, 4 May 1934, p. 9.

Table 14. 'Principal picture successes' in 1933, *Film Weekly*

Title (inc. year of release)
Calvacade (1933)
Forty-Second Street (1933)
The Good Companions (1933)*
I Am a Fugitive from a Chain Gang (1932)
I Was a Spy (1933*)
King Kong (1933)

Maid of the Mountains (1932)*
The Private Life of Henry VIII (1933)*
Sleepless Nights (1932)*
Smilin' Through (1932)
Tell Me Tonight (1932)*

Source: *Film Weekly*, 29 December 1933, pp. 4–5.
* denotes a British production

Table 15. 'Big Money' stars in 1933, *Film Weekly*

Lionel Barrymore	Jan Kiepura
Wallace Beery	Charles Laughton
Madeleine Carroll	Jessie Matthews
Edmund Gwenn	Paul Muni
Jean Harlow	Spencer Tracy
Katharine Hepburn	Lee Tracy
Leslie Howard	Mae West

Source: *Film Weekly*, 29 December 1933, pp. 4–5.

Table 16. Award of Merit 1933, *Picturegoer* – male stars

Rank	Star	Title (inc. year of release)
1	Clive Brook	*Calvacade* (1933)
2	Ronald Colman	*Cynara* (1932)
3	Gary Cooper	*A Farewell to Arms* (1932)
4	Conrad Veidt	*I Was a Spy* (1933)*
5	Paul Muni	*I Am a Fugitive from a Chain Gang* (1932)
6	Leslie Howard	*Smilin' Through* (1932)
7	Walter Huston	*Gabriel Over the White House* (1933)
8	George Arliss	*The Working Man* (19323)
9	John Barrymore	*A Bill of Divorcement* (1932)
10	Edmund Gwenn	*The Good Companions* (1933)*

Source: *Picturegoer*, 28 April 1934, pp. 12–13.
* denotes a British production

Table 17. Award of Merit 1933, *Picturegoer* – female stars

Rank	Star	Title (inc. year of release)
1	Norma Shearer	*Smilin' Through* (1932)
2	Diana Wynyard	*Calvacade* (1933)
3	Madeleine Carroll	*I Was a Spy* (1933)*
4	Greta Garbo	*Grand Hotel* (1932)
5	Marlene Dietrich	*Blonde Venus* (1932)
6	Anna Neagle	*Bitter Sweet* (1933)*
7	Katharine Hepburn	*Christopher Strong* (1933)
8	Kay Francis	*One Way Passage* (1932)
9	Cicely Courtneidge	*Soldiers of the King* (1933)*
10	Sylvia Sidney	*Madame Butterfly* (1932)

Source: *Picturegoer*, 28 April 1934, pp. 12–13.

* denotes a British production

Table 18. Very good films in 1933, Bernstein questionnaire report

Rank	Title (inc. year of release)
1	*Calvacade* (1933)
2	*The Private Life of Henry VIII* (1933)*
3	*I Was a Spy* (1933)
4	*Tugboat Annie* (1933)
5	*The Kid from Spain* (1932)
6	*Voltaire* (1933)

Source: Bernstein questionnaire report, 1934, p. 18.

* denotes a British production

Table 19. Most popular film stars in 1933, Bernstein questionnaire report

Rank	Male	Female
1	George Arliss	Norma Shearer
2	Clark Gable	Marie Dressler
3	Wallace Beery	Greta Garbo
4	Clive Brook	Kay Francis
5	Robert Montgomery	Marlene Dietrich
6	Ronald Colman	Katharine Hepburn

Source: Bernstein questionnaire report, 1934, p. 1.

1934

Table 20. Best British films of 1934, *Film Weekly*

Rank	Title (inc. year of release)
1	*Blossom Time* (1934)
2	*The Private Life of Henry VIII* (1933)
3	*Evergreen* (1934)
4	*Catherine the Great* (1934)
5	*The Constant Nymph* (1933)
6	*Man of Aran* (1934)
7	*Little Friend* (1934)
8	*Friday the Thirteenth* (1933)
9	*Sorrell and Son* (1933)
10	*The Wandering Jew* (1933)

Source: *Film Weekly*, 5 April 1935, p. 11.

Table 21. Best performance in a British film in 1934, Film Weekly

Rank	Performer	Title (inc. year of release)
1	Charles Laughton	*The Private Life of Henry VIII* (1933)
2	Conrad Veidt	*The Wandering Jew* (1933)
3	Nova Pilbeam	*Little Friend* (1934)
4	Elisabeth Bergner	*Catherine the Great* (1934)
5	Jessie Matthews	*Evergreen* (1934)
6	Brian Aherne	*The Constant Nymph* (1933)
7	Victoria Hopper	*The Constant Nymph* (1933)
8	Richard Tauber	*Blossom Time* (1934)
9	Evelyn Laye	*Evensong* (1934)
10	H.B. Warner	*Sorrell and Son* (1933)

Source: *Film Weekly*, 5 April 1935, p. 11.

Table 22. Award of Merit 1934, *Picturegoer* – male stars

Rank	Star	Title (inc. year of release)
1	Clark Gable	*It Happened One Night* (1934)
2	William Powell	*The Thin Man* (1934)
3	Charles Laughton	*The Private Life of Henry VIII* (1933)*
4	Fredric March	*The Barretts of Wimpole Street* (1934)
5	George Arliss	*The House of Rothschild* (1934)
6	Charles Laughton	*The Barretts of Wimpole Street* (1934)

7	John Gilbert	*Queen Christina* (1934)
8	Conrad Veidt	*The Wandering Jew* (1933)*
9	Conrad Veidt	*Jew Süss* (1934)*
10	Leslie Howard	*Berkeley Square* (1933)

Source: *Picturegoer*, 15 June 1935, pp. 8–9.

* denotes a British production

Table 23. Award of Merit 1934, *Picturegoer* – female stars

Rank	Star	Title (inc. year of release)
1	Greta Garbo	*Queen Christina* (1934)
2	Norma Shearer	*The Barretts of Wimpole Street* (1934)
3	Nova Pilbeam	*Little Friend* (1934)*
4	Myrna Loy	*The Thin Man* (1934)
5	Claudette Colbert	*It Happened One Night* (1934)
6	Jessie Matthews	*Evergreen* (1934)*
7	Katharine Hepburn	*Little Women* (1933)
8	Margaret Sullavan	*Only Yesterday* (1933)
9	Elizabeth Bergner	*Catherine the Great* (1934)*
10	Maureen O'Sullivan	*The Barretts of Wimpole Street* (1934)

Source: *Picturegoer*, 15 June 1935, pp. 8–9.

* denotes a British production

1935

Table 24. Best British films of 1935, *Film Weekly*

Rank	Title (inc. year of release)
1	*The Thirty-Nine Steps* (1935)
2	*The Scarlet Pimpernel* (1935)
3	*Nell Gwynn* (1934)
4	*The Man Who Knew Too Much* (1934)
5	*Sanders of the River* (1935)
6	*Escape Me Never* (1935)
7	*The Clairvoyant* (1935)
8	*Jew Süss* (1934)
9	*Scrooge* (1935)
10	*Heart's Desire* (1935)

Source: *Film Weekly*, 2 May 1936, p. 15.

Table 25. Best performance in a British film in 1935, *Film Weekly*

Rank	Performer	Title (inc. year of release)
1	Elisabeth Bergner	*Escape Me Never* (1935)
2	Robert Donat	*The Thirty-Nine Steps* (1935)
3	Leslie Howard	*The Scarlet Pimpernel* (1935)
4	Anna Neagle	*Nell Gwynn* (1934)
5	Leslie Banks	*Sanders of the River* (1935)
6	Conrad Veidt	*Jew Süss* (1934)
7	Peter Lorre	*The Man Who Knew Too Much* (1934)
8	Claude Rains	*The Clairvoyant* (1935)
9	Peggy Ashcroft	*The Thirty-Nine Steps* (1935)
10	Raymond Massey	*The Scarlet Pimpernel* (1935)

Source: *Film Weekly*, 2 May 1936, p. 15.

Table 26. Award of Merit 1935, *Picturegoer* – male stars

Rank	Star	Title (inc. year of release)
1	Leslie Howard	*The Scarlet Pimpernel* (1935)*
2	Gary Cooper	*The Lives of a Bengal Lancer* (1935)
3	Robert Donat	*The Count of Monte Cristo* (1934)
4	Franchot Tone	*The Lives of a Bengal Lancer* (1935)
5	Robert Donat	*The Thirty-Nine Steps* (1935)*
6	Victor McLaglen	*The Informer* (1935)
7	Freddie Bartholomew	*David Copperfield* (1935)
=8	Clark Gable	*China Seas* (1935)
=8	Ronald Colman	*Clive of India* (1935)
9	Charles Laughton	*Ruggles of Red Gap* (1935)
10	W.C. Fields	*David Copperfield* (1935)

Source: *Picturegoer*, 8 August 1936, pp. 12–13.
* denotes a British production

Table 27. Award of Merit 1935, *Picturegoer* – female stars

Rank	Star	Title (inc. year of release)
1	Elisabeth Bergner	*Escape Me Never* (1935)
2	Greta Garbo	*The Painted Veil* (1934)
3	Katharine Hepburn	*The Little Minister* (1934)

4	Anna Neagle	*Nell Gwyn* (1934)*
5	Bette Davis	*Of Human Bondage* (1934)
6	Anne Shirley	*Anne of Green Gables* (1934)
7	Joan Crawford	*Forsaking All Others* (1934)
8	Miriam Hopkins	*Becky Sharpe* (1935)
9	Shirley Temple	*The Little Colonel* (1935)
=10	Claudette Colbert	*Private Worlds* (1935)
=10	Grace Moore	*One Night of Love* (1934)

Source: *Picturegoer*, 8 August 1936, pp. 12–13.

* denotes a British production

Table 28. Most popular British film actors in 1935,
Alexander Korda's national film ballot

Rank	Star(s)
1	Charles Laughton
2	George Arliss
3	Cedric Hardwicke
4	Robert Donat
5	Jack Hulbert
6	Leslie Howard
7	Tom Walls
8	Jack Buchanan
9	Gordon Harker
10	Conrad Veidt
11	Leslie Banks
12	Clive Brook

Source: *News Chronicle*, 7 November 1935.

1936

Table 29. Best British films of 1936, *Film Weekly*

Rank	Title (inc. year of release)
1	*The Ghost Goes West* (1935)
2	*Tudor Rose* (1936)
3	*Peg of Old Drury* (1935)
4	*The Passing of the Third Floor Back* (1935)
5	*Secret Agent* (1936)
6	*Turn of the Tide* (1935)

7	*Ourselves Alone* (1936)
8	*Rhodes of Africa* (1936)
9	*Things to Come* (1936)
10	*The Amateur Gentleman* (1936)

Source: *Film Weekly*, 8 May 1937, p. 11.

Table 30. Best performance in a British film in 1936, *Film Weekly*

Rank	Performer	Title (inc. year of release)
1	Nova Pilbeam	*Tudor Rose* (1936)
2	Robert Donat	*The Ghost Goes West* (1935)
3	Anna Neagle	*Peg of Old Drury* (1935)
4	Conrad Veidt	*The Passing of the Third Floor Back* (1935)
5	René Ray	*The Passing of the Third Floor Back* (1935)
6	Walter Huston	*Rhodes of Africa* (1936)
7	Peter Lorre	*The Secret Agent* (1936)
8	Oscar Homolka	*Rhodes of Africa* (1936)
9	Douglas Fairbanks Jr	*The Amateur Gentleman* (1936)
10	John Lodge	*Ourselves Alone* (1936)

Source: *Film Weekly*, 8 May 1937, p. 11.

Table 31. Award of Merit 1936, *Picturegoer* – male stars

Rank	Star	Title (inc. year of release)
1	Gary Cooper	*Mr Deeds Goes to Town* (1936)
2	Ronald Colman	*A Tale of Two Cities* (1935)
3	Robert Donat	*The Ghost Goes West* (1935)*
4	Errol Flynn	*Captain Blood* (1935)
5	Charles Laughton	*Mutiny on the Bounty* (1935)
6	Paul Muni	*The Story of Louis Pasteur* (1936)
7	Clark Gable	*Mutiny on the Bounty* (1935)
8	Spencer Tracy	*Fury* (1936)
9	Leslie Howard	*The Petrified Forest* (1936)
10	Fredric March	*The Dark Angel* (1935)

Source: *Picturegoer*, 12 March 1938, pp. 8–9.
*denotes a British production

Table 32. Award of Merit 1936, *Picturegoer* – female stars

Rank	Star	Title (inc. year of release)
1	Nova Pilbeam	*Tudor Rose* (1936)*
2	Greta Garbo	*Anna Karenina* (1935)
3	Bette Davis	*Dangerous* (1935)
=4	Claudette Colbert	*Under Two Flags* (1936)
=4	Merle Oberon	*The Dark Angel* (1935)
5	Marlene Dietrich	*Desire* (1936)
6	Anna Neagle	*Peg of Old Drury* (1935)*
7	Jean Arthur	*Mr Deeds Goes to Town* (1936)
8	Luise Rainer	*Escapade* (1935)
9	Jeanette MacDonald	*Rose Marie* (1936)
=10	Claudette Colbert	*She Married Her Boss* (1935)
=10	Katharine Hepburn	*Sylvia Scarlet* (1935)

Source: *Picturegoer*, 12 March 1938, pp. 8–9.

*denotes a British production

Table 33. 'Box Office Winners' in 1936, *Kinematograph Weekly*

Biggest money maker: *Mr Deeds Goes to Town*

Runner-up: *Mutiny on the Bounty*

Most popular British film: *The Ghost Goes West**

Most popular and consistent star: Shirley Temple

Other box office successes: *Rose Marie, Captain January, The Littlest Rebel, A Tale of Two Cities, Follow the Fleet, These Three, First A Girl*, Modern Times, Under Two Flags, It's Love Again*, The Secret Agent*, Queen of Hearts*, Come Out of the Pantry*, Boys Will Be Boys*, China Seas, Broadway Melody of 1936, She Married Her Boss, Ourselves Alone, Living Dangerously, Anna Karenina, I Give My Heart*, The Dark Angel*

Source: *Kinematograph Weekly*, 14 January 1937, p. 40A.

* denotes a British production

Table 34. 'The British All-Star Money Makers of 1936',
International Motion Picture Almanac

Rank	Star(s)
1	Shirley Temple
2	Fred Astaire/Ginger Rogers
3	Gracie Fields
4	Clark Gable
5	Laurel and Hardy
6	Jessie Matthews
7	James Cagney
8	Wallace Beery
9	Greta Garbo
10	Norma Shearer

Source: *International Motion Picture Almanac*, 1937–1938, p. 1093.

Table 35. Most popular film stars in 1936, Bernstein questionnaire report

Rank	Male	Female
1	Gary Cooper	Norma Shearer
2	Clark Gable	Myrna Loy
3	Charles Laughton	Greta Garbo
4	Robert Taylor	Ginger Rogers
5	Ronald Colman	Claudette Colbert
6	William Powell	Shirley Temple

Source: Bernstein questionnaire report, 1937, p. 1.

Table 36. 'Outstanding' films in Bernstein questionnaire report

Rank	Title (inc. year of release)
1	*Mutiny on the Bounty* (1935)
2	*The Lives of a Bengal Lancer* (1935)
3	*Mr Deeds Goes to Town* (1936)
4	*Under Two Flags* (1936)
5	*David Copperfield* (1935)
6	*Captain Blood* (1935)

Source: Bernstein questionnaire report, 1937, p. 29.

1937

Table 37. 'Box Office Winners' in 1937, *Kinematograph Weekly*

Biggest money maker: *Lost Horizon*

Most successful output: MGM

Most popular and consistent star: Shirley Temple

Winning British stars: Gracie Fields, George Formby

January: *San Francisco, Windbag the Sailor, Anthony Adverse, Showboat*

February: *Gorgeous Hussy, Sabotage*, My Man Godfrey, Dodsworth, Charlie Chan at the Race Track, His Lordship**

March: *The Great Ziegfeld, Romeo and Juliet, Dimples, Keep Your Seats Please*, Craig's Wife*

April: *Libelled Lady, Good Morning, Boys*, Dishonour Bright, The General Died at Dawn, Love on the Run, The Great Barrier*, Theodora Goes Wild*

May: *Three Smart Girls, Come and Get It, Cain and Mabel, Banjo on My Knee**

June: *The Plainsman, Charlie Chan at the Opera, Love From a Stranger**

July: *Jungle Princess, Espionage*, Feather Your Nest*, Black Legion, The Magnificent Brute*

August: *Wings of the Morning*, Stowaway, One in a Million, Dark Journey*, Man in Possession*

September: *After the Thin Man, Camille, King Solomon's Mines*, Elephant Boy*, A Day at the Races, Lloyds of London, On the Avenue, Shall We Dance, The Charge of the Light Brigade*

October: *Lost Horizon, The Frog*, They Gave Him a Gun, Seventh Heaven, Maytime*

November: *Night Must Fall, I Met Him in Paris, Charlie Chan at the Olympics, His Affair, Saratoga, Storm in a Teacup*, Under the Red Robe*

December: *Victoria the Great*, Wee Willie Winkie, Tarzan and the Green Goddess, Captains Courageous*

Source: *Kinematograph Weekly*, 13 January 1938, p. 49.

* denotes a British production

Table 38. Best British films of 1937, *Film Weekly*

Rank	Title (inc. year of release)
1	*Victoria the Great* (1937)
2	*Wings of the Morning* (1937)
3	*Farewell Again* (1937)
4	*Fire Over England* (1937)
5	*Storm in a Teacup* (1937)

6	*Love from a Stranger* (1936)	
7	*Elephant Boy* (1937)	
8	*The Great Barrier* (1937)	
9	*Rembrandt* (1936)	
10	*Dark Journey* (1937)	

Source: *Film Weekly*, 2 July 1938, p. 5.

Table 39. Best performance in a British film in 1937, *Film Weekly* – actors

Rank	Performer	Title (inc. year of release)
1	Anton Walbrook	*Victoria the Great* (1937)
2	Basil Rathbone	*Love from a Stranger* (1936)
3	Charles Laughton	*Rembrandt* (1936)
4	Rex Harrison	*Storm in a Teacup* (1937)
5	Conrad Veidt	*Dark Journey* (1937)
6	Laurence Olivier	*Fire Over England* (1937)
7	Leslie Banks	*Farewell Again* (1937)
8	John Lodge	*Sensation* (1936)
9	Sabu	*Elephant Boy* (1937)
10	Emlyn Williams	*Broken Blossoms* (1936)

Source: *Film Weekly*, 2 July 1938, p. 5.

Table 40. Best performance in a British film in 1937, *Film Weekly* – actresses

Rank	Performer	Title (inc. year of release)
1	Flora Robson	*Fire Over England* (1937)
2	Anna Neagle	*Victoria the Great* (1937)
3	Annabella	*Wings of the Morning* (1937)
4	Diana Churchill	*The Dominant Sex* (1937)
5	Ann Harding	*Love from a Stranger* (1936)
6	Dolly Haas	*Broken Blossoms* (1936)
7	Vivien Leigh	*Storm in a Teacup* (1937)
8	Elisabeth Bergner	*Dreaming Lips* (1937)
9	Miriam Hopkins	*Men Are Not Gods* (1936)
10	Sylvia Sidney	*Sabotage* (1936)

Source: *Film Weekly*, 2 July 1938, p. 5.

Table 41. Award of Merit 1937, *Picturegoer* – male stars

Rank	Star	Title (inc. year of release)
1	Spencer Tracy	*Captains Courageous* (1937)
2	Anton Walbrook	*Victoria the Great* (1937)*
3	Ronald Colman	*Lost Horizon* (1937)
4	Errol Flynn	*The Charge of the Light Brigade* (1936)
5	Leslie Howard	*Romeo and Juliet* (1936)
6	Gary Cooper	*The Plainsman* (1936)
7	Robert Montgomery	*Night Must Fall* (1937)
8	Spencer Tracy	*San Francisco* (1936)
9	Clark Gable	*San Francisco* (1936)
10	Robert Taylor	*Camille* (1937)

Source: *Picturegoer*, 14 May 1938, pp. 10–11.

* denotes a British production

Table 42. Award of Merit 1937, *Picturegoer* – female stars

Rank	Star	Title (inc. year of release)
1	Anna Neagle	*Victoria the Great* (1937)*
2	Greta Garbo	*Camille* (1937)
3	Norma Shearer	*Romeo and Juliet* (1936)
4	Deanna Durbin	*Three Smart Girls* (1936)
5	Jeanette MacDonald	*Maytime* (1937)
6	Flora Robson	*Fire Over England* (1937)
7	Annabella	*Wings of the Morning* (1937)*
8	Irene Dunne	*Theodora Goes Wild* (1936)
9	Luise Rainer	*The Great Ziegfeld* (1936)
10	Katharine Hepburn	*Quality Street* (1937)

Source: *Picturegoer*, 14 May 1938, pp. 10–11.

* denotes a British production

1938

Table 43. 'Box Office Winners' in 1938, *Kinematograph Weekly*

Biggest money maker: *Snow White and the Seven Dwarfs*

Runner-up: *A Yank at Oxford**, *Captains Courageous*

Most popular and consistent star: Shirley Temple

Most successful output: MGM

Winning British stars: George Formby, Gracie Fields

January: *A Star is Born, The Good Earth, Oh, Mr Porter*, Knight Without Armour*, Kid Galahad, Big City, Way Out West*

February: *Firefly, Keep Fit*, Souls at Sea, Stella Dallas, Dr Syn*, The Squeaker**

March: *The Prisoner of Zenda, One Hundred Men and a Girl, Ali Baba Goes to Town, Stage Door, Leave it to Me*, The Rat*, Non-Stop New York**

April: *Marie Walewska, Dead End, The Awful Truth, Heidi, The Return of the Scarlet Pimpernel*, Angel*

May: *Wells Fargo, The Last Gangster, Dead Men Tell No Tales*, Submarine DI, Man Proof, Alcatraz Island*

June: *Bad Men of Brimstone, Damsels in Distress, You're a Sweetheart, Tarzan's Revenge, Mademoiselle Docteur**

July: *I See Ice*, The Buccaneer, Boy of the Streets*

August: *Rebecca of Sunnybrook Farm, The Housemaster*, Vessel of Wrath*, South Riding*, Owd Bob*, A Slight Case of Murder, Mannequin, The Baroness and the Butler*

September: *Snow White and the Seven Dwarfs, A Yank at Oxford*, The Hurricane, Mad About Music, Test Pilot, Convict 99*, Tovarich, Bluebeard's Eighth Wife, The Girl of the Golden West*

October: *The Drum*, Alf's Button Afloat*, In Old Chicago, Three Comrades, Joy of Living, The Terror**

November: *The Crowd Roars, Blockade, The Adventures of Marco Polo, The Boy From Barnardo's, There's Always a Woman, Vivacious Lady*

December: *Sixty Glorious Years*, Little Miss Broadway, Hey! Hey! U.S.A.!*, Three Men and a Girl, Spawn of the North, Love Finds Andy Hardy, Crime School, This Man is News*, Sing You Sinners*

Source: *Kinematograph Weekly*, 12 January 1939, p. 61.

* denotes a British production

Table 44. Best British films of 1938, *Film Weekly*

Rank	Title (inc. year of release)
1	*Pygmalion* (1938)
2	*Sixty Glorious Years* (1938)
3	*South Riding* (1938)
4	*The Lady Vanishes* (1938)
5	*A Yank at Oxford* (1937)
6	*The Drum* (1938)
7	*Bank Holiday* (1938)
8	*The Housemaster* (1938)
9	*The Edge of the World* (1937)
10	*This Man is News* (1938)

Source: *Film Weekly*, 24 June 1939, p. 5.

Table 45. Best performance in a British film in 1938, *Film Weekly* – actors

Rank	Performer	Title (inc. year of release)
1	Ralph Richardson	*South Riding* (1938)
2	Leslie Howard	*Pygmalion* (1938)
3	Will Fyffe	*Owd Bob* (1938)
4	Otto Kruger	*The Housemaster* (1938)
5	Anton Walbrook	*Sixty Glorious Years* (1938)
6	Barry K. Barnes	*This Man is News* (1938)
7	Robert Taylor	*A Yank at Oxford* (1937)
8	Charles Laughton	*Vessel of Wrath* (1938)
9	Emlyn Williams	*Dead Men Tell No Tales* (1938)
10	Laurence Olivier	*The Divorce of Lady X* (1938)

Source: *Film Weekly*, 24 June 1939, p. 5.

Table 46. Best performance in a British film in 1938, *Film Weekly* –
actresses

Rank	Performer	Title (inc. year of release)
1	Wendy Hiller	*Pygmalion* (1938)
2	Anna Neagle	*Sixty Glorious Years* (1938)
3	Margaret Lockwood	*Bank Holiday* (1938)
4	Edna Best	*South Riding* (1938)
5	Nova Pilbeam	*Young and Innocent* (1937)

6	Elsa Lanchester	*Vessel of Wrath* (1938)
7	Valerie Hobson	*This Man is News* (1938)
8	Diana Churchill	*The Housemaster* (1938)
9	Vivien Leigh	*A Yank at Oxford* (1937)
10	May Whitty	*The Lady Vanishes* (1938)

Source: *Film Weekly*, 24 June 1939, p. 5.

Table 47. Award of Merit 1938, *Picturegoer* – male stars

Rank	Star	Title (inc. year of release)
1	Charles Boyer	*Marie Walewska* (1937)
2	Spencer Tracy	*Test Pilot* (1938)
3	Robert Taylor	*A Yank at Oxford* (1937)*
4	Ronald Colman	*The Prisoner of Zenda* (1937)
5	Fredric March	*A Star is Born* (1937)
6	Paul Muni	*The Life of Emile Zola* (1937)
7	Anton Walbrook	*Sixty Glorious Years* (1938)*
8	Barry K. Barnes	*This Man is News* (1938)*
9	Clark Gable	*Test Pilot* (1938)
10	Franchot Tone	*Three Comrades* (1938)

Source: *Picturegoer*, 6 May 1939, pp. 8–9.
* denotes a British production

Table 48. Award of Merit 1938, *Picturegoer* – female stars

Rank	Star	Title (inc. year of release)
1	Margaret Sullavan	*Three Comrades* (1938)
2	Greta Garbo	*Marie Walewska* (1937)
3	Bette Davis	*Jezebel* (1938)
4	Deanna Durbin	*Mad About Music* (1938)
5	Anna Neagle	*Sixty Glorious Years* (1938)*
6	Luise Rainer	*The Good Earth* (1937)
7	Katharine Hepburn	*Stage Door* (1937)
8	Deanna Durbin	*One Hundred Men and a Girl* (1937)
9	Janet Gaynor	*A Star is Born* 1937)
10	Alice Faye	*In Old Chicago* (1938)

Source: *Picturegoer*, 6 May 1939, pp. 8–9.
* denotes a British production

1939

Table 49. 'Box Office Winners' in 1939, *Kinematograph Weekly*

Biggest money maker: *The Citadel**, *The Lion Has Wings**

Most popular and consistent star: Deanna Durbin

Most successful output: MGM

Winning British stars: Gracie Fields, George Formby

Biggest all-time turn-up: *Pygmalion**

January: *Pygmalion**, *The Adventures of Robin Hood**, *That Certain Age*, *The Amazing Doctor Clitterhouse*, *Too Hot to Handle*, *Alexander's Ragtime Band*, *The Lady Vanishes**, *St. Martins' Lane**

February: *It's in the Air*, *Boys Town*, *Marie Antoinette*, *Stablemates*, *Yellow Sands**, *Carefree*, *If I Were King*, *I am the Law*

March: *The Citadel**, *You Can't Take it with You*, *Keep Smiling*, *Thanks for the Memory*, *Old Bones of the River**, *Suez*, *Submarine Patrol*, *Racket Busters*, *Men with Wings*, *Young in Heart*, *Four Daughters*, *The Return of the Frog**

April: *The Dawn Patrol*, *Out West with the Hardies*, *The Great Waltz*, *The Cowboy and the Lady*, *Kentucky*, *Stolen Life**, *Just Around the Corner*

May: *Stand Up and Fight*, *Sweethearts*, *The Ware Case**, *Young Dr Kildare*, *Angels with Dirty Faces*, *Four's a Crowd*, *Trade Winds*, *Service de Luxe*

June: *Topper Takes a Tip*, *The Sisters*, *They Made Me a Criminal*, *Honolulu*, *Storm Over Bengal*

July: *Trouble Brewing**, *The Adventures of Huckleberry Finn*, *Wings of the Navy*, *Tailspin*, *Fast and Loose*

August: *Love Affair*, *Oklahoma Kid*, *Captain Fury*, *Q Planes**, *Sergeant Madden*, *The Little Princess*, *East Side of Heaven*, *Jesse James*, *The Outsider**, *Ask a Policeman**

September: *The Four Feathers**, *Idiot's Delight*, *Ice Follies*, *Made for Each Other*, *The Hound of the Baskervilles*, *The Face at the Window**

October: *Gunga Din*, *Three Smart Girls Grow Up*, *The Hardy's Ride High*, *The Story of Irene and Vernon Castle*, *Dark Victory*, *Beau Gate*, *Stagecoach*, *Jamaica Inn**, *The Mikado**

November: *The Lion Has Wings**, *Goodbye Mr Chips,**, *Shipyard Sally**, *Confessions of a Nazi Spy*, *Dodge City*, *Union Pacific*, *Nurse Edith Cavell**, *Wuthering Heights*, *Calling Dr Kildare*, *It's a Wonderful World*, *Only Angels Have Wings*, *The Four Just Men**

December: *Tarzan Finds a Son*, *Andy Hardy Gets Spring Fever*, *Man of Conquest*, *Under Pup*, *Stanley and Livingstone*, *This Man in Paris**, *Man About Town*, *The Sun Never Sets*, *Spies of the Air**, *Five Came Back*

Source: *Kinematograph Weekly*, 11 January 1940, p. E1.

* denotes a British production

Table 50. Award of Merit 1939, *Picturegoer and Film Weekly* – male stars

Rank	Star	Title (inc. year of release)
1	Robert Donat	*Goodbye Mr Chips* (1939)*
2	Laurence Olivier	*Wuthering Heights* (1939)
3	Ralph Richardson	*The Four Feathers* (1939)*
4	Charles Boyer	*Love Affair* (1939)
5	Errol Flynn	*The Dawn Patrol* (1938)
6	David Niven	*The Dawn Patrol* (1938)
7	Spencer Tracy	*Boys' Town* (1938)
8	Conrad Veidt	*The Spy in Black* (1939)*
9	Leslie Howard	*Pygmalion* (1938)*
10	Kenny Baker	*The Mikado* (1939)*

Source: *Picturegoer*, 18 May 1940, pp. 12–13.
* denotes a British production

Table 51. Award of Merit 1939, *Picturegoer and Film Weekly* – female stars

Rank	Star	Title (inc. year of release)
1	Bette Davis	*Dark Victory* (1939)
2	Wendy Hiller	*Pygmalion* (1938)*
3	Deanna Durbin	*Three Smart Girls Grow Up* (1939)
4	Merle Oberon	*Wuthering Heights* (1939)
5	Elisabeth Bergner	*A Stolen Life* (1939)*
6	Anna Neagle	*Nurse Edith Cavell* (1939)*
7	Greer Garson	*Goodbye Mr Chips* (1939)*
8	Norma Shearer	*Marie Antoinette* (1938)
9	Irene Dunne	*Love Affair* (1939)
10	Claire Trevor	*Stagecoach* (1939)

Source: *Picturegoer*, 18 May 1940, pp. 12–13.
* denotes a British production

Table 52. 'The British All-Star Money Makers of 1939',

International Motion Picture Almanac

Rank	Stars	British stars	'Western' moneymakers
1	Deanna Durbin	George Formby	Bill Boyd
2	Mickey Rooney	Gracie Fields	Gene Autry
3	Shirley Temple	Robert Donat	Dick Foran
4	Robert Taylor	Will Hay	George O'Brien
5	Jeanette MacDonald	Anna Neagle	Buck Jones
6	Spencer Tracy	Leslie Howard	Ken Maynard
7	Errol Flynn	Charles Laughton	The Three Mesquiteers
8	George Formby	Gordon Harker	Tim McCoy
9	Nelson Eddy	Ralph Richardson	Bob Baker
10	Gary Cooper	Will Fyffe	Tex Ritter

Source: *International Motion Picture Almanac*, 1940–1941, pp. 834–835.

Appendix II:
Sidney Bernstein questionnaires, 1932 and 1934
Pre-report material

Source: Sidney Berstein Collection, Special Collections, British Film Institute, London

Table I. Favourite male film stars, 1932: class comparison

Rank	Working-class votes	Middle-class votes	Rank
1	Ronald Colman	Ronald Colman	1
2	George Arliss	Clive Brook	2
3	Clive Brook	George Arliss	3
4	Robert Montgomery	Maurice Chevalier	4
5	John Boles	Robert Montgomery	5
6	Maurice Chevalier	John Boles	6
7	Jack Holt	Ralph Lynn	7
8	Charles Farrell	Tom Walls	8
9	Tom Walls	William Powell	9
10	William Powell	George Bancroft	10
11	Ralph Lynn	Wallace Beery	11
12	Lew Stone	Gary Cooper	12
13	Wallace Beery	Lew Stone	13
14	Ramon Novarro	Ramon Novarro	14
15	Jack Buchanan	Jack Holt	15
16	George Bancroft	Charles Farrell	16
17	Gary Cooper	Walter Huston	17
18	Walter Huston	Jack Buchanan	18

Table 2. Favourite female film stars, 1932: class comparison

Rank	Working-class votes	Middle-class votes	Rank
1	Norma Shearer	Norma Shearer	1
2	Constance Bennett	Marie Dressler	2
3	Marie Dressler	Constance Bennett	3
4	Ruth Chatterton	Ruth Chatterton	4
5	Janet Gaynor	Janet Gaynor	5
6	Joan Crawford	Jeanette MacDonald	6
7	Greta Garbo	Greta Garbo	7
8	Jeanette MacDonald	Ann Harding	8
9	Ann Harding	Joan Crawford	9
10	Marlene Dietrich	Marlene Dietrich	10
11	Madeleine Carroll	Madeleine Carroll	11
12	Kay Francis	Kay Francis	12

Table 3. All-time favourite films, 1932: class comparison

Rank	Working-class votes	Middle-class votes	Rank
1	*Ben-Hur*	*Ben-Hur*	1
2	*The Hunchback of Notre Dame*	*The Four Horsemen of the Apocalypse*	2
3	*The Four Horsemen of the Apocalypse*	*Seventh Heaven*	3
4	*Seventh Heaven*	*Beau Geste*	4
5	*Beau Geste*	*The Hunchback of Notre Dame*	5
6	*Over the Hill*	*Way Down East*	6
7	*The Kid*	*The Ten Commandments*	7
8	*The Covered Wagon*	*The Gold Rush*	8
9	*Way Down East*	*Sorrell and Son*	9
10	*The Ten Commandments*	*The Kid*	10
11	*The Gold Rush*	*The Covered Wagon*	11
12	*Sorrell and Son*	*Orphans of the Storm*	12
13	*Vaudeville*	*Scaramouche*	13
14	*Metropolis*	*The Sheik*	14
15	*Birth of a Nation*	*Smilin' Through*	15
16	*Broken Blossoms*	*Vaudeville*	16
17	*The Sheik*	*Shoulder Arms*	17
18	*Orphans of the Storm*	*Metropolis*	18
19	*Shoulder Arms*	*Over the Hill*	19
20	*Scaramouche*	*The Merry Widow*	20
21	*The Merry Widow*	*Birth of a Nation*	21
22	*Smilin' Through*	*Broken Blossoms*	22

Table 4. Attendances sheet, 'working-class' cinemas, 1932
(numbers in parentheses refer to 'wandering public')

Title	Edmonton Empire	West Ham Kinema	East Ham Rialto	Plumstead Kinema	Shrewsbury King's
Warm Corner	(47)	(35)	3917* (76)	(48)	3057* (28)
Canaries Sometimes Sing	(45)	(35)	(64)	3781* (64)	9598 (56)
Reducing	6513* (71)	6510* (50)	9894* (95)	4923* (90)	(42)
Madame Satan	6976* (56)	7016* (42)	3883* (60)	4622++ (69)	(42)
Almost a Honeymoon	5605* (54)	(36)	(72)	(53)	(39)
Africa Speaks	5945* (56)	(57)	(83)	4068* (15)	(45)
Hook, Line and Sinker	(35)	7798* (40)	6620* (81)	(50)	3782* (33)
Sin Takes a Holiday	7204* (56)	(40)	(54)	4642* (71)	(30)
The Sleeping Cardinal	(18)	7443* (36)	4414* (45)	4195* (37)	3715* (26)
Dracula	8602* (62)	(65)	(87)	6107* (83)	3624* (38)
The Middle Watch	(45)	5532* (46)	5153* (75)	(39)	(10)
Plunder	15231 (72)	(46)	(76)	11732 (85)	(50)
The Man Who Came Back	(41)	10272* (48)	8935* (76)	(67)	(37)
Charley's Aunt	15175 (91)	(61)	(92)	11744 (82)	(56)
Inspiration	6841* (52)	9237* (43)	(42)	5471* (65)	4178* (37)
Yankee at King Arthur's Court	(27)	7506* (44)	(59)	(16)	4242* (33)
Min and Bill	15592 (94)	6301* (73)	5844* (111)	12544 (98)	(42)
Viennese Nights	(33)	4190* (32)	8192* (60)	(57)	4324* (44)
Monte Carlo	11953 (76)	(60)	(69)	9753 (93)	(39)
Dance, Fools, Dance	(40)	6222* (56)	(50)	6279* (70)	3567* (36)
Cimarron	(41)	(27)	(56)	(74)	3455* (30)
New Moon	5256* (39)	7704* (37)	(40)	(67)	(36)
P.C. Josser	(22)	7484* (44)	8491* (71)	(48)	(33)
Animal Crackers	(37)	(29)	(57)	(24)	(4)
Tons of Money	12863 (80)	(57)	(84)	9382 (91)	(58)
Resurrection	12576 (65)	7194* (45)	5481 * (67)	(42)	3095* (33)
The Woman Between	(15)	4196* (17)	(56)	(19)	3434* (22)
Hell's Angels	16652 (86)	(75)	(97)	13603 (110)	(56)
East Lynne	(46)	6931* (58)	5191* (78)	(48)	(41)

Title	Edmonton Empire	West Ham Kinema	East Ham Rialto	Plumstead Kinema	Shrewsbury King's
Feet First	(51)	(34)	5374* (95)	(74)	(37)
City of Song	(7)	(36)	(35)	4165* (66)	(35)
Sports of Kings	12576 (67)	(34)	(43)	4956* (68)	(43)
The Criminal Code	(27)	(35)	(65)	(19)	1849* (4)
Tom Sawyer	(41)	(40)	5831* (75)	4893* (66)	3338* (35)
One Heavenly Night	11399 (72)	(60)	(70)	9426 (98)	(45)
Born to Love	12771 (78)	10367* (62)	(52)	(65)	(41)
Trader Horn	16583 (89)	5729* (74)	4665* (112)	13418 (98)	(46)
City Lights	17479 (79)	8588 (67)	4263* (76)	13268 (100)	5631 (57)
Devil to Pay	13728 (76)	(60)	(74)	10781 (93)	(43)
Jail Birds	(38)	9313* (51)	6758* (74)	6097* (85)	4494* (49)
Sous Les Toits de Paris	(16)	(14)	(16)	(12)	(4)
Hallelujah	(29)	(9)	(12)	(12)	(4)
Loose Ends	(21)	7805* (37)	6653* (58)	(36)	(33)
Blue Angel	(39)	(23)	(57)	(50)	(10)
King of Jazz	(54)	(49)	(72)	(67)	(16)
The Dawn Patrol	14329 (73)	9127* (61)	6410* (100)	12782 (92)	(49)
Whoopee!	16257 (77)	(55)	(85)	14851 (99)	(43)
Raffle	12311 (70)	1724+ (50)	1750+ (82)	10107 (83)	(46)
Strangers May Kiss	11854 (83)	(54)	(67)	4387* (97)	(50)

Note: + one day; ++ two days; * three days; others six days

Table 5. Attendances sheet, 'middle-class' cinemas, 1932
(numbers in parentheses refer to 'wandering public')

Title	Tooting Granada	Willesden Empire	Enfield Rialto	Waltham-stow Granada	Leyton-stone Rialto	Shrews-bury Empire
Warm Corner	4234+ (234)	8659* (233)	13139 (99)	(222)	8795* (138)	(60)
Canaries Sometimes Sing	(174)	7811* (250)	(67)	(257)	9158* (145)	(102)
Reducing	(248)	8691* (275)	6690* (86)	23669 (444)	19922 (193)	9051 (94)
Madame Satan	(194)	7766* (212)	4475* (61)	23236 (310)	6881* (115)	10141 (85)
Almost a Honey-moon	(201)	(191)	6990* (84)	(221)	10224* (125)	8908 (95)
Africa Speaks	(206)	13685* (277)	3746* (100)	(264)	15568 (162)	10125 (92)
Hook, Line and Sinker	(178)	9768* (192)	(34)	(176)	(56)	(45)
Sin Takes a Holiday	(183)	9401* (227)	4160* (73)	24450 (293)	7622* (107)	5783 (63)
The Sleeping Cardinal	(82)	(68)	5165* (51)	(107)	(29)	(34)
Dracula	(229)	11293* (270)	11044 (95)	(293)	10632* (148)	(60)
The Middle Watch	(208)	(187)	(62)	(218)	(92)	(25)
Plunder	4062+ (247)	19740 (305)	15610 (125)	31321 (417)	21308 (183)	9085 (99)
The Man Who Came Back	(149)	(197)	7197* (74)	30353 (294)	(76)	8471 (65)
Charley's Aunt	(272)	17299 (320)	13760 (94)	27892 (400)	10801* (157)	11405 (94)
Inspiration	(167)	(121)	(63)	24102 (313)	9301* (120)	(59)
Yankee at King Arthur's Court	(289)	(247)	(50)	(213)	(67)	(76)
Min and Bill	(284)	19777 (355)	13145 (116)	32153 (441)	18657 (203)	10010 (92)
Viennese Nights	(156)	9076* (146)	(25)	(199)	(80)	(60)
Monte Carlo	31920 (309)	14216 (300)	11095 (108)	(279)	16539 (181)	9960 (95)
Dance, Fools, Dance	(180)	8101* (221)	(30)	(205)	9942* (143)	(49)
Cimarron	(207)	(226)	(71)	(220)	(84)	(48)

Title	Tooting Granada	Willesden Empire	Enfield Rialto	Waltham- stow Granada	Leyton- stone Rialto	Shrews- bury Empire
New Moon	(120)	7458* (197)	5165* (48)	38085 (327)	(49)	9553 (62)
P.C. Josser	4272+ (166)	(88)	(41)	24102 (303)	(52)	10029 (70)
The Last Parade	(121)	14017 (248)	7008* (69)	(161)	17582 (136)	(42)
Animal Crackers	(142)	(129)	(47)	15574 (324)	(65)	(13)
Tons of Money	4125+ (233)	15488 (337)	14317 (133)	26662 (421)	17582 (191)	10635 (112)
Resurrection	(146)	19500 (270)	14317 (96)	(164)	18711 (163)	(45)
The Woman Between	(39)	(91)	(21)	(67)	(42)	(41)
Hell's Angels	31648 (359)	17292 (357)	13371 (117)	30525 (403)	18388 (202)	12637 (92)
East Lynne	40774 (310)	(242)	(60)	(287)	(98)	8728 (87)
Feet First	37795 (299)	(171)	(82)	(251)	(87)	8437 (80)
City of Song	(131)	(120)	(44)	15574 (236)	(34)	7279 (61)
Sports of Kings	3750+ (137)	14017 (286)	12682 (101)	21516 (333)	18738 (171)	8477 (101)
The Criminal Code	37795 (262)	(180)	(38)	(179)	(32)	(10)
Tom Sawyer	42385 (294)	7074* (226)	12682 (100)	(197)	(31)	(46)
One Heavenly Night	(230)	10038* (276)	11573 (108)	(307)	15380 (192)	10442 (102)
Born to Love	42385 (284)	(219)	(72)	(260)	18736 (161)	8026 (77)
Trader Horn	(269)	20639 (354)	14891 (128)	34549 (423)	24811 (210)	11236 (90)
City Lights	44312 (320)	(284)	6051* (119)	35386 (412)	22709 (198)	16228 (106)
Devil to Pay	30971 (264)	19497 (317)	11285 (112)	30151 (435)	18711 (197)	11834 (86)
Jail Birds	44312 (323)	20615 (322)	13362 (114)	29523 (379)	20005 (189)	(56)
Sous Les Toits de Paris	(63)	(73)	(26)	(14)	(45)	(12)
Hallelujah	(40)	(55)	10918 (68)	(45)	(17)	(11)

Title	Tooting Granada	Willesden Empire	Enfield Rialto	Waltham-stow Granada	Leyton-stone Rialto	Shrews-bury Empire
Loose Ends	(131)	(123)	(25)	(149)	(36)	8942 (79)
Blue Angel	(176)	(184)	7193* (85)	(212)	(92)	(26)
King of Jazz	(302)	(285)	(97)	(334)	(131)	(34)
The Dawn Patrol	(226)	6241++ (306)	(69)	3213+ (338)	14705 (162)	9041 (84)
Whoopee!	(249)	18899 (328)	13927 (93)	(301)	18053 (178)	9805 (86)
Raffles	(259)	16225 (290)	12833 (103)	24767 (366)	16764 (167)	10334 (102)
Strangers May Kiss	(205)	8300* (289)	10658 (141)	28263 (459)	9274* (187)	7979 (99)

Note: + one day; ++ two days; * three days; others six days

Table 6. Film dislikes, 1932

Title	Seen		Disliked		Percentages	
	m	f	m	f	m	f
Warm Corner	570	660	40	62	7.0	9.4
Canaries Sometimes Sing	580	679	94	77	16.2	11.3
Reducing	708	980	62	78	8.8	8.0
Madame Satan	526	724	100	110	19.0	15.2
Almost a Honeymoon	520	641	89	116	17.1	18.1
Africa Speaks	676	741	69	50	10.2	6.7
Hook, Line and Sinker	468	452	109	104	23.2	23.0
Sin Takes a Holiday	461	736	113	145	24.5	19.7
The Sleeping Cardinal	269	264	41	36	15.2	13.6
Dracula	737	743	225	252	30.5	33.9
The Middle Watch	470	537	73	68	15.5	12.7
Plunder	797	908	38	69	4.8	7.6
The Man Who Came Back	433	691	145	237	33.5	34.3
Charley's Aunt	776	943	123	119	15.9	12.6
Inspiration	401	681	110	150	27.4	22.0
Yankee at King Arthur's Court	556	565	86	115	15.5	20.4
Min and Bill	868	1041	47	61	5.4	5.9
Viennese Nights	348	544	28	32	8.0	5.9
Monte Carlo	720	879	117	131	16.3	14.9
Dance, Fools, Dance	456	624	60	79	13.2	12.7
Cimarron	554	530	54	60	9.7	11.3
New Moon	415	607	77	114	18.6	18.8

Title	Seen		Disliked		Percentages	
	m	f	m	f	m	f
The Last Parade	461	515	32	55	6.9	10.7
Animal Crackers	421	450	147	215	34.9	47.8
Tons of Money	813	964	80	99	9.8	10.3
Resurrection	451	685	167	169	37.0	24.7
The Woman Between	174	256	47	67	27.0	26.1
Hell's Angels	951	1003	139	157	14.6	15.7
East Lynne	537	818	101	130	18.8	15.9
Feet First	619	642	203	221	32.8	34.4
City of Song	333	472	86	110	25.8	23.3
Sports of Kings	637	727	55	90	8.6	12.4
The Criminal Code	423	434	20	27	4.7	6.2
Tom Sawyer	503	648	79	104	15.7	16.1
One Heavenly Night	617	943	209	244	33.9	25.9
Born to Love	551	820	131	199	23.8	24.3
Trader Horn	916	977	60	62	6.6	6.3
City Lights	848	970	300	281	35.4	29.0
Devil to Pay	815	1042	19	41	2.3	3.9
Jail Birds	810	873	163	163	20.1	18.7
Sous Les Toits de Paris	198	227	52	79	26.2	34.8
Hallelujah	143	159	46	42	32.2	26.4
Loose Ends	290	438	59	92	20.3	21.0
Blue Angel	436	518	92	173	21.1	33.4
King of Jazz	655	886	109	165	16.6	18.6
The Dawn Patrol	774	786	32	36	4.1	4.6
Whoopee!	729	865	49	79	6.7	9.1
Raffles	706	912	92	110	13.0	12.1
Strangers May Kiss	728	1003	182	204	25.0	20.3

Table 7. Favourite male film stars, 1934: class comparison

Rank	Working-class votes	Middle-class votes	Rank
1	George Arliss	George Arliss	1
2	Clark Gable	Clark Gable	2
3	Clive Brook	Wallace Beery	3
4	Wallace Beery	Robert Montgomery	4
5	Ronald Colman	Clive Brook	5
6	Jack Hulbert	Ronald Colman	6
7	Robert Montgomery	Lionel Barrymore	7
8	Lionel Barrymore	Jack Hulbert	8
9	Charles Laughton	Charles Laughton	9
10	Warner Baxter	Tom Walls	10
11	Herbert Marshall	Fredric March	11
12	Tom Walls	Conrad Veidt	12
13	Conrad Veidt	Warner Baxter	13
=14	Leslie Howard	Leslie Howard	14
=14	Jack Buchanan	Herbert Marshall	15
16	Jack Holt	Jack Holt	16
17	Fredric March	Eddie Cantor	17
18	Maurice Chevalier	Jack Buchanan	18
19	Eddie Cantor	Maurice Chevalier	19

Table 8. Favourite female film stars, 1934: class comparison

Rank	Working-class votes	Middle-class votes	Rank
1	Marie Dressler	Norma Shearer	1
2	Norma Shearer	Marie Dressler	2
3	Greta Garbo	Greta Garbo	3
4	Kay Francis	Marlene Dietrich	4
5	Gracie Fields	Kay Francis	5
=6	Marlene Dietrich	Katharine Hepburn	6
=6	Janet Gaynor	Gracie Fields	7
8	Katharine Hepburn	Claudette Colbert	8
9	Jean Harlow	Joan Crawford	9
10	Claudette Colbert	Janet Gaynor	10
11	Jessie Matthews	Jean Harlow	11
12	Cicely Courtneidge	Cicely Courtneidge	12
13	Joan Crawford	Diana Wynyard	13
=14	Diana Wynyard	Madeleine Carroll	14
=14	Joan Blondell	Jessie Matthews	15
16	Madeleine Carroll	Joan Blondell	16

Table 9. Favourite male film stars, 1934: age preferences

Age group	Under 21		21–40		40–60		Over 60		No age	
Star	m	f	m	f	m	f	m	f	m	f
Arliss	83	103	147	178	56	121	10	22	4	7
Gable	47	142	69	144	10	34	4	8	-	7
Beery	59	39	119	65	27	32	3	4	1	-
Brook	28	48	65	98	32	53	3	12	1	3
Montgomery	45	88	52	106	4	23	-	7	-	1
Colman	30	41	63	103	10	35	1	9	-	3
Hulbert	66	41	50	50	16	35	4	6	3	4
Barrymore	31	30	60	68	19	32	3	8	1	1
Laughton	33	29	77	53	8	12	1	2	-	3
Walls	36	15	40	42	26	24	7	7	-	1
Baxter	14	47	21	68	2	23	2	6	-	-
March	16	56	30	54	1	16	-	1	-	2
Veidt	26	27	45	54	9	7	1	4	-	-
Marshall	8	21	24	76	6	26	1	4	2	2
Howard	6	37	21	64	5	24	-	4	-	1
Holt	24	22	34	33	14	14	2	2	-	-
Buchanan	19	22	13	37	11	21	3	6	-	1
Cantor	31	13	33	21	3	9	2	-	-	-
Chevalier	21	27	16	18	4	10	4	8	-	1

Table 10. Favourite female film stars, 1934: age preferences

Age group	Under 21		21–40		40–60		Over 60		No age	
Star	m	f	m	f	m	f	m	f	m	f
Shearer	70	159	157	269	39	97	8	25	2	3
Dressler	69	104	149	178	41	98	7	17	1	3
Garbo	39	116	80	153	23	56	3	10	1	-
Francis	39	51	81	120	20	44	2	14	2	3
Dietrich	45	70	90	98	19	38	2	4	3	1
Hepburn	29	90	50	84	10	26	4	7	1	4
Fields	45	61	37	59	26	43	3	11	1	3
Gaynor	32	89	37	55	4	26	3	9	-	1
Crawford	21	54	46	68	15	23	1	4	-	-
Colbert	25	48	53	64	6	27	1	4	-	1
Harlow	60	61	48	34	6	10	1	2	-	-
Courtneidge	21	31	23	45	18	31	3	9	1	3
Wynyard	15	29	15	52	20	23	3	6	-	-
Matthews	34	28	30	31	10	16	2	4	-	2
Blondell	26	28	30	35	6	7	1	-	-	-
Carroll	18	21	31	41	6	6	-	-	1	5

Appendix III:
Patterns of literature popularity

Source: All material taken from Ronald F. Batty, *How to Run a Twopenny Library* (London: John Gifford, 1938).

Names in bold are mentioned in more than one genre category.

Novels

Michael Arlen

Vicki Baum

Rex Beach

Neil Bell

Arnold Bennett

Phyllis Bentley

Ursula Bloom

Ethel Boileau

John Buchan

Pearl S. Clark

Gideon Clark

J. Conrad

A.J. Cronin

Lewis Cox

Clemence Dane

Ricjard Dehan

Maurice Dekobra

O. Douglas

Theodore Dreiser

Rosita Forbes

Louis Golding

Winifred Graham

A.P. Herbert

Robert Hichens

James Hilton

Joseph Hocking

Michael Home

Fanny Hurst

Baroness Von Hutten

Naomi Jacob

Robert Keable

Sinclair Lewis

Eric Linklater

D.M. Locke

William J. Locke

Rose Macaulay

Patrick Macgill

Denis Mackail

Compton Mackenzie

Stephen McKenna

Beverley Nicols

Kathleen Norris

Katie O'Brien

Gertrude Page

Eden Phillpotts

J.B. Priestley

Ernest Raymond

Cecil Roberts

M. De La Roche

B.K. Seymour

R.C. Sherriff

Lady Eleanor Smith

Sheila Kaye-Smith

Helen Z. Smith

H. De Vere Stacpoole

G.B. Stern

A.G. Street

Netta Syrett

Sylvia Thompson

M. Walsh

Susan Ertz
L. Feutalwanger
Gilbert Frankau
John Galsworthy
Anthony Gibbs
Sir Philip Gibbs

Ethel Mannin
W. Somerset Maugham
L.G. Moberley
L.M. Montgomery
C. Morgan
R.H. Mottram

Russell Thorndike
Hugh Walpole
Dennis Wheatley
Pamela Wynne
Dornford Yates
F. Brett Young

Love and romance

Cecil Adair
Ruby M. Ayres
Faith Baldwin
Jean Barre
Rex Beach
Dorothy Black
Charlotte M. Brame
Elizabeth Carfrae
Barbara Cartland
H.M.E. Clamp
Isabel Clark
Sophie Cole
Joan Conquest
Lewis Cox
Victoria Cross
Simon Dare
Warwick Deeping
Ethel M. Dell
Anne Duffield
Alice Eustace
Jeffery Farnol
Louise Gerand
Elinor Glyn

Maysie Greig
Helena Grose
Mabel Barnes Grundy
Ian Hay
Anne Hepple
Muriel Hine
E.M. Hull
Joan Kennedy
Margaret Kennedy
Annabel Lee
Sheila MacDonald
Netta Muskett
Rachel Swete Macnamara
Louise Jordan Miln
L.M. Montgomery
Emmeline Morrison
Geoffrey Moss
Baroness Orczy
Gertrude Page
Margaret Pedler
Margaret Peterson
Marjorie M. Price
Kathlyn Rhodes

Grace S. Richmond
Florence Riddell
Denise Robins
Effie Adelaide Rowlands
Berta Ruck
Rafael Sabatini
Oliver Sandys
Juanita Savage
E.W. Savi
Renee Shane
H. De Vere Stacpoole
Nora K. Strange
Joan Sutherland
Annie S. Swan
Paul Trent
Valentine
Olive Wadsley
Marjorie Warby
Dolf Wyllarde
Pamela Wynne
Dornford Yates

Detective and mystery

A.J. Alan
H. Adams
L. Allan

S.S. Van Dine
F. Everton
Richard Essex

Vernon Loder
Philip Macdonald
Wyndham Martyn

M. Allingham

John Arnold

Francis Beeding

E.C. Bentley

Anthony Berkely

Ben Bolt

John C. Brandon

M. Burton

John Dickson Carr

Leslie Charteris

Agatha Christie

G.D.H. Cole

M. Cole

Gilbert Collins

J.J. Connington

Freeman Wills Crofts

Roland Daniel

Earl Derr Biggers

Carter Dickson

George Dihot

Gerard Fairlie

J. Jefferson Farjeon

John Ferguson

Errol Fitzgerald

J.S. Fletcher

Brian Flynn

R. Austin Freeman

Erle S. Gardner

Arthur Gask

Francis Gerard

Anthony Gilbert

Sinclair Gluck

Bruce Graeme

C.F. Gregg

Henry Holt

Sydney Horler

Francis Iles

Edgar Jepson

Harry Stephen Keeler

Milward Kennedy

A.E.W. Mason

Walter S. Masterman

E. Phillips Oppenheim

Frank L. Packard

Ellery Queen

John Rhode

Sax Rohmer

R. Rodd

Anthony Rolls

Dorothy L. Sayers

SeaMark

Bram Stoker

Sir Basil Thomson

Gerald Vermer

Roy Vickers

E. Charles Vivian

J.M. Walsh

Valentine Williams

Western

Robert Ames Bennett

Buck Billings

Max Brand

F.R. Buckley

R.O. Case

Jackson Cole

Eli Colter

Dane Coolidge

Courtney Ryder Cooper

Hamilton Craigie

C. Culley

Ridgwell Cullum

C. Dangerfield

Hal Dunning

W.B.M. Ferguson

Jackson Gregory

Zane Grey

A.G. Hales

Ernest Haycox

James B. Hendryx

W.D. Hoffman

George M. Johnson

Alan Le May

William Colt MacDonald

E.B. Mann

Gary Marshall

Amos Moore

Clarence Mulford

G.W. Ogden

H. Pendexter

W. Macleod Raine

Wallace Q. Reid

F.C. Robertson

Geo. B. Rodney

Charles Wesley Sanders

Charles Alden Seltzer

J.S. Sisco

Charles H. Snow

Oliver Strange

W.C. Tuttle

Clem Yore

Gordon Ray Young

Daniel Ward

Adventure

Luke Allan	**Jeffery Farnol**	**Rafael Sabatini**
A. Armstrong	Rupert Grayson	'Sapper'
Bartimeus	Peter B. Kyne	'Taffrail'
Ottwell Binns	Jack London	Louis Tracy
Ben Bolt	Stephen Maddock	Gordon Volk
John Buchan	V. Markham	Edgar Wallace
Edgar Rice Burroughs	L.W. Meynell	P.C. Wren
A.D. Divine	Talbot Mundy	
Henry Edmonds	**Baroness Orczy**	

Modern novels

Richard Aldington	Eve Ellin	Mary Mitchell
Carmen Barnes	Warner Fabian	Liam O'Flaherty
Vera Brittain	Ernest Hemingway	Evadne Price
Eve Chaucer	Aldous Huxley	Marguerite Steen
D.H. Clark	Norah C. James	L.A.G. Strong
Colette	F.A. Kumner	Evelyn Waugh
Vina Delmar	D.H. Lawrence	Mae West
Jean Devanny	Margery Lawrence	
J. Van Druten	R. Lehmann	

Air and war stories

R. Aldington	**Ian Hay**	Graham Seton
Covington Clarke	Flying Officer W.E. Johns	E.W. Springs
Humphrey Cobb	W.F. Morris	Capt. A.O. Pollard
Col. Laurence Driggs	W. Saint-Maude	
Gilbert Frankau	George E. Rochester	

Humorous

K.R.G. Browne	Keble Howard	A.A. Thomson
Joan Butler	W.W. Jacobs	Ben Travers
Richmal Crompton	Herbert Jenkins	P.G. Wodehouse
Ian Hay	Jerome K. Jerome	**Dornford Yates**

Author rankings (I)

Source: All material taken from T.E. Callender, 'The Twopenny Library', *Library Association Record,* March 1933.

Rank	Author (inc. titles available)
1	Edgar Wallace (100)
2	Warwick Deeping (41)
3	E.P. Oppenheim (38)
4	P.G. Wodehouse (32)
5	A.G. Hales (28)
6	Margaret Peterson (26)
7	Joan Sutherland (25)
=8	Ruby M. Ayres (24)
=8	Edgar Rice Burroughs (24)
=8	W.J. Locke (24)
11	Ethel M. Dell (23)
12	Sax Rohmer (18)
=13	Richmal Crompton (14)
=13	Jeffery Farnol (14)
15	Elinor Glyn (13)
16	Marie Corelli (9)

Author rankings (2)

Source: All material taken from Garfield Howe, 'What the Public Likes', *The Bookseller,* 19 June 1935.

Rank	Author (inc. titles available)
1	Edgar Wallace (101)
2	E.P. Oppenheim (75)
=3	J.S. Fletcher (56)
=3	E.M. Savi (56
5	Warwick Deeping (46)
6	Sydney Horler (45)
7	P.G. Wodehouse (72)
8	A.G. Hales (38)
9	Denise Robins (36)

10	Kathleen Norris (34)
11	F.E. Mills Young (33)
=12	Charlotte M. Brame (31)
=12	Paul Trent (31)
=14	Sophie Cole (26–30)
=14	Ethel M. Dell (26–30)
=14	Zane Grey (26–30)
=14	H. Rider Haggard (26–30)
=14	W.J. Locke (26–30)
=14	Margaret Peterson (26–30)
=14	E. Adelaide Rowlands (26–30)
=14	Rafael Sabatini (26–30)
=14	Joan Sutherland (26–30)
=23	Ruby M. Ayres (21–25)
=23	Jeffery Farnol (21–25)
=23	Louise Gerard (21–25)
=23	Sax Rohmer (21–25)
=27	Edgar Rice Burroughs (16–20)
=27	Elizabeth Carfrae (16–20)
=27	Marie Corelli (16–20)
=27	Richmal Crompton (16–20)
=27	'Sapper' (16–20)
=32	Elinor Glyn (10–15)
=32	Deirdre O'Brien (10–15)
=32	Marjorie M. Price (10–15)
=35	Charles Garvice (0–8)
=35	Nat Gould (0–8)

Select bibliography

Primary sources have been fully referenced in the footnotes or in the text. Those wanting more detailed bibliographical information should consult my PhD thesis, *Working-Class Taste in 1930s Britain: A Comparative Study of Film and Literature*, University of Portsmouth, 2007.

Books

Aldcroft, Derek H., *The Inter-War Economy: Britain, 1919–1939*, London, 1970

Altick, Richard D., *The English Common Reader: A Social History of the Mass Reading Public 1800–1900*, second edition, London, 1967

Ang, Ien, *Watching Dallas: Soap Opera and the Melodramatic Imagination*, London, 1985

August, Andrew, *The British Working Class 1832–1940*, Harlow, 2007

Barker, J., Brown, R., and Greer, W., *The Cinemas of Portsmouth*, Horndean, 1981

Baxter, John, *Hollywood in the Thirties*, London, 1968

Bayley, Stephen, *Taste: The Secret Meaning of Things*, London, 1991

Beauman, Nicola, *A Very Great Profession: The Woman's Novel 1914–1939*, London, 1983

Beaven, Brad, *Leisure, Citizenship and Working-Class Men in Britain 1850–1945*, Manchester, 2005

Benson, John, *The Working Class in Britain, 1850–1939*, second edition, London, 2003

Berry, David, *Wales and Cinema: The First Hundred Years*, Cardiff, 1994

Black, Alistair, *The Public Library in Britain 1914–2000*, London, 2000

Bourdieu, Pierre, *Distinction: A Social Critique of the Judgement of Taste*, London, 1984

Bourdieu, Pierre, *The Field of Cultural Production: Essays on Art and Literature*, London, 1993

Branson, Noreen and Heinemann, Margot, *Britain in the Nineteen Thirties*, London, 1971

Connor, Steven, *Theory and Cultural Value*, Oxford, 1992

Davies, Andrew, *Leisure, Gender and Poverty. Working-Class Culture in Salford and Manchester: 1900–1939*, Milton Keynes, 1992

Davies, Walter Haydn, *The Right Place – The Right Time (Memories of Boyhood Days in a Welsh Mining Community)*, Llandybie, 1972.

Dickinson, Margaret and Street, Sarah, *Cinema and State: The Film Industry and the Government 1927–84*, London, 1985

Drotner, Kirsten, *English Children and their Magazines, 1751–1945*, London, 1988

Eco, Umberto, *The Role of the Reader*, London, 1981

Ferguson, Marjorie, *Forever Feminine: Women's Magazines and the Cult of Femininity*, London, 1983

Fine, Ben and Leopold, Ellen, *The World of Consumption*, London, 1993

Francis, Hywel and Smith, David, *The Fed: A History of the South Wales Miners in the Twentieth Century*, London, 1980

Franklin, Ashley, *A Cinema Near You: 100 Years of Going to the Pictures in Derbyshire*, Derby, 1996

Geertz, Clifford, *The Interpretation of Cultures*, New York, 1973

Glynn, Sean and Oxborrow, John, *Interwar Britain: A Social and Economic Recovery*, London, 1976

Gomery, Douglas, *Shared Pleasures: A History of Movie Presentation in the United States*, London, 1992

Harper, Sue, *Picturing the Past: The Rise and Fall of the British Costume Film*, London, 1994

James, Louis, *Fiction for the Working Man, 1830–50: A Study of the Literature Produced for the Working Classes in Early Victorian Urban England*, second edition, Middlesex, 1974

Jones, Stephen G., *Workers at Play: A Social and Economic History of Leisure, 1918–1939*, London, 1986

Jones, Stephen G., *The British Labour Movement and Film, 1918–1939*, London, 1987

Kaplan, Cora, *Sea Changes: Culture and Feminism*, London, 1986

Kirk, Neville, *Change, Continuity and Class: Labour in British Society, 1850–1920*, Manchester, 1998

Kuhn, Annette, *An Everyday Magic: Cinema and Cultural Memory*, London, 2002

Landy, Marcia, *British Genres: Cinema and Society, 1930–1960*, Princeton, 1991

Light, Alison, *Forever England: Femininity, Literature and Conservatism Between the Wars*, London, 1991

Low, Rachael, *The History of the British Film: Films of Comment and Persuasion of the 1930s*, London, 1979

Low, Rachael, *The History of British Film 1929–1939: Film-Making in 1930s Britain*, London, 1997

McAleer, Joseph, *Popular Reading and Publishing in Britain, 1914–1950*, Oxford, 1992

McKibbin, Ross, *The Ideologies of Class: Social Relations in Britain 1880–1950*, Oxford, 1991

Miles, Peter and Smith, Malcolm, *Cinema, Literature and Society: Elite and Mass Culture in Interwar Britain*, London, 1987

Miller, Daniel, *Material Culture and Mass Consumption*, Oxford, 1987

Miskell, Peter, *A Social History of the Cinema in Wales, 1918–1951: Pulpits, Coal Pits and Fleapits*, Cardiff, 2006

Neale, Steve, *Genre and Hollywood*, Florence, 1999

Pollard, Sidney, *The Development of the British Economy, 1914–1990*, fourth edition, London, 1992

Radway, Janice, *Reading the Romance: Women, Patriarchy and Popular Literature*, London, 1987

Ray, Robert B., *A Certain Tendency of the Hollywood Cinema, 1930–1980*, Princeton, 1985

Richards, Jeffrey, *The Age of the Dream Palace: Cinema and Society in Britain 1930–1939*, London, 1984

Richards, Jeffrey and Sheridan, Dorothy, eds, *Mass-Observation at the Movies*, London, 1987

Richardson, H.W., *Economic Recovery in Britain, 1932–9*, London, 1967

Robertson, James C., *The British Board of Film Censors: Film Censorship in Britain, 1896–1950*, London, 1985

Robertson, James C., *The Hidden Cinema: British Film Censorship in Action*, London, 1989

Rose, Jonathan, *The Intellectual Life of the British Working Classes*, London, 2001

Savage, Mike and Miles, Andrew, *The Remaking of the British Working Class, 1840–1940*, London, 1994

Sedgwick, John, *Popular Filmgoing in 1930s Britain: A Choice of Pleasures*, Exeter, 2000

Smith, Sarah, *Children, Cinema and Censorship: From Dracula to Dead End*, London, 2005

Springhall, John, *Youth, Popular Culture and Moral Panics: Penny Gaffs to Gangsta Rap, 1830–1996*, New York, 1999

Stacey, Jackie, *Star Gazing: Hollywood and Female Spectatorship*, London, 1994

Stead, Peter, *Film and the Working Class: The Feature Film in British and American Society*, London, 1989

Stedman Jones, Gareth, *Languages of Class*, Cambridge, 1983

Stevenson, John, *British Society 1914–45*, second edition, London, 1990

Stevenson, John and Cook, Chris, *Britain in the Depression: Society and Politics, 1929–1939*, second edition, London, 1994

Storey, John, *Cultural Theory and Popular Culture: An Introduction*, third edition, London, 2001

Storey, John, *Cultural Consumption and Everyday Life*, London, 2003

Sutton, David, *A Chorus of Raspberries: British Film Comedy 1929–1939*, Exeter, 2000

Symons, Julian, *The Thirties: A Dream Revolved*, London, 1975

Szanto, George, *Narrative Taste and Social Perspectives: The Matter of Quality*, Basingstoke, 1987

Thompson, John B., *Ideology and Modern Culture: Critical Social Theory in the Era of Mass Communication*, London, 1990

Tinkler, Penny, *Constructing Girlhood: Popular Magazines for Girls Growing Up in England, 1920–1950*, London, 1995

Turner, Graeme, *Film as Social Practice*, second edition, London, 1993

Webb, R.K., *The British Working-Class Reader 1790–1848: Literacy and Social Tension*, London, 1955

White, Cynthia L., *Women's Magazines, 1693–1968*, London, 1970

Williams, Raymond, *Problems in Materialism and Culture*, London, 1980

Williams, Raymond, *Keywords: A Vocabulary of Culture and Society*, second edition, London, 1988

Winfield, Sam, *Dream Palaces of Derby*, Derby, 1995

Worpole, Ken, *Dockers and Detectives. Popular Reading: Popular Writing*, London, 1983

Articles in books

Bennett, Tony, 'Popular Culture and the "Turn to Gramsci"', in John Storey, ed., *Cultural Theory and Popular Culture: A Reader*, second edition, London, 1998, pp. 217–224.

Boyd, Kelly, 'Knowing Your Place: The Tension of Manliness in Boys' Papers, 1918–1939', in Michael Roper and John Tosh, eds, *Manful Assertions: Masculinities in Britain Since 1800*, London, 1991, pp. 145–167.

Calder, Angus, 'Mass-Observation 1937–1949', in M. Bulmer, ed., *Essays on the History of British Sociological Research*, London, 1985, pp. 121–136.

Chapman, James, 'Celluloid Shockers', in Jeffrey Richards, ed., *The Unknown 1930s: An Alternative History of the British Cinema, 1929–1939*, London, 1998, pp. 75–97.

Ellis, John, 'British Cinema as Performance Art; *Brief Encounter, Radio Parade of 1935*, and the Circumstances of Film Exhibition', in Justine Ashby and Andrew Higson, eds, *British Cinema, Past and Present*, London, 2000, pp. 95–109.

Ferro, Marc, 'The Fiction Film and Historical Analysis', in Paul Smith, ed., *The Historian and Film*, Cambridge, 1976, pp. 80–94.

Fiske, John, 'The Popular Economy', in John Storey, ed., *Cultural Theory and Popular Culture: A Reader*, second edition, London, 1998, pp. 504–521.

Frith, Simon, 'The Good, the Bad, and the Indifferent: Defending Popular Culture from the Populists', in John Storey, ed., *Cultural Theory and Popular Culture: A Reader*, second edition, London, 1998, pp. 570–586.

Guy, Stephen, 'Calling All Stars: Musical Films in a Musical Decade', in Jeffrey Richards, ed., *The Unknown 1930s: An Alternative History of the British Cinema, 1929–1939*, London, 1998, pp. 99–118.

Harper, Sue, 'Studying Popular Taste: British Historical Films in the 1930s', in Richard Dyer and Ginette Vincendeau, eds, *Popular European Cinema*, London, 1992, pp. 101–111.

Harvey, Sylvia, 'The "Other Cinema" in Britain; Unfinished Business in Oppositional and Independent Film, 1929–1984', in Charles Barr, ed., *All Our Yesterdays: 90 Years of British Cinema*, London, 1986, pp. 225–251.

Hobsbawm, E. J., 'The Making of the Working Class 1870–1914' in E. J. Hobsbawm, *Worlds of Labour: Further Studies in the History of Labour*, London, 1984, pp. 194–213.

Hollows, Joanne and Jankovich, Mark, 'Popular Film and Cultural Distinctions', in Joanne Hollows and Mark Jankovich, eds, *Approaches to Popular Film*, Manchester, 1995, pp. 1–14.

Hughes, William, 'The Evaluation of Film as Evidence', in Paul Smith, ed., *The Historian and Film*, Cambridge, 1976, pp. 49–79.

McDonald, Paul, 'Star Studies', in Joanne Hollows and Mark Jankovich, eds, *Approaches to Popular Film*, Manchester, 1995, pp. 79–97.

McFarlane, Brian, 'A Literary Cinema? British Films and British Novels', in Charles Barr, ed., *All Our Yesterdays: 90 Years of British Cinema*, London, 1986, pp. 120–142.

McGuigan, Jim, 'Trajectories of Cultural Populism', in John Storey, ed., *Cultural Theory and Popular Culture: A Reader*, second edition, London, 1998, pp. 587–599.

Medhurst, Andy, 'Music Hall and British Cinema' in Charles Barr, ed., *All Our Yesterdays: 90 Years of British Cinema*, London, 1986, pp. 168–188.

Miller, Daniel, 'Consumption as the Vanguard of History: A Polemic by Way of Introduction', in Daniel Miller, ed., *Acknowledging Consumption: A Review of New Studies*, London, 1995, pp. 1–57.

Morley, David, 'Theories of Consumption in Media Studies', in Daniel Miller, ed., *Acknowledging Consumption: A Review of New Studies*, London, 1995, pp. 296–328.

Petley, Julian, 'Cinema and State', in Charles Barr, ed., *All Our Yesterdays: 90 Years of British Cinema*, London, 1986, pp. 31–46.

Reid, Betty, 'The Left Book Club in the Thirties', in Jon Clark, Margot Heinemann, David Margolies and Carol Snee, eds, *Culture and Crisis in Britain in the Thirties*, London, 1979, pp. 193–207.

Richards, Jeffrey, 'British Film Censorship', in Robert Murphy, ed., *The British Cinema Book*, London, 1997, pp. 167–177.

Spicer, Andrew, 'Jack Buchanan: The "Man About Town" of British musical-comedies in the 1930s', in Ian Conrich and Estella Tincknell, eds, *Film's Musical Moments*, Edinburgh, 2006, pp. 71–83.

Tinkler, Penny, 'Women and Popular Literature', in June Purvis, ed., *Women's History: Britain, 1850–1945: An Introduction*, London, 1995, pp. 131–156.

Vincent, David, 'Reading in the Working-Class Home', in J.K. Walton and J. Walvin, eds, *Leisure in Britain, 1780–1939*, Manchester, 1983, pp. 207–226.

Willis, Andy, 'Cultural Studies and Popular Film', in Joanne Hollows and Mark Jankovich, eds, *Approaches to Popular Film*, Manchester, 1995, pp. 173–191.

Wood, Linda, 'Julius Hagen and Twickenham Film Studios', in Jeffrey Richards, ed., *The Unknown 1930s: An Alternative History of the British Cinema, 1929–1939*, London, 1998, pp. 37–55.

Wright, Iain, 'F. R. Leavis, the *Scrutiny* Movement and the Crisis', in Jon Clark, Margot Heinemann, David Margolies and Carole Snee, eds, *Culture and Crisis in Britain in the Thirties*, London, 1979, pp. 37–65.

Journal articles

Allen, Steven W., 'Will Hay and the Cinema of Consensus', *Journal of British Cinema and Television*, 3:2, 2006, pp. 244–265.

Baggs, Christopher, 'How Well Read was My Valley? Reading, Popular Fiction, and the Miners of South Wales, 1875–1939,' *Book History*, 4, 2001, pp. 277–301.

Baggs, Christopher, '"Carnegie Offered Money and Lots of South Wales Refused to Have it: It was Blood Money": Bringing Public Libraries to the South Wales Valleys 1870 to 1939', *Library History*, 17:3, 2001, pp. 171–179.

Baggs, Christopher, '"The Whole Tragedy of Leisure in Penury": The South Wales Miners' Institute Libraries during the Great Depression', *Libraries and Culture*, 39:2, 2004, pp. 115–136.

Bakker, Gerben, 'Building Knowledge about the Consumer: The Emergence of Market Research in the Motion Picture Industry', *Business History*, 45:1, 2003, pp. 101–127.

Barnett, V., 'Popular Novelists and the British Film Industry, 1927–1932', *Journal of European Economic History*, 36:1, 2007, pp. 73–100.

Glancy, Mark, 'Temporary American Citizens? British Audiences, Hollywood Films and the Threat of Americanization in the 1920s', *Historical Journal of Film, Radio and Television*, 26:4, 2006, pp. 461–484.

Harper, Sue, 'A Lower Middle-Class Taste Community in the 1930s: Admissions Figures at the Regent Cinema, Portsmouth, UK', *Historical Journal of Film, Radio and Television*, 24:4, 2004, pp. 565–587.

Harper, Sue, 'Fragmentation and Crisis: 1940s Admissions Figures at the Regent Cinema, Portsmouth, UK', *Historical Journal of Film, Radio and Television*, 26:3, 2006, pp. 361–394.

Harper, Sue and Porter, Vincent, 'Moved to Tears: Weeping in the Cinema in Post-war Britain', *Screen*, 37:2, 1996, pp. 152–173.

Hogenkamp, Bert, 'Miners' Cinemas in South Wales in the 1920s and 1930s', *Llafur*, 4:2, 1985, pp. 64–76.

James, Robert, '*Kinematograph Weekly* in the 1930s: Trade Attitudes Towards Audience Taste', *Journal of Popular British Cinema and Television*, 3:2, 2006, pp. 229–243.

James, Robert, '"A Very Profitable Enterprise": South Wales Miners' Institute Cinemas in the 1930s', *Historical Journal of Film, Radio and Television*, 27:1, 2007, pp. 27–61.

Kuhn, Annette, 'Cinema-Going in Britain in the 1930s. Report of a Questionnaire Survey', *Historical Journal of Film, Radio and Television*, 19:4, 1999, pp. 531–543.

Miskell, Peter, 'Seduced by the Silver Screen: Film Addicts, Critics and Cinema Regulation in Britain in the 1930s and 1940s', *Business History*, 47:3, 2005, pp. 433–448.

Mulvey, Laura, 'Visual Pleasure and Narrative Cinema', *Screen*, 16:3, 1975, pp. 6–18.

Poole, Julian, 'British Cinema Attendance in Wartime: Audience Preference at the Majestic, Macclesfield, 1939–1946', *Historical Journal of Film, Radio and Television*, 7:1, 1987, pp. 15–34.

Richards, Jeffrey, 'The British Board of Film Censors and Content Control in the 1930s: Images of Britain', *Historical Journal of Film, Radio and Television*, 1:2, 1981, pp. 95–116.

Ridgwell, Stephen, 'South Wales and the Cinema in the 1930s', *Welsh History Review*, 17:4, 1995, pp. 590–615.

Ridgwell, Stephen, 'The People's Amusement: Cinema and Cinemagoing in 1930s Britain', *Historian*, 1996, 52, pp. 18–21.

Ridgwell, Stephen, 'Pictures and Proletarians: South Wales Miners' Cinemas in the 1930s', *Llafur*, 7:2, 1997, pp. 69–80.

Rose, Jonathan, 'Marx, Jane Eyre, Tarzan: Miners' Libraries in South Wales, 1923–52', *Leipziger Jahrbuch zur Buchgeschichte*, 4, 1994, pp. 187–207.

Sedgwick, John, 'Cinemagoing in Portsmouth during the 1930s', *Cinema Journal*, 46:1, 2006, pp. 52–84.

Stearns, Peter N., 'The Effort at Continuity in Working-Class Culture', *Journal of Modern History*, 52:4, 1980, pp. 626–655.

Tegel, Susan, 'The Politics of Censorship: Britain's "Jew Süss" (1934) in London, New York and Vienna', *Historical Journal of Film, Radio and Television*, 15:2, 1995, pp. 219–244.

Todd, Selina, 'Flappers and Factory Hands: Youth and Youth Culture in Interwar Britain', *Historical Compass*, 4:4, 2006, pp. 715–730.

Unpublished theses

Baggs, Christopher, 'The Miners' Libraries of South Wales from the 1860s to 1939', PhD thesis, Aberystwyth University, 1995

Miskell, Peter, 'Pulpits, Coal Pits and Fleapits: A Social History of the Cinema in Wales 1918–1951, PhD thesis, Aberystwyth University, 2000

Walker, Colin Peter, 'Municipal Enterprise: A Study of the Interwar Municipal Corporation of Portsmouth 1919–1939', MA dissertation, University of Portsmouth, 2003

Film catalogues

American Film Institute Catalog
Gifford, Dennis, *The British Film Catalogue 1895–1985*, London, 1986
Halliwell's Film and Video Guide 2003, London, 2002

Internet resources

http://www.imdb.com, accessed on 31 March 2006
http://www.newbridge-memo.net/jewel/index.html, accessed on 22 February 2006

Index

Lightning Source UK Ltd.
Milton Keynes UK
UKOW04f0718180314

228307UK00001B/15/P